Rupert Brooke
a reappraisal and selection

Rupert Brooke, 1910
Photographer: V. H. Mottram

Rupert Brooke

a reappraisal and selection

from his writings, some hitherto unpublished

Timothy Rogers

NEW YORK
BARNES & NOBLE, INC.

29373

Published in Great Britain *1971*
Published in the United States of America *1971*
by Barnes & Noble Inc., New York, N.Y.
© Timothy Rogers *1971*
ISBN 0 389 04114 9

Printed in Great Britain

Contents

List of illustrations

Preface and acknowledgments

Rupert Brooke has always appealed to young readers. I was eleven or twelve when I first came across him – 'The Soldier' and 'Grantchester' I remember from that time – and perhaps two years older when I read Sir Edward Marsh's *Memoir*. When my turn came to give a paper to the school literary society, he seemed an obvious choice. In preparing it I corresponded with a number of his friends; and one of them, Lady Violet Bonham Carter, asked if I was writing a life of him. The idea then of writing any sort of book appealed to me, so from that moment I *was*. The paper was delivered, and its subsequent publication in *The Poetry Review* (vol. xxxvi, no. 1, 1945) was accompanied by a note that 'our contributor is about to publish *A Richer Dust*, a biography of Rupert Brooke'. From this time I can date my researches.

Six months between national service and university were spent in gathering material, and I met then many of his surviving friends. After twenty years, I may now make public my thanks to Sir Edward Marsh, Dr Hugh (later Lord) Dalton, Walter de la Mare, Frances Cornford, Gwen Raverat, Professors Edward J. Dent, J. B. Trend and Albert Rutherstan, Sir Geoffrey Keynes, Sir John Sheppard, and Arthur Waley. Among those with whom I corresponded at that time were John Masefield, Wilfred Gibson, Dudley Ward, Professor M. A. Lewis, Duncan Grant, and Cathleen Nesbitt. Comparison with the acknowledgments in Christopher Hassall's *Rupert Brooke* (1964) will show two things: the omission of many key names from my list; the omission of many no less important from his, for by the time he came to write his biography many of them had died.

No one was more helpful to me than the late Frances Cornford, who pulled my first version to pieces, helped me to rebuild it, and then tried hard to get me to publish it. When, some sixteen years later, Hassall's biography appeared, I realized how right I had been to withhold it, for his was a far more thorough work than mine, and drew upon some sources of which I had not even been aware. And yet, while I must gratefully acknowledge here my indebtedness to Hassall, there are, as I shall show, reasons why even his should not be the last word.

To Sir Geoffrey Keynes, as friend, editor and bibliographer of Brooke, and as his senior trustee, I owe an especial debt. It will be clear from some of what follows that we have had our differences about Brooke; but these make me all the more conscious of my obligation to him: without his permission to include unpublished and copyright material, this book would have been a less worthy tribute to the man whom each of us respects.

I must thank the Provost and Fellows of Brooke's old college, King's, for their hospitality during a busy fortnight of the summer vacation; and in particular Dr A. N. L. Munby, Librarian of the college, for his kindness and help.

Some of the letters are reprinted by permission of Faber and Faber Ltd and Harcourt Brace Jovanovich, Inc. from *The Letters of Rupert Brooke*, edited by Geoffrey Keynes, © 1968 the Rupert Brooke Trustees. Much of the second section of the introduction was contained in my review of Hassall's biography in *The Times Literary Supplement* (28 May 1964), and part of the fifth section is taken from my review of the Penguin *Georgian Poetry* in the same paper (23 February 1962): I am grateful to the Editor for allowing me to reprint these. I am likewise grateful to the Editor of *English*, who printed an article of mine (Autumn 1968) which led directly to the recrudescence of my earlier study.

Among friends of Brooke's whom I have met more recently, no one has been more helpful than Miss Cathleen Nesbitt. It has been a great encouragement to hear from one who was so close to him in his last years that I have 'got nearer to his personality than anyone [she has] read'. To her and to Frances Cornford above all his friends must belong the chief credit for that.

1

Introduction

For all the enduring popularity of his poems, Rupert Brooke is at most a minor figure in English literature. Yet he has already attracted to himself a formidable body of biographical and critical attention, and a disproportionate amount of his own writing has been published. Why then, it may be asked, another book of and about him? The short answer is that no writer, major or minor, has been so widely misjudged and misrepresented, not only by his denigrators but by many of those who would call themselves his friends.

I have attempted within the compass of a single book to bring together the best of his writing, both in verse and prose, and to suggest (chiefly by doing so) a fairer basis for his appraisal. I would not claim to have replaced the fuller collections of his writing: the interested and the curious will wish to search further, and I have suggested in the short Bibliography some ways of their doing so. But I have hoped neither to overstate nor overburden. How often in the reviews of Hassall's biography (550 pages) and the Keynes edition of the *Letters* (700 pages) did one hear the charge of dullness! Brooke could be foolish, perverse, uncritical, embittered, cynical, egotistical, and many other things which the myth-makers would not recognize, but he was never, I think, dull. If I have allowed him in these pages to seem so, the fault is mine.

But it would be naïve to suppose that any reader now can come freshly to Brooke. Before presenting the writing, one must try to remove some of the misconceptions, for one cannot, as he himself said, 'smell flowers through a blanket'.

'If his fame survives the blare of trumpets that has purported to declare it to the world in the past few years, there will be proof enough that he has, after all, written poetry fit to endure.' This was said of Brooke in 1919, but the trumpets have continued to sound for him like the annual dirge for Linus. Not for *him*, perhaps, but for a beautiful young poet (see photographs by Sherril Schell) who played cricket for Rugby School, danced dream-dances on tip-toe for college balls at Cambridge, played simple tunes on a pan-pipe at Grantchester, wooed 'Mamua' in Tahiti, volunteered for service in a war whose praise he sang in five famous sonnets, and died off the island of Theseus and Achilles, on the day of Wordsworth, Vaughan, Shakespeare and St George.

The Shelleyan (or Schellian) Brooke is part of the truth. He was – there seemed to be no other word for it among his contemporaries – beautiful. Galsworthy had 'rarely seen a man more beautiful'; Yeats called him 'the most beautiful young man in England'. Frances Cornford, though she resented others using the word to describe him (it 'somehow managed to give a quite wrong impression of him'), did so herself, for 'it was an essential thing about him, how "lovely and pleasant" he was to look upon'. And, aware of this, Brooke liked to present himself at times as the beautiful young poet. On his first meeting with Henry James, 'I did the fresh boyish stunt, and it was a great success.' And when James said later, 'I do not see why he need be a poet', he was echoing (though probably without knowing it) the *Punch* parody of Wilde: 'Why should he ever trouble to *be* anything? Why couldn't he be content to exist beautifully?' Brooke once asked Gwen Raverat: 'Will you please disarrange my hair; I've got to read poetry to some old ladies.' And he himself suggested to Sherril Schell the neo-classical pose for that famous swan-neck photograph (his Cambridge friends used to call it 'your favourite actress'). While playing the poet-hero, however, Brooke would be laughing at himself. It was as though at times he was saying: '*Rupert* would say that; I must say it'; '*Rupert* would wear that'; but there was present a dread lest anyone should take him too seriously. And when one of his biographers, Maurice Browne, writes: 'When twenty-first century realists try to disentangle the man from the myth . . . they will be attempting a difficult task: the man *was* the myth', he is making that very mistake, and effecting only, in Brooke's own words, to 'praise all the bad about [him], and hush the good away.'

Sir Edward Marsh's *Memoir* has long been one of the chief sources of biographical information. Written four months after

Brooke's death in 1915, its publication was delayed until 1918 because of difficulties with Brooke's formidable mother. Much of the story of their differences is told in Marsh's *A Number of People*; but the biography of Marsh by Christopher Hassall retells it more fully, and clarifies one matter of importance. Marsh has been blamed for the 'Young Apollo' myth ('150 pages of gold' was a contemporary judgment of the *Memoir*). When Mrs Brooke returned his draft copy of the *Memoir* it was bespattered with the word 'apple-pie'. The remark that 'Rupert left Rugby in a blaze of glory' was altered to 'Rupert left Rugby in July'. She complained that 'Eddie always seems to be thinking of Rupert's *fame*, and I can't stand it'. But it is clear now that, by her expurgations, she was herself unwittingly no less responsible than he for the golden legend.

The *Memoir* gave what was expected at the time: a memorial of a public reputation. *The Cambridge Review* declared: 'A legend has been endorsed. This life slips by like a panorama of earth's loveliest experiences.' In his concern to guide Brooke's posthumous career even as he had guided him in life, Marsh no more than hints at the less lovely experiences (of which, indeed, he may have been largely ignorant), and gives little insight into the harder qualities of Brooke's character. Nor in one other respect was he the ideal biographer, because his relationship was that of an older to a younger man. Sometimes Brooke's zestfulness is seen through a mature filter, and the equal balance of friendship is all but disturbed by patronage. When Brooke leaves with Denis Browne for the Royal Naval Division's camp:

> I saw them off . . . from Charing Cross – excited and a little
> shy, like two new boys going to school – happy and
> handsome in their new uniforms, and especially proud of
> their caps, which had very superior badges.

And an exact contemporary would not have seen Brooke (as the Herald in the *Eumenides*) as a 'radiant youthful figure in gold and vivid red and blue, like a Page in the Riccardi Chapel'.

A more serious weakness of the *Memoir* was suggested by Brooke's mother. In her short introduction to it she wrote of her 'great desire to gain the collaboration of some of his contemporaries at Cambridge and during his young manhood, for I believe strongly that they knew the largest part of him'. She had wished, it seems, for a conglomerate of obituary notices by representative spokesmen for the various paths he had trodden, and tried hard to get such a book compiled. It was impossible, partly because so many of his contemporaries had also been killed. But the implication of her remark is clear; and for its truth it is necessary only to refer to the brief account Hugh Dalton wrote for the *Memoir* (Marsh gives most of it), or to the accounts, published and unpublished, of Frances Cornford, Jacques and Gwen Raverat, Sir John Sheppard and Sybil Pye.

A longer study of Brooke, Arthur Stringer's *Red Wine of Youth*, appeared in 1948. Twenty-three years previously an American journalist and adventurer, Richard Halliburton, had obtained from the less reticent of Brooke's surviving friends material for a biography which he did not live to write; and by access to this material Stringer was able to supplement what is otherwise little more than a paraphrase of Brooke's letters. He claims to distinguish between mask and face; he refers to 'the cellophane with which . . . [Brooke] sought to protect the vulnerable wares of the heart', to 'the old device of sheathing the fine blade of feeling in a scabbard of flippancy', and to the need for protecting 'the inner meat of emotion with a shielding bur of cynicism'; but he seldom penetrates the cellophane, scabbard or bur to reveal the true Brooke. He does not subscribe to the popular misconception of him as an essentially happy young man, and sees through the surface gaiety to the inner brooding, often unhappy, spirit – possibly, even, neglecting too much the gay Brooke who was such a rare companion. But what is almost entirely neglected is that laughing self-deprecatory quality which is the key to a true understanding. He quotes from a letter to Jacques Raverat Brooke's description of meeting his ideal woman, and telling her 'that the Earth was crowned with windflowers and dancing down the violet ways of Spring, that Christ had died and Pan was risen, and that her mouth was like the sunlight on a gull's wings'. And there he ends the quotation, with a reference to 'the mercurial young poet', omitting Brooke's final remark: 'As a matter of fact I believe I said, "Hullo! isn't it rippin' weather?" '

No less unfair to his subject are the bowdlerizations, and the attempts to improve the phrasing of original letters. Brooke wrote to Marsh from the Montreal Express:

Now I'm shut up in my upper half of the sleeping berth!
I'm empty but a little easier. Beneath me sleeps – oh,
a mattress and a plank between us! – a fat old lady.

Stringer gives:

> Now I'm shut up in the upper half of my sleeping berth.
> I'm emptier but a little easier. Oh, a mattress and a
> plank between us – me and a fat old lady.

It is hard to have confidence in a biographer who takes such liberties with his material, or in the critical judgment of one who can refer to Brooke periphrastically as 'the author of "The Soldier" and "Menelaus and Helen" '. There are numerous small errors of fact, interpolations of fancy, mistakes in chronology, quotations wrongly attributed. What is most serious is that truth is still further obscured by luxuriances of style. Frances Cornford spoke of its 'complete crass *vulgarity*'. Poor Sir Edward Marsh found himself counting references to 'the genial Eddie'. The figure who emerges from the text – 'The Apollonian youth', 'the wandering singer', 'the Cambridge Romeo', 'the poet of Grantchester', 'the son of Warwickshire', 'the carefree Epicurean', the 'brooding blue-domer', 'the island-hopper', 'the loquacious and long-haired King's student', 'the tawny-headed poet', 'the golden-haired officer' – is, surely, the *reductio ad absurdum* of the myth.

III

It is true that the Hassall biography (1964) and the *Letters* (1968) have done something to replace the myth with the man; but each of these official and monumental works suffers on the one hand from including too much that is trivial and on the other from an unfortunate censorship. Sir Geoffrey Keynes was Brooke's contemporary as a schoolboy at Rugby, where he had for him an 'adoration' (the word is Lytton Strachey's) to which he has been loyal throughout his life. One of the many influences of Brooke for which all readers of Donne, Blake, Jane Austen, Hazlitt, and Evelyn must be grateful is that his friendship started Sir Geoffrey on a lifelong interest in bibliography. His Brooke bibliography is more complete than anyone else could have hoped to make, for it includes anonymous and pseudonymous writings dating from Brooke's earliest contributions to Rugby magazines. But Sir Geoffrey now in his eighties, belongs to a generation which believed that certain private matters should not be published whatever might be their literary or historical importance. It must be said in fairness that others of Brooke's friends urged (and practised) still greater reticence about him. But the consequence has been that the published correspondence is hopelessly incomplete; there are three hundred excisions (for various reasons) from the fewer than six hundred published letters, and some of the closest friendships are unchronicled. It may be thought that by such treatment more questions are posed than answered. It may also be thought by a younger generation that no skeletons at present concealed could be more shocking than the uncensored antisemitism, however mild, and however typical of the upper classes in Brooke's day. (He shared this trait with writers such as Hulme, Pound and Eliot, as well as with Hilaire Belloc who chiefly infected him.)

I have not made it my business to probe in these dark corners; I doubt if it would have been possible if I had tried. A later biographer (his book, *The Handsomest Young Man in England*, might more truly be called a picturebook with notes, many of them inaccurate) has suggested: 'it will never be possible to make a clear description of Brooke's personality without reference to the correspondence between James Strachey and Noel Olivier, between Gwen Darwin and Ka Cox, and between Rupert Brooke and Michael Sadler, and lastly, between Frances Cornford and Brooke'. I do not know; these things may be. I do know that Brooke's letters to Katharine Cox are in the Library of King's College, Cambridge, sealed by the trustees; that his letters to James Strachey (bits of which are quoted by Hassall, but none included in the *Letters*) are now in New York Public Library, and that Sir Geoffrey would allow their publication 'only over his dead body'. Brooke, it seems, was the self-appointed sexual adviser to Strachey, a homosexual, who had been his contemporary at preparatory school, and remained a friend until 1912 when Brooke broke dramatically with Bloomsbury. That he made sexual advances to Brooke is likely, and likely that Brooke repelled them. I have not crossed the Atlantic to seek further, but have heard at third-hand that Brooke comes out quite well from these encounters. I refer briefly and (in part) conjecturally to such matters in my next chapter.

It may be wondered why it should be necessary to concern oneself with Brooke's life at all: what matters, surely, is in the poems. The answer is partly, as has been suggested, that the life has been obscured by the myth, which has in turn obscured the poems, and that to free them from that encumbrance one must try to see the man. But it is further true, and a possible weakness of the poems, that they are inseparably a part of their author. Trelawny wrote of Shelley: 'To form a just idea of his poetry, you should have witnessed his daily life; his words and actions best illustrated his writings.' Edward Thomas wrote of Brooke: 'No one who knew him could easily separate him from his poetry: not that they were the same, but that the two inextricably mixed and helped one another.' Brooke's poems belong to the class of personal revelations. 'They share his secrets with the world,' wrote Walter de la Mare, 'as if a boy had turned out the astonishing contents of his pockets just before going to bed.' Some of them might have been taken from a private diary; and I know of only one, apart from the obvious flights of fancy, in which Brooke did not himself experience the incidents he relates. The writing of poetry was for him, indeed, not an act of dedication, but a convenient means of self-expression; his poems are a record of life as he reacted to it.

In my outline of Brooke's life I have done little more than note the main events and what I take to be his chief characteristics. I have tried to correct some inaccuracies and wrong emphases in Hassall, but cannot claim to provide more than an appendix to what will be, if not the definitive, for many years the most authoritative life.

IV

In a way inseparable from the 'beautiful young poet' myth, and yet requiring separate notice, is the aura which clings to Brooke as a 'war poet'. The '1914' sonnets first appeared in December 1914 in the fourth (and last) instalment of the quarterly, *New Numbers*. On Easter Sunday 1915, 'The Soldier' was quoted in St Paul's by Dean Inge: *The Times* reported the sermon, and gave the sonnet in full. *The Cambridge Magazine* (ironically, one day after Brooke's death) included a précis of Dean Inge:

> The enthusiasm of a pure and elevated patriotism, free
> from hate, bitterness, and fear, had never found a
> nobler expression. And yet it fell somewhat short of
> Isaiah's vision and still more of the Christian hope.
> It was a worthy thought that the dust out of which
> the happy warrior's body was once compacted was

consecrated for ever by the cause for which he died.
Yet was there not a tinge of materialism in such an
idea?

Brooke received a cutting from *The Times*, and his last recorded
remark was a regret that the Dean hadn't thought him as good as
Isaiah.

The first tentative jottings of four of the '1914' sonnets were
made in a small field-notebook. Interspersed among them are notes
from military lectures – 'Every officer should be easily found',
'German explosive shells carry further back than forward', 'Keep
strict discipline' – and personal memoranda – 'Thompson, Officers'
Mess, doesn't make his bed up', 'Wanted: 1 curtain . . . table . . .
chairs'. It is well that the beginnings of these idealistic sonnets
should be thus preserved among tokens of a more practical concern.
At the same time they are poems, not of war, but of preparation for
war (Brooke's first title for 'The Soldier' was 'The Recruit'). The
attitude to war expressed in them recalls Lord Reading's picture of
him in August 1914 at a parade in Regent's Park:

> . . . clad in civilian clothes but equipped with rifle
> and haversack, and he had crowned this hybrid 'turnout'
> with a rakish, challenging, wide-brimmed black felt
> hat, worn with the air of an ancient Greek turned
> modern Mexican, which was the Poet's latest gesture
> of freedom before capitulating to the uniform drab.

The late Professor J. B. Trend suggested that contemporary
leaders in *The Morning Post* might have prompted Brooke's attitude
in the sonnets and been the source of some of the expressions in
them. We may not accept this suggestion as it stands; Brooke was
always capable of thinking for himself, nor at the height of his
enthusiasm would he have succumbed to and reiterated the naïve
sentiments expressed in that newspaper. But the articles do show
that many of his ideas were 'in the air' at the time. Expressions that
'manly animosities of war' are preferable to the sloth, selfishness
and cowardice of 'a shameful peace' ('. . . war is not altogether an
evil: it cleans and purifies: it invigorates . . .'), that 'the soul of
England is the soul of the sum of Englishmen living and dead', and
that all people are 'parts of a great whole, whose destiny and interest

are of inﬁnitely higher importance than their own' – all these are
exactly reflected in the sonnets.

They are reflected, too, in the writings of other poets at this
time, in none more than in the jubilant John Freeman's:

A common beating is in the air –
The heart of England throbbing everywhere.
And all her roads are nerves of noble thought,
And all her people's brain is but her brain;
Now all her history
Is part of her requickened consciousness –
Her courage rises clean again.

It is well to remember, too, that the feelings of those two poets
who, more vividly than any, were to express the later mood of dis-
illusion, were very different in the early months. Wilfred Owen at
the outset felt a sense of 'new crusade and modern knightliness'. In
the summer of 1915, shortly after Brooke's death, Siegfried Sassoon
could write in 'Absolution':

The anguish of the earth absolves our eyes
Till beauty shines in all that we can see.
War is our scourge; yet war has made us wise,
And, fighting for our freedom, we are free.

Horror of wounds and anger at the foe,
And loss of things desired; all these must pass.
We are the happy legion, for we know
Time's but a golden wind that shakes the grass.

Brooke, like Tennyson in 'Blow, Bugle, blow' and Henley in
'England, my England', called on bugles to maffick the 'rich dead';
Owen was later to ask, 'What passing bells for these who die as
cattle?' But Brooke's only glimpse of war had been at Antwerp,
where the long sad columns of Belgian refugees had greatly moved
him. After Antwerp he wrote: 'it's a bloody thing, half the youth of
Europe, blown through pain to nothingness' – a phrase which an-
ticipates Owen (cf. 'The Parable of the Old Man and the Young').
In another letter he writes to Cathleen Nesbitt: 'All those people at
the front who are fighting – muddledly enough – for some idea
called England – it's some faint shadowing of the things you can

give that they have in their heart to die for' ('Whatever hope is yours, Was my life also'). His friend and fellow officer, Patrick Shaw-Stewart, wrote a month after Brooke's death: 'There was another heap of dead in front of the trench, and at dawn a lark got up from there and started singing – a queer contrast. Rupert Brooke could have written a poem on that, rather his subject.' The young Isaac Rosenberg was to do almost that in 'Returning, we hear the larks'.

The truth is, surely, that no one could have written more bitterly, more ironically, more truly of war than Rupert Brooke. There is small doubt that he would have done so, had he lived: he was acutely sensitive to the sorrows and the beastliness of war; his early 'realistic' vein was always near the surface. It could be that in later disillusionment he might have regretted those early paeans. Some of his friends believed he would. Edward Dent wrote a fortnight after Brooke's death:

> It was grotesquely tragic – what a characteristic
> satire he would have written on it himself! – that
> he should have died (at Lemnos, too!) just after a
> sudden and rather factitious celebrity had been
> obtained by a few poems which, beautiful as they are in
> technique and expression, represented him in a phase
> that could only have been temporary.

D. H. Lawrence repudiated the sonnets for himself but recognized that they were true for Brooke: 'It is terrible to think that there are opposing truths – but so it is.' Brooke's view of the truth would, no doubt, have changed, but he could have looked back on the sonnets as the faithful expression of a then prevailing mood. He captured the thoughts and feelings of the moment, and gave eloquent expression to them. 'Rupert expressed us *all*,' said Henry James, 'at the highest tide of our actuality.' But the moment was to pass: the simple rhetoric became outmoded, the attitude of mind suspect.

v

Apart from the predictable reaction against the '1914' sonnets, there was in the years following the war a reaction against all things 'Georgian'. 'Georgian Poetry' had been more of a business venture than a literary movement. Brooke, who with Edward Marsh was its prime mover, declared that the England of 1912 'must be bom-

barded' with the claims of its neglected poets, and was prepared to
use his own rapidly growing influence 'as brazenly as a commercial
traveller'. It was said that on the day the first volume was published
the Prime Minister's car was waiting outside Bumpus's at opening
time, and that Brooke's strategy was to be seen in it. It is certain
that the first edition of five hundred copies was sold out on the
first day (Asquith buying two of them); and the third volume was
to sell over nineteen thousand copies. What anthology of present-
day verse could equal that?

Its aim, in which it was supremely successful, was to create a
large reading public for poetry. The best of the thirty-six contributors to the five volumes differed widely in their methods and
achievements; and the qualities suggested by the label 'Georgian' –
and later so much derided – are most obviously shown in the
writings of the weaker poets. Marsh can be excused for writing
as the *envoi* in the final volume:

> It is natural that the poets of a generation should have
> points in common; but to my fond eye those who have graced
> these collections look as diverse as sheep to their shepherd.

Contributors to the series had included: W. H. Davies, Ralph
Hodgson, Walter de la Mare, John Masefield, Harold Monro,
James Stephens, J. E. Flecker, Isaac Rosenberg, Siegfried Sassoon,
D. H. Lawrence, Robert Graves and Edmund Blunden – a pretty
variegated flock.

But literary history is concerned less with diversity than with
points in common. And, for the vaticide, a label is a convenience;
he can dispatch his victims in number instead of singly. Which is
indeed what was attempted. A writer in the Cambridge magazine
Granta (in 1929) was groping towards this:

> One still lacks a succinct formula in which to dismiss
> [Georgian Poetry]. Its main faults are that it is
> facile, sentimental, socially and politically non-
> significant, fit for people of all ages, and above all,
> popular.

And W. H. Auden mirrored more succinctly the change in taste:

> For gasworks and dried tubers, I forsook
> The clock at Grantchester, the English rook.

It may be said that Mr Auden at least acknowledges this stage on his personal journey. Others who have 'recovered from an adolescent "phase" of Brooke' have, in Christopher Hassall's words, 'lived ever afterwards in a state of resentful convalescence'. It has sometimes been forgotten, too, how many of the Georgians, including Brooke, were in revolt against their immediate predecessors. Lawrence himself wrote of the first volume:

> The time to be impersonal has gone. We start from
> the joy we have in being ourselves, and everything
> must take colour from that joy. It is the return of
> the blood, that has been held back, as when the
> heart's action is arrested by fear. Now the warmth
> of the blood is in everything, quick, healthy,
> passionate blood.

But it is not my purpose to give more than an outline here of the Georgians and their fortunes. This has been admirably done by Robert H. Ross in a pioneer study, *The Georgian Revolt* (*1910–22*). Professor Ross writes:

> ... perhaps no group of poets since the Pre-Raphaelites
> has suffered more, or more ignominiously, from the
> widespread acceptance of oversimplified stereotypes
> and critical half-truths, even among readers who should
> know better. Often the Georgians have been
> misrepresented because of the ignorance of their subsequent
> critics, but even more often have they been the victims
> of pure political spleen. Many of the major Georgian
> poets surely deserve rescue from the almost universal
> obloquy which the weaknesses of a few of the brethren
> have drawn down upon the heads of the entire body. The
> law of poetic averages alone – to say nothing of careful
> reading – would suggest to an unbiased observer that not
> every poet published in the five volumes of *Georgian
> Poetry* was a glib, pseudo-pastoral lark-lover.

He suggests that, whereas with the first two volumes (1912 and 1915) 'Georgian' implied vigour, revolt and youth, after 1917 it was to imply retrenchment, escape, and enervation. Borrowing a label of Alec Waugh's, which was subsequently taken up by Herbert Palmer and others, he distinguishes between the first generation Georgians and the 'neo-Georgians' who were to succeed them. It was these last who were to be satirized by Osbert Sitwell in 'The Jolly Old Squire, or Way-Down in Georgia', the two 'heroes' of which were Edward Shanks and J. C. Squire (who gave his name to 'The Squirearchy'). The Prologue to the 'Mime-Drama' concludes:

> Now in the Play which follows you shall see
> The mighty Goddess Mediocrity
> Contrive that naughty Satan's overthrow.
> Meanwhile blow bugles, blow red trumpets, blow!

Except in that last line, Brooke does not appear to be a particular target of Sir Osbert's wit. But it might be said in retaliation that these lines of Sir Osbert's from 'Church Parade' are not so very far from the manner of his butt:

> The round contentment in their eyes
> Betrays their favourite surmise,
>
> That all successful at a trade
> Shall tread an eternal Church Parade,
>
> And every soul that's sleek and fat
> Shall wear a heavenly top-hat.

Is this not John Rump in Grantchester?

The Sitwells with their anthology *Wheels* were certainly among the noisiest of the Georgians' critics; but far more important in the poetic revolution of the 1910s was the work of Ezra Pound and T. S. Eliot. Brooke had reviewed Pound's *Personae* for *The Cambridge Review* in 1909, a little condescendingly perhaps (was he not an American? – had he not fallen 'under the dangerous influence of Whitman'? – Brooke was never reconciled to *vers libre*), but with early percipience none the less: 'one cannot but feel a note of exultation that is rare enough in modern poetry'; 'It is important to remember his name.' It was Brooke, indeed, who persuaded Marsh to invite Pound to contribute to the first *Georgian Poetry* anthology. (Pound would have done so had the poems Marsh asked for been available, and offered himself for the second.) Later he wrote a slightly obscure epigram on Brooke, the point of which, as he explained in letters, was that, even when a South Sea island princess fell madly in love with him, the handsome young Englishman would go on writing Petrarchan sonnets. There is no doubt that the two poets had great differences (and delighted in them: they once crossed swords over Lascelles Abercrombie in the pages of *The Poetry Review*). But in a letter to Harriet Monroe (editor of *Poetry*, Chicago) immediately after Brooke's death Pound writes of him as 'the best of all that Georgian group' (a view exactly echoed by John H. Johnston in *English Poetry of the First World War*). And five months later he writes to the same correspondent:

> Now that his friends have taken to writing sentimental
> elegies about his long prehensile toes, it might seem
> time for him to be protected by people like myself who
> knew him only slightly . . .
> And for God's sake if there was anything in the man,
> let us dissociate him from his surviving friends.
> Something ought to be done to clear him from the
> stain of having been quoted by Dean Inge, and to save
> him from friends who express their grief at his death
> by writing such phrases as (yes, here it is verbatim):
> 'in fact Rupert's mobile toes were a subject for the
> admiration of his friends'.

Like Pound, Eliot had few affinities with the Georgians (even Monro had refused to publish 'Prufrock': it could not have fallen within Marsh's far narrower canons of acceptance). He wrote of them in a critical note to Monro's *Collected Poems* that he could remember only 'a small number of poems by two or three men'. It is likely, though, that Brooke was one of those remembered. Mr B. C. Southam has suggested recently that Eliot may have had Brooke's 'The Old Vicarage, Grantchester' in mind in the opening of 'The Waste Land': 'there are considerable likenesses in detail and design; and it is likely that Eliot would be expecting the reader to catch the essential dissimilarity between their two views of life, as glimpsed through their accounts of Spring memories and awakenings' (B. C. Southam, *A Student's Guide to the Selected Poems of T. S. Eliot*, 1968). Certainly Eliot quoted from 'Grantchester' in his 'Reflections on Contemporary Poetry' in *The Egoist*, and wrote interestingly of 'The Fish':

> The Georgian love of Nature is on the whole less
> vague than Wordsworth's, and has less philosophy

behind it: for Wordsworth had a philosophy, though ill
apprehended from foreign teachers; the Georgian
plays more delicately with his subject, and in his
style has often more in common with Stevenson. On
the other hand, not having abstractions to fall back
upon, the modern poet, when he diverts his attention
from birds, fields, and villages, is subject to lapses
of rhetoric from which Wordsworth, with his complete
innocence of other emotions than those in which he
specialized, is comparatively free. Thus Rupert
Brooke, after a number of lines which show a really
amazing felicity and command of language, in 'The
Fish', descends to:

> O world of lips, O world of laughter,
> When hope is fleet and thought flies after . . .

retrieved happily by another fine passage at the end.

In Eliot's own early writings there are some suggestions, if only
slight, of kinship. In his decadent phase at Rugby, Brooke had been
much attached to a simile he made up about the moon: 'The moon
was like an enormous yellow scab on the livid flesh of some leper.'
Eliot shows a similar delight in the disgusting. In the original
edition of *Ara vos Prec* there is a poem which he later took pains to
suppress, retaining only a shorter French version. The poem as it
first stood described a honeymoon couple in bed at Ravenna, hot,
sweaty, flea-bitten. It ascends to a climax with these lines about the
moon:

> A washed-out smallpox cracks her face
> Her hand twists a paper rose,
> That smells of dust and Eau de Cologne,
> She is alone
> With all the old nocturnal smells.

There is evidence in the better known poems of a shared delight
in polysyllables for satirical effect (Brooke: 'Teleologically unperturbed', 'Intolerable consanguinity'; Eliot: 'Polyphilopro-
genitive The sapient sutlers of the Lord'). Brooke's Smet-Smet,
the Hippopotamus Goddess, would seem to have some 'consanguinity' with Eliot's 'broad-backed Hippopotamus', the Established

Church. Again, as Mr G. S. Fraser has observed, we are sometimes struck by imagery in Brooke's poems that 'seems to foretell a coming shift of taste:

> Heart, you are restless as a paper scrap
> That's tossed down dusty pavements by the wind.

This was the sort of thing Mr Eliot was to notice, though he would use it as a symbol, not as a simile.' Most important, the poets had a common bond in their new found admiration for Donne. Eliot reviewed the Grierson edition for *The Times Literary Supplement*; Brooke for *The Nation*. Eliot wrote: 'Soul and body are what Donne has to offer, with their subtle and secret interactions . . .'; Brooke: 'He was the one English love-poet who was not afraid to acknowledge that he was composed of body, soul, and mind . . .'. Eliot's review – unfortunately for my thesis – preceded Brooke's by a fortnight.

It was a letter from Eliot in *The Times Literary Supplement* attacking the idea of anthologies which started a correspondence on that subject. In the following week a letter by Robert Graves (who had then appeared in the third and fourth Georgian anthologies) makes obvious allusion to his difficulties as a 'Georgian':

> A poet who once gets marked by the reviewers
> with the ranch-brand of the anthology in which
> he first appears is thereafter made to suffer
> for the failings of the other weaker members
> of the herd, with whom he may have nothing further
> in common.

– feelings which did not prevent his allowing himself to appear in volume five.

Graves was to say some fierce things about 'neo-Georgians' but he wrote with equal strength on Brooke's behalf:

> How wrong about Rupert: we all look up to him as
> to our elder brother and have immense admiration
> for his work from any standpoint, especially his
> technique upon which we all build. I know it is
> fashionable in some low quarters to pretend to
> dislike him; but nobody does really, least of
> all R. N[ichols]; S. S[assoon]; or R. G[raves].

The fashion has persisted, and in some quite high quarters: hence this recital of contrary evidence. Much more could be said, but at this point it would seem right to close. Time and Professor Ross have provided a new generation with a truer perspective.

2
Life

Rupert Chawner Brooke was born at Rugby on 3 August 1887. His father, William Parker Brooke, was a Rugby schoolmaster, whose academic career as a classical scholar and Fellow of King's College, Cambridge, his son was to emulate. In 1892 he became housemaster of School Field. Rupert's mother, Mary Ruth Cotterill, was a lady of stern character, decorous and autocratic. In later years he called her the Ranee (a name suggested by the Brookes of Sarawak, with whom, however, they were unconnected); this was testimony alike to her regal bearing and to his good-humoured acceptance of it.

He was the second of three brothers. Dick, who was six years older, died after a short illness in January 1907. His death meant much to Rupert, then in his first year at King's; in 'The Call' (*P.W.* 164),[1] the first of his poems to be published in Cambridge, he fancies a reunion with him. Alfred, three years younger, followed Rupert to King's, and there was a close bond between them: Sir John Sheppard, who knew each well, was emphatic that 'if Alfred were excluded from the family circle, it would be out of focus'. He was killed two months after Rupert while serving as a lieutenant in the Post Office Rifles. One of his last injunctions to his mother had been that she should on no account believe the sentiments of the '1914' sonnets: war was horrible.

A second child, a girl, had died in infancy. Mrs Brooke, who was often shrewd in assessing character but pitifully ignorant of psy-

[1] Poems *not* included in my selection are thus referred to their page in *The Poetical Works of Rupert Brooke*, ed. Geoffrey Keynes.

chology, allowed Rupert to know how deeply she had hoped for another daughter before his birth. He was to write later:

> I am here because at Fettes, in the seventies, Willie Brooke and May Cotterill got thrown together. And then they had a son and a daughter, and the daughter died, and while the mother was thinking of her daughter another child was born, and it was a son, but in consequence of all this very female in parts – sehr dichterisch – me.

As Hassall comments, there was nothing effeminate about him; but the fascination that there might be, and the fear that others might suppose there was, made him concerned both to convince himself and to persuade others of his virility.

Brooke loathed his local preparatory school, Hillbrow, but he made a number of good friends there, including James Strachey, the younger brother of Lytton, who was his academic sparring-partner. He entered Rugby at fourteen at the house which had been his home. Marsh quotes Hugh Russell-Smith, a friend and contemporary at School Field:

> He was in all things more than loyal to his father, but he never made it awkward for the rest of us. His sense of fun saw him through, and it helped us a good deal to know that he would not misinterpret all the little pleasantries that boys make at the expense of their Housemaster. The result was a sort of union between the Housemaster and the House, which made very much for good.

It is possible to think, however, that this close tie with home, especially with the dominating Ranee, made difficulties for Brooke, both then and later. In 1911 in Munich he was very excited by a performance of *John Gabriel Borkman*. 'Do you know the play . . .?' he asked Jacques Raverat. 'Therein is a youth who will fly from his mother in order to LIVE (it happens in Norway also).'

His school career was successful but not outstanding. He did the sort of things expected then (as now) of an English public schoolboy: captained his house, played cricket and football for the school (though not especially well), wrote poems for the school prize ('The Bastille', *P.W.* 174, was successful), won a medal for prose with an essay on 'England's Debt to William III', read literary papers to the Upper Bench, and spoke in the Debating Society.

Not until page 96 of his biography does Hassall allow him to leave Rugby; here a few glimpses from contemporary sources must suffice.

The Meteor, the Rugby magazine, contains this account of his prowess on the rugby field:

> R. C. Brooke (11 st. 2 lb.) – A reliable centre three-quarter, who, though not brilliant, is usually in his place, and makes good openings. He tackles too high.

Is it too fanciful to apply this comment to his school career, even to his life? – 'not brilliant . . . usually in his place . . . makes good openings'. Again from *The Meteor*, a report of his maiden speech in the Debating Society, opposing the motion that 'This House laments the present condition of the Daily Press':

> Mr. R. C. Brooke . . . said that the proposers of the motion were pessimists; they had presented no ideal. The daily papers should be light and easy to read. The modern crowd must be educated from blatancy upwards. Murders and police news were the substitutes for romance. A good murder deserved two columns. Macbeth was the story of a murder, the Iliad the result of a kind of divorce case.

There is a like provocativeness in his own account of a very different occasion: a paper to the sixth form literary society, Eranos, on Swinburn's *Atalanta in Calydon*:

> The usual papers we have on such subjects as Hood or Calverley – 'something to make you laugh' . . . I saw my opportunity, and took it. 'Have I not', I said, 'many a time and oft been bored beyond endurance by such Philistines? Now my revenge comes; I shall be merciless.' So I prepared a very long and profound paper full of beautiful quotations, and read it to them for a long time, and they were greatly bored. They sat round in chairs and slumbered uneasily, moaning a little; while I in the centre ranted fragments of choruses and hurled epithets upon them. At length I ended with Meleager's last speech, and my voice was almost husky with tears; so that they awoke, and wondered greatly, and sat up, and yawned, and entered into a

discussion on *Tragedy*, wherein I advanced the most wild
and heterodox and antinomian theories, and was very
properly squashed. So, you see, even in Rugby the
Philistines don't get it their own way always.

I have read the paper: it is indeed long, and it is possible to sympathize just a little with the Rugby philistines.

One of the self-confessed philistines was Lord Reading (though, as Brooke's junior by several years, he would not have been present for *Atalanta*). Recalling that Brooke was not widely popular outside his house, he attributed this, not to a subconscious envy of his greater accomplishments, nor to a resentment that so many gifts should have been showered upon one being, but rather to a vague feeling that he did not come from the same mould as the rest, that he was somehow unusual; and 'at school the unusual is always sinister'.

Looking back on those days . . ., I am more than ever
convinced that his hair was to blame: very thick, very
golden, and by our cropped and prosaic standards
scandalously long, it was at once the symbol for him of his
own singularity and the focus to us of our faint hostility.

One remembers the attitude to Shelley of his fellow Etonians. But the non-conformity was not treated with such suspicion by everyone. To return to the loyal Russell-Smith:

. . . gradually most of us in the House came under his spell.
We accepted his literary interests. He was so straightforward
and unaffected and natural about them, and he took our
chaff so well, that we couldn't have helped doing so.
Perhaps they amused most of us, but one or two – and
those the most unlikely – were occasionally found clumsily
trying to see what there really was in such things.

Brooke's own attitude to school is well typified in a note to his father from a junior master, carefully preserved by Parker Brooke among his son's school reports:

Dear Brooke,
I fear I must complain of Rupert for bribing a musician
to play during my 4th lesson.

II

The recipient of Brooke's thoughts on his *Atalanta* paper was St
John Lucas, an important influence in these early years. His family
were neighbours of the Brookes, but he had gone to Haileybury
and read law at Oxford; and at the time of Brooke's first letter to
him in 1905 he was in his mid-twenties and a barrister at the
Middle Temple. His first interest, though, was in poetry and contemporary – especially 'decadent' – literature. He edited *The Oxford
Book of French Verse* (which Brooke was to review enthusiastically
in *The Cambridge Review*), and introduced Brooke to the poems of
Baudelaire. The phase of 'decadence' which was to possess Brooke
for some years was certainly encouraged by Lucas, to whom he
played up in conversation and in the mannered but self-mocking
letters which survive.

In his last term at Rugby Brooke wrote in a manner designed to
please Lucas:

> I am infinitely happy. I am writing nothing. I am content
> to live. After this term is over, the world awaits. But I do
> not now care what will come then. Only, my present
> happiness is so great that I fear the jealous gods will requite
> me afterwards with some terrible punishment, death perhaps
> – or life.

He left home and school for Cambridge in 1906, and a nostalgia
for the life that was past made much of his first year there unhappy.
But he early developed interests which were to be important to his
own life, and in some small part to history.

One interest was in the drama. He was never a good actor: on
stage his movements had an awkwardness, his voice a huskiness,
which were uncharacteristic of him. In his first term he was demoted
from the part of Hermes in the *Eumenides*, but his appearance for
one brief minute as Herald seems to have been one of the evening's
successes. 'I stand in the middle of the stage,' he wrote to his
mother, 'and pretend to blow a trumpet, while somebody in the
wings makes a sudden noise. The part is not difficult.'

In the autumn of the following year Brooke, with his friend and
namesake Justin Brooke (President of the Amateur Dramatic Club)
and a number of actor friends, combined to produce Marlowe's
Dr Faustus, the inaugural production of what was to become the

Marlowe Society. Justin Brooke, the most experienced of them, played Faustus, and Rupert Mephistopheles.

Even more important for Brooke was the next venture of the Marlowe group: a production of *Comus* as part of Christ College's celebration of the Milton Tercentenary. As the Attendant Spirit, he managed to look picturesque; and a reviewer in *The Athenaeum* thought him 'the best of the performers, and a better reciter of blank verse than we have heard of late anywhere'. But it was chiefly the preparatory work which interested him. He studied all matters from theatre-construction to textual criticism. The experience deepened his devotion to Milton's poetry (he told Frances Cornford that when he took a volume of Milton from the shelf he found his hand trembling to think of what was in it); it deepened his sense of drama and music; and, as Edward Dent said, it assisted the development of an ideal, ever present in his mind, of 'young Cambridge, as the source from which the most vital movements in literature, art, and drama were to spring'.

The ideal of Young Cambridge suggests two other interests of this time. In the second volume of his *Autobiography*, Bertrand Russell includes a letter from himself to Lady Ottoline Morrell, written after reading Marsh's *Memoir*. Marsh 'goes building up the respectable legend', and it makes Russell 'very sad and very indignant'.

It hurts reading of all that young world swept away –
Rupert and his brother and Keeling and lots of others – in
whom one foolishly thought at the time that there was
hope for the world – they were full of life and energy and
truth . . .

Russell had come to know Brooke well on his election to the Apostles. Marsh, who had himself been an Apostle, wrote of 'that old, great, secret, but vaguely famous Brotherhood from which the membership of Tennyson and others of the illustrious has lifted a corner of the veil'.

A fellow Apostle was Geoffrey Keynes's elder brother, Maynard, the economist. In the second of his *Two Memoirs*, Lord Keynes was to recall the influence upon himself and his contemporaries of the philosopher, G. E. Moore, who was a presiding spirit over the Society. Moore's *Principia Ethica*, which had been published in 1903, was 'not only overwhelming; . . . it was exciting, exhilarating, the beginning of a renaissance, the opening of a new heaven on a new earth, we were the forerunners of a new dispensation, we were not afraid of anything.' Although infected by the general enthusiasm for his method, the Apostles seemed to share little of the philosophical spirit Moore was so eager to foster, and seized rather upon the incidental answers he provided. As Keynes says, 'We accepted Moore's religion, so to speak, and discarded his morals.' Brooke was concerned in particular with Moore's question of what was *'good in itself'*, and accepted his conclusion that metaphysics, 'as the investigation of a supposed supersensible reality', had no logical bearing on the answer. What mattered were 'states of mind' and which of them were good or bad – a question which seemed to depend finally upon one's intuition. Moore's answer that 'By far the most valuable things, which we know or can imagine, are certain states of consciousness, which may be roughly described as the pleasures of human intercourse and the enjoyment of beautiful objects' was carried a stage further by Brooke, who made it the basis of what he hesitatingly called his 'Mysticism'. An expression of this mysticism may be found in the letter to F. H. Keeling (chapter 3). There are hints of it in the hitherto unpublished paper to the Apostles which I have included in chapter 6.

The other interest suggested by the ideal of Young Cambridge was Brooke's active concern with politics. In speaking of these times, with a youthful enthusiasm he retained throughout his life, the late Lord Dalton recalled how he and Brooke and their contemporaries thought of their generation as far superior to any that had preceded it (a sentiment no less apparent in the witness of Keynes and Russell). Dalton had been converted from a Conservative tariff reformer to a Fabian socialist largely through the influence of Frederick (Ben) Keeling, a Wykehamist in his third year at Trinity, whose posthumous *Letters and Recollections* (introduced by H. G. Wells) is one of the political documents of the period. Over the chimney-piece of Keeling's rooms hung an enormous poster depicting the workers of the world surging forward with clenched fists, and under it the legend 'Forward the day is breaking'. Dalton always maintained that the lines from Brooke's 'Second Best' (*P.W.* 144):

> Yet, behind the night,
> Waits for the great unborn, somewhere afar,
> Some white tremendous daybreak

1 Rupert Brooke, 1906

2 Rupert Brooke writing in the garden of the Old Vicarage, Grantchester

3   Rupert Brooke and Dudley Ward (left) on the river at Grantchester

4   Rupert Brooke at Lulworth,
      c. 1910

foretold the dawning of a Socialist state. If so, it is the only political reference in the published poems; though Dalton recalled that Brooke was at one time seriously planning an epic poem on modern wealth and poverty, culminating in a triumphant Social Revolution, but found the theme intractable.

Brooke was cautious in his approach to the Fabians. 'I'm not your sort of Socialist,' he told Dalton; 'I'm a William Morris sort of Socialist.' Like Morris, he at first neglected economics, and his theme was Morris's Civilization:

> The attainment of peace and order and freedom, of
> goodwill between man and man, of the love of truth and
> the hatred of injustice, and by consequence the attainment
> of the good life which these things breed.

But, said Dalton, the subtle influence of the Webbs – 'the funny old, silly old Webbs' – soon showed him the intellectual limitations of Morris; and, 'though he never studied the fine points of economics, he came to talk very good sense on the larger economic questions'. He became a full member of the Society in 1908, and its President in 1909, being one of the most effective in its history, and securing as many new members by his presence at a meeting as woud the; most persuasive pamphlet. He attended the Fabian Summer Sclhools and his notes on the *Minority Report of the Poor Law Commission* (he went on a caravan tour to popularize it) show both meticulous concern and passionate involvement. It was said that if one chanced to meet him in the street when there was talk of an industrial dispute, he would be as well versed in the complications of social questions as in the obscurities of Donne.

But it was through the meetings of another society that Dalton first came to know him well. In their first term a small group of Kingsmen, 'Atheist Exquisites and Anarchist Bedlamites', formed itself for a weekly paper followed by discussion. The *Objects* of the Carbonari – for that was the awesome name they chose for themselves – were 'the production of minor poets and strong, silent politicians'; *Qualifications* for membership were 'Culture: long hair: old pumps (or carpet-slippers)'; and for *Subscriptions*, all payments were to be made in kind, 'verse and epigrams preferred'. Arthur Waley, one of the dozen hirsute and slippered members, recalled that on many a summer evening he and Brooke and Dalton would cycle out of Cambridge to a favourite clump of

elm trees. There they would read Swinburne's poems by the light
of a cycle lamp, to be woken at dawn by the warm, sickly smell of
cow-breath on their faces.

No one has written more vividly of Brooke at this time than
Dalton in the record he prepared for Marsh's *Memoir*. But Marsh
omits this account of the Carbonari:

> Generally at our meetings a paper was read, and then
> everyone had to speak, the order of speaking being decided
> by drawing lots. When everyone had spoken, the reader of the
> paper replied and the discussion ceased to be regulated.
> Politics, in the narrow sense, were barred, but everything
> else was permitted. His contributions to our discussions were
> informal and conversational, typical of what such contributions
> should be. His own papers were some fantastic, some
> satirical, some merely critical and expository.

Dalton remembered in particular Brooke's reading 'The Romantic
History and Surprising Adventures of John Rump', a satire in the
manner of Belloc's *Emmanuel Burden*, from which I have included
(chapter 8) the verse Epilogue in Heaven. On another occasion H. G.
Wells was principal speaker when the Carbonari debated 'the
family' in Brooke's rooms, anticipating by some sixty years the
thoughts of a later Provost of King's.

For some of his friends, for Kingsmen such as J. T. Sheppard
(later Sir John Sheppard, Provost) and Goldsworthy Lowes Dickinson, the ideal of Young Cambridge was more ambitiously linked
to a Classical Ideal. This was founded on a belief that Greek art
and Greek culture were the highest expressions of man's divine
nature, and that the problems of the modern world were not only
the same as those of ancient Greece, but best approached in the
manner of Plato's *Dialogues*. Cambridge was seen as a modern
Athens, where Phaedrus would talk with Socrates, not on the
banks of the Ilissus, but beside the Cam. Needless to say, the
Young Apollo of Mrs Cornford's epigram became for these idealists
a perfect citizen of their Republic; just as the memorial tributes
of such as Gilbert Murray gave later currency to the picture of a
young Athenian. Needless to say, too, Brooke played up to their
expectations of him, while refusing to take himself entirely seriously
in this – or any other – role.

III

At Cambridge, as at Rugby, the Classics were not indeed first among Brooke's interests. His Second in the Classical Tripos at the end of his third year was none the less a disappointment. Hassall suggests that it was debated whether his papers did not more properly belong to a still lower class; but Frances Cornford recalled that her husband had recommended him for a First: it seems that he was more inclined than his fellow examiners to judge the little Brooke had written by its quality.

When Brooke's tutor advised that he should give up the Classics and concentrate on English literature, and set him as an immediate object an essay for the Charles Oldham Shakespeare scholarship, he eagerly concurred. Accepting the further advice that he should protect himself from a social life which was beginning to overwhelm him, he took lodgings at The Orchard, Grantchester, and worked hard on his first essay on Webster with which he won the scholarship. He claimed that he did not really begin to live until he went out of College: it was his first escape from institutional life.

In the Christmas holiday following his move he went to Switzerland, with a skiing party of his friends, and, returning through Basle, contracted food poisoning. He arrived in Rugby with a high fever to find that his father was even more seriously ill after a cerebral haemorrhage. After a short illness, Parker Brooke died, and was buried on the very day of the school's return. Rupert found himself deputizing for his father in the house, and forwent his plans for the term at Cambridge.

'What,' he asked, 'is the whole duty of a housemaster? To prepare the boys for confirmation, and turn a blind eye on sodomy.' He found himself well suited to housemastering, with 'a bluff Christian tone that is almost wholly pedagogic'. Also the boys remembered 'I used to play for the school at various violent games, and respect me accordingly'.

He returned to Grantchester in May, and divided his time between the various societies, the University library and The Orchard. He was working at this time on a monograph, *Puritanism as Represented or Referred to in the Early English Drama up to 1642*, for which he won the Harness Prize.

The following year, after three months in Munich, he moved to the Old Vicarage, next door to The Orchard. He loved this shabby house with its wild garden, a labyrinth of flowers and weeds, in which he walked 'like a fly crawling on the score of the Fifth Symphony'. Always he felt most at peace in wild surroundings; and, on visiting once a more formal garden in which white lilies were displayed against a green and silver background of fig-tree boughs, he admitted its impressiveness, but complained that it made him feel uncomfortable, 'as if the Angel Gabriel might pop out at any moment and announce something'. In a corner of the garden was a tumble-down rococo building of clunch and tiles. And beyond it, beneath a canopy of trees, there flowed the 'yet unacademic stream' (its status is unchanged) which, rejoining the other half of the river further down, flowed in Brooke's day through an old mill, since destroyed by fire. The ruins of Chaucer's Trumpington Mill – the 'phantom mill' of Brooke's poem – are further upstream.

Sybil Pye, in her admirable account of these Grantchester days (much misquoted by Hassall), has recalled the long discussions held in the Old Vicarage garden, in which all subjects were touched on if few conclusions reached. One quality especially was apparent in Brooke: 'that docility and gentleness which has well been called "the necessary midwife of genius" '.

> Never was there a more sympathetic opponent: he had a
> way sometimes of working the last speaker's opinion into his
> own reply in such a manner that his dissension appeared merely
> a comment on some conclusion already reached.

This gentleness in discussion, and his unwillingness to take the lead in it, recalled the words of Keats that 'Man should not dispute or assert, but whisper results to his neighbour'.

His chief work during the latter part of 1911 was a fellowship dissertation on *John Webster and the Elizabethan Drama* which he finished with difficulty. He appeared as a negro slave in *The Magic Flute*, and scribbled hard in a dressing-room when not wanted on the stage. He was also preparing the poems for the only book to be published in his lifetime; and, in the brief intervals of Webster, corresponded with his publisher, 'who's always discovering new indecencies in my poems and demanding omissions'. When the *Poems* appeared in December, he wrote:

> I've an insistent queer feeling of having got rid of poems
> I've written and published – of having cut the umbilical

cord – that they're now just slightly more anybody's concern than mine, and that everybody else has an equal right and a faintly greater opportunity of understanding them.

He elsewhere confessed to feeling 'that degrading ecstasy that I have always despised in parents whose shapeless offspring are praised for beauty'.

IV

Some of the early poems, such as 'The Hill', were written about and for Brooke's first love, Noel Olivier. Up to the time of her death (in April 1969), Dr Noel Olivier Richards steadfastly refused publication of the letters Brooke had written her: without them, and those to her sisters, it is impossible to judge the importance of their relationship. Noel was the youngest of the four daughters of Sir Sydney Olivier (later Lord Olivier), who had been Governor of Jamaica and was a keen Fabian. In May 1907 Sir Sydney had been invited to address the Cambridge Fabians, and it was at a supper party in Ben Keeling's rooms before the meeting that Brooke first met Noel, then a girl of fifteen and a half, and still at school at Bedales. Their frequent meetings over several years, often secretly contrived, were to mean much to each of them; for a short time, it seems, they were unofficially 'engaged'. But, from whatever motives, her sisters seemed determined that Noel should not become committed at so early an age. When Brooke offered her the dedication of his *Poems*, she refused. Their last recorded meeting was in the November before his death.

Of greater consequence to both parties, and indeed to others, was Brooke's love for Katharine Cox. Some sixty of his letters to her have been published at least in part, though others have been deemed too bitter ever to appear. Hassall said several times (though never, I think, in print) that Brooke's letters to her were among the best he wrote, a judgment which cannot be fully supported by those selected for the *Letters*. In his biography he traced, though not completely one feels, the turbulent course of their relationship, without some knowledge of which the published correspondence would be hard to follow.

Katharine Cox, known to all her friends as Ka, was by four months Brooke's senior. While she was still a child she had lost her mother, and had shared with her elder sister responsibility for the home and family, a younger sister and a father to whom she was devoted. Her father's death in 1905, the year before she went up to Newnham, was an emotional deprivation from which she never fully recovered.

She and Brooke met during their first year at Cambridge: one of the revolutionary achievements of the Fabians (of which she was to be elected Treasurer) was in being almost the first society to break down the rigid barriers between men's and women's colleges. She was a plain but none the less attractive young woman, warm and motherly in her affections, and wide in her sympathies. 'To be with her,' said Frances Cornford, 'was like sitting in a green field of clover . . . She accepted everybody without criticism, as she did the weather, and then gave out, not knowing how much she was giving.' It was no doubt a craving for that 'sleepy mother-comfort' he writes of in 'A Memory' (though this was of another love) that led Brooke after several years of platonic friendship to look upon her with a different feeling. But his full passion seems to have been first roused by jealousy.

The occasion was a reading party at Lulworth in December 1911. He had finished his fellowship dissertation only a week or so before, and was in a state of near exhaustion. Two days after Christmas he arrived at lodgings with Lytton Strachey, other members of the party, including Ka, being accommodated near by. Strachey had let the painter, Henry Lamb, know of Ka's presence there, and Lamb joined them on the afternoon of the 30th. That evening his friends noticed that Brooke was unusually silent and solitary, while Ka and Lamb went walking on the sea-shore. On the following day she confided in Brooke what he had had reason to fear for some weeks, that she thought herself to be in love with Lamb. We may accept the conjecture of Hassall, firmly based if delicately understated, that it was 'natural for idealistic love, poisoned by jealous fears, to ascribe the motives of a libertine to its prospering rival'. Brooke was his mother's son, and nowhere is the Ranee's puritanism more apparent than in his jealous, protective urge to keep Ka unspotted by the world. Many of his letters from this time forth speak of a revulsion from dirtiness, a hunger for cleanness. The pedagogic tone, if neither bluff nor Christian, expressed itself in fearful warnings and injunctions both to her and to their mutual friends. Even the published extracts from his letters are painful witness to the confusions, revulsions and self-loathing which were to result from this emotional crisis.

Desperately, and forgetting Noel, he made his own bid, and asked Ka to marry him. She, of course, refused; but, as ever accommodating, and concerned for his peace of mind, she agreed to be his companion in Munich. Brooke left Lulworth on the verge of a nervous breakdown; a London specialist prescribed complete rest, and he spent a month of turmoil, tended for three weeks by the watchful Ranee in an hotel at Cannes.

At the end of January he escaped from his protesting mother, met Ka at Verona, and went with her from there to Munich. She was not in love with him, indeed she was in love with Lamb; but she nursed him as lovingly as any mother – he was still in a pitiful state of health – and for a time he seemed to be regaining strength. They were living together now as lovers; and she chose her moment – it was when they were leaving Munich for Starnberg in mid-February – to confess that while he had been pouring out his feelings to her in daily letters from Cannes, she had been continuing her relationship with Lamb. His reaction was far fiercer than she could have anticipated. He relapsed into the state in which she had seen him in Lulworth less than two months previously. Four days later they cut short their stay, and returned hurriedly to England.

Brooke was shocked and humiliated to think that Ka had allowed herself to be loved by him while her true affections were elsewhere. She, who had acted out of pity and compassion – one might say therapeutically – became now the victim of his passionate resentment. From the South Seas he was to write in 'Waikiki':

Of two that loved – or did not love – and one
Whose perplexed heart did evil, foolishly,
A long while since, and by some other sea.

And in a last letter to her in 1915 ('I suppose you are about the best I can do in the way of a widow'):

My dear, my dear, you did me wrong: but I
have done you very great wrong.

As he fell out of love with her – fell at first into a sort of deadness of feeling – so, with the perversity of human nature, she found herself falling in love with him. There were trials and failures, forgivenesses and recriminations. From this time, it seems, Brooke could never be sure again of his love for any woman. Desperately as he longed for marriage, and widely – though not promiscuously – as he loved and was loved, he could never finally commit himself.

But his bitterness was not directed only at Ka Cox. Lytton Strachey, who had invited Lamb to Lulworth and had been present with him and Ka on subsequent occasions, was cast as Pandarus (with what probable injustice one may judge from Michael Holroyd's biography of him). Brooke cut Strachey dead, in public, in the foyer at Drury Lane, and broke not only with him but with his brother James and others of his Bloomsbury and Cambridge friends. Nor was this the only cause of his resentment. In an unpublished paper on Shakespeare, written much under the influence of Frank Harris, Brooke described him as 'a hysterical decadent creature, who was almost driven mad by conflicting motives of lust, love, snobbery and hate'. This, he claimed, was the consequence of Shakespeare's boy-friend's falling in love with his girl-friend. 'Pure sodomy,' he says in the same paper, 'is a pretty affectation in the young, but if it is anything more, leads to secondrateness, sentimentality, fluff, gentle dilettante slush.' How near he himself may have been to the intellectual decision to become a passive homosexual is suggested by his later vehemence against 'hermaphroditism' as he called it. But ultimately it revolted him. It was of James Strachey, arriving late at a camp, that he wrote the lines:

> In the half-light he was out of place,
> And infinitely irrelevant at dawn.

In a passage of psychologizing, Hassall summed up the effect on Brooke of his relations with Katharine Cox:

> [He] never lived to regain that wholesome objectivity and
> balance which restores the sense of proportion after a period
> of breakdown. The injury had gone too deep. His condition
> remained – in this one sphere of memory and association
> alone – what scientists who chart the mind would have us
> call paranoiac.

The word is not too strong to be supported even by the published evidence. Even the discreet, loyal Geoffrey Keynes refers, in his biographical preface to the letters of 1912, to 'his mind being at times possessed by so frenzied a jealousy of Lamb's influence in Katharine's life that he seemed to his friends to be almost out of his mind'.

In his preface to the letters of the following year, Sir Geoffrey refers to Brooke's asking Marsh to arrange a meeting with Cathleen Nesbitt, then a promising young actress on the London stage. 'In her company his more normal feelings revived, and she was from thenceforward to play the main part in his emotional life.' Strangely, his first surviving letter to her is omitted from Sir Geoffrey's selection, an omission I have been happy to supply. Miss Nesbitt recalls that she was conscious of 'a great searching and "aliveness" [in Brooke] that could never be satisfied, at all events in his youth, by one woman only'. Some of the later poems were written for her: 'Doubts', which he wrote one afternoon while she was sleeping off a toothache; 'Safety', which he sent her after she had read aloud to him Donne's 'Anniversarie'. From the South Seas he scribbled 'a charming silly little poem [unpublished] on a picture postcard of a Samoan girl guide called Kathleen'. She replied with a mock 'Complaint of a maiden awaiting a real "pome" from her lover'; and he sent her 'Retrospect', without a letter. That poem, as Hassall suggests, is 'in effect an elegy to the memory of the "mother-quiet" of Ka'; but it is possible to see in it also the 'still delight' of his new love. Miss Nesbitt remembered how they had once talked of Donne's 'Extasie', and of 'how much nearer to that feeling love was in its very beginnings before the awareness of desire, just as the dawn was more breathless just before the sun had fully risen.'

V

Among all Brooke's friends no one was more understanding than Frances Cornford. It was to her in particular that he confided his feelings for Katharine Cox, and she who did most by her love for each of them to console and reassure. He wrote to his close friend, Dudley Ward:

> Frances Cornford, who is the only decent person in this country who knows about it all, and understands, and is good, is a great blessing. She turns out to be a fine person. The only emotion I have nowadays is thankfulness for what good people there are.

And in the same letter:

> Frances wants me to go to America or somewhere for a year for Ka's sake, for mine, and for everybody's. America means,

if possible, some physical work and little or no mental.
California ...

Almost a year was to pass between his acceptance of this good
advice and his sailing for America in May 1913. His journey was
partly financed by the *Westminster Gazette* for which paper he was
commissioned to write a series of travel letters. The selection from
these which I have included in chapter 4 must be allowed to cover
the early part of his journeyings, and the article on Samoa in the
same chapter together with letters to Edmund Gosse and Violet
Asquith in chapter 3, to speak briefly for his time in the South Seas.
There he found happiness in a simpler life, and wrote some of his
finest poems. How prophetically had he written in a manuscript
note of 1906: 'The life of the poet is made up of tragedies: they
begin with an infatuation and end with a sonnet sequence'! In
Tahiti, where he spent three months, he met the Mamua of 'Tiare
Tahiti', a native girl of Mataia called Taatamata, who became his
mistress. He wrote from there to Cathleen Nesbitt:

> Will it come to your having to fetch me? The boat's ready
> to start; the brown lovely people in their bright clothes are
> gathered on the old wharf to wave her away. Everyone has
> a white flower behind their ear. Mamua has given me one.
> Do you know the significance of a white flower worn over the
> ear? A white flower over the right ear means 'I am looking
> for a sweetheart.' And a white flower over the left ear
> means 'I have found a sweetheart.' And a white flower over
> each ear means 'I have one sweetheart, and am looking for
> another.' A white flower over each ear, my dear, is dreadfully
> the most fashionable way of adorning yourself in Tahiti.

He returned to England via America, spending a few days in
Chicago with Maurice Browne, who ran the Little Theatre there
and was to be the first producer, after Brooke's death, of his one-act
play, *Lithuania*. Browne's account of these days and of the homeward voyage on which he accompanied him can be found in his
Recollections. His actress wife, Ellen van Volkenberg, wrote in her
diary of the voyage:

> Mr. Brooke is having sighs and eyes cast at him; even a
> married woman took a snapshot of him today because he has
> 'such a noble head'. A young girl two tables down from us

gazes at him, awestruck and beautifully melancholy. When
I told him of her adoration, he remarked 'How dull'.

I quote this anecdote, so typical of many, because it gives one part
of a truth which – however magnified in the legend – cannot be
ignored.

On his return in early June of 1914 there followed two months of
gaiety, spent mostly in London, and with Marsh as master of many
of the ceremonies. Brooke's revulsion from 'Bloomsbury' had been
compensated by his introduction through Marsh to some of his
most interesting contemporaries. Of older writers he had met
Henry James, who had been lured to Cambridge in the May Week
of 1909. He had sat next to Shaw at a Fabian dinner, and met Yeats,
and Hardy, and Belloc (whom he greatly admired). Through Marsh
he met his fellow 'Georgians'; and through him, too, met Winston
Churchill to whom Marsh was secretary, and the circle of friends
that centred on 10 Downing Street while Asquith was Prime
Minister. Violet Asquith (Lady Violet Bonham Carter, and later
Baroness Asquith of Yarnbury) became an especial friend; her
brother, Arthur (Oc), was to be with him on the Dardanelles
expedition. Lady Violet was to lose another brother, Raymond,
to whom she was devoted, and many of the close friends of her
circle. Some twenty-five years before her own death in 1969 she
discussed Brooke's beliefs and thoughts about death. 'I don't
think he was a dogmatic atheist (though I certainly should not have
described him as a "believer"). He had too much imagination to
dismiss the Unknown. I think he groped, like most of us, in regions
of the spirit, but his beliefs were not crystallized in a faith. He was
still exploring life.' To the end of her life, Lady Violet cherished a
belief that people who died young would grow in some new world
to what they might have been.

Two days before the declaration of war, Brooke wrote to Marsh:

> I feel as if I had left London for ages. I *did* enjoy July.
> It's now a far and lovely vision . . . All things are past. Do
> you have a Brussels-before-Waterloo feeling that we'll all –
> or some – meet with other eyes in 1915? . . .

He was staying with the Cornfords in Cley, Norfolk, when war was
declared. There is a suggestion of his feelings at the time in his
essay 'An Unusual Young Man' (by which he is represented in

The Oxford Book of English Prose), but the essay seems both to over-dramatize and over-simplify. His first reaction to the idea of war, in common with those other intellectuals who protested in *The Times*, had been of disgust. He regarded a possible war as the foolish expression of imperialism, and quarrelled so violently about this with his French friend Jacques Raverat that, for a time, they were not on speaking terms. But the change of attitude, when it came, was the more forceful. Brooke may have started by reluctantly accepting the event, and thinking, in the words of the Unusual Young Man, 'Well, if Armageddon's *on*, I suppose one should be there.' But the acceptance, once made, served him as a means to a personal fulfilment; and the wanderer in the middle mist could now become a crusader, with the 'central purpose of my life, the aim and end of it . . ., the thing God wants of me' being, quite simply, 'to get good at beating Germans'.

With others of his Cambridge contemporaries, including Ben Keeling, he joined the Artists' Rifles, and began drilling with them in London. But Keeling – who refused three times to leave the ranks because of his belief in 'civic equality' – wrote somewhat bitterly towards the end of August:

> Rupert Brooke has dropped out. He wants a commission after all, and thinks he can get one through pushing in various quarters.

He hoped at first for a Territorial commission through Cambridge. But in September Winston Churchill offered him a commission in the Royal Naval Division.

As sub-lieutenant he found a new role to play. The authoritarian side of his character – the Brooke of the Sixth Form at Rugby, the pedagogic schoolmaster, the White Man among the Fijians – a side which he had never taken wholly seriously, became dominant. He was fatherly to his men, and he treated their roughness with an amused tolerance. He writes of a kit check:

> I soon found that questions about some of the articles on the lists were purely academic. 'How many handkerchiefs have you?' The first two men were prompted to say 'none'.
> The third was called Cassidy. 'How many phwatt, sorr?' 'Handkerchiefs.' – '?' – 'Handkerchiefs, man, handkerchiefs.' (*In a hoarse whisper to the Petty Officer*) 'Phwat

does he mane?' P.O. (*in a stage whisper*), 'Ter blow your
nose with, you bloody fool.' Cassidy (rather indignant),
'None, sorr!' They were dears, and very strong, some of
them.

We may hear also in that last comment the tone of the young don
of King's.

On October 4th the Brigade left for Antwerp to help in the
relief of the Belgians. On reaching the city, 'everyone cheered and
flung themselves on us, and gave us apples and chocolate and flags
and kisses, and cried *Vivent les Anglais* and "Heep! Heep! Heep!" '
At Vieux Dieux they relieved part of the First Brigade which had
been brought back from the trenches in front of the town; and the
scene in the town square – filled with British and Belgian troops,
staff officers shouting, dispatch riders roaring through, and an
endless stream of refugees from the outlying villages humbly making
their way from certain to uncertain disaster – was memorable. The
sight of the exhausted Belgian troops was the Brigade's first introduction to the realities of war. And Brooke wrote of the refugees:

I'll never forget that white-faced, endless procession in the
night, pressed aside to let the military – us – pass, crawling
forward at some hundred yards an hour, quite hopeless, the
old men crying, and the women with hard drawn faces.

His experience served to strengthen his resolve; and he wrote
later:

. . . apart from the tragedy – I've never felt happier or
better in my life than in those days in Belgium. And now
I've the feeling of anger at a seen wrong – Belgium – to
make me happier and more resolved in my work. I know
that whatever happens, I'll be doing some good, fighting to
prevent *that*.

On the evening of the 8th, after two days spent mostly in the trenches,
came the withdrawal; and the Division started on its homeward
march under conditions of great hardship.

The Division was stationed next at Blandford Camp in Dorset.
From there Brooke went on leave shortly after Christmas, and
finished at Rugby the five sonnets '1914' which had had their
beginnings before the Antwerp Expedition. He also visited London,

staying first with Marsh and then with the Prime Minister, and recapturing something of past gaiety.

On February 29th, the Division embarked at Avonmouth, and sailed the same day for the Dardanelles. Brooke wrote, 'I've never been so happy in my life'; and realized suddenly that 'the ambition of my life has been – since I was two – to go on a military expedition against Constantinople.'

After a short stay in Malta and a week in Lemnos, the Division landed at Port Said and was given three days' leave. It was during this time that he contracted amoebic dysentery, and joined a fellow sufferer, Patrick Shaw-Stewart, in the Casino Hotel. Sir Ian Hamilton offered him a post as his Aide-de-Camp, but he refused to leave his men. Shaw-Stewart wrote: 'Rupert and I were trundled on board the Grantully Castle when the battalion pushed off rather hastily about April 11, this time meaning business.' His eagerness to go proved fatal. He never regained his strength completely; and when, less than a fortnight later, he lay comatose with acute blood-poisoning, the doctors on the French hospital ship held that nothing but a strong constitution could have saved him. He himself wrote on the day he embarked:

> . . . while I shall be well, I think, for our first thrust into
> the fray, I shall be able to give my Turk, at the utmost, a
> kitten's tap. A diet of arrowroot doesn't build up violence.
> I am as weak as a pacifist.

After two or three days in his cabin, he began to get up and go about. A table was formed in the dining saloon, under the presidency of one of the ship's officers, 'who was occasionally,' wrote Shaw-Stewart, 'a little surprised at our conversation. I subsequently happened to hear that this table was known to the others as "the Latin Club".' The conversation ranged from the little ways of Byzantine emperors to the correct way of dealing with Turkish prisoners; and 'we were convinced that the campaign would most unfortunately be ended in a month by the R.N.D. occupying the entire Gallipoli peninsula and setting its foot on the neck of the Turks'.

On April 17th they landed at Skyros. Brooke seemed quite well till the 20th, when there was a Division field day, and he went to bed immediately after dinner. He stayed in bed the next day with pains in his back and head and a steadily mounting temperature;

and was transferred on the day after that (the 22nd) to the French hospital ship, *Duguay-Trouin*. On the afternoon of the 23rd, with a school friend, Denis Browne, beside him, he died, and was buried the same evening on Skyros.

A cable was sent to the Admiralty from Lemnos. Winston Churchill wrote an obituary for *The Times*. But the most fitting memorial was composed by Brooke himself in the fragment of a last elegy:

> What he is yet,
> Not living, lives, hath place in a few minds ...
>   He wears
> The ungathered blossom of quiet; stiller he
> Than a deep well at noon, or lovers met;
> Than sleep, or the heart after wrath. He is
> The silence following great words of peace.

3
Letters

In his twentieth year Brooke wrote to Geoffrey Keynes: 'Even more than yourself I attempt to be "all things to all men"; rather "cultured" among the cultured, faintly athletic among athletes, a little blasphemous among blasphemers, slightly insincere to myself . . .'. One of the most fascinating experiences in speaking to his friends has been to find how each had known – and treasured as 'the real Rupert' – a different person. And something of this chameleon quality (we remember Keats on the 'Camelion Poet' who has no identity, but 'lives in gusto') comes through in his letters.

Hugh Dalton was not alone among Brooke's friends in finding him 'the best letter-writer I have ever known'; certainly almost all his correspondents seem to have kept his letters, and the big Keynes edition is a mere selection. All but two of the thirteen letters I have included here appear in Keynes (and some also in Edward Marsh's *Memoir*: Brooke's first editor had always a keen perception of quality). The first of the letters, that to St John Lucas, had been destined for the *Memoir*, but it was one of Mrs Brooke's excisions, a target for her 'applepies'. 'You seem to forget,' she told Marsh, 'that Rupert was a schoolmaster's son, and that I am a schoolmaster's widow.' Time may, I think, be held to have removed that objection. The first of the two letters to Cathleen Nesbitt appeared (in garbled form) in Stringer's *Red Wine of Youth*, but was omitted both from Hassall's biography and the Keynes *Letters*. Though not (as Stringer claimed) his first letter to her, it was certainly one of the earliest, and pre-dates any of the published ones. I have included as a companion piece the hitherto unpublished note to her from the Aegean which was to be opened in the event of his death. With the other letters I have followed the text of the Keynes edition, except that I have taken the opportunity to correct one or two small inaccuracies.

To St John Lucas   *The Liberal Publication Department*
Rugby
[*January 1906*]

Dear St. John,

Many thanks for your patience in displaying to me the wonders of the wicked city. I found my headmasters[1] flourishing exceedingly. By themselves they are shy, frightened individuals; but when they foregather in large numbers they become very rowdy. Most of the day they spent in discordant religion in the Chapel; but I managed to chat with a few for some quiet minutes: I was very patient and gentle. I told them many things they did not know before. They went away a little dazed. I am now hopelessly involved in politics. Every night I go down to the Liberal Club and cheer, from 10 to 12 p.m., at the results of the polls. I am even editing an election paper, '*The Rugby Elector*', which appears on alternate days in the Liberal interest. It is full of cheap and low gibes at Steel-Maitland, which proceed from my middle-class imagination. The whole thing is ridiculously English.

The Rugby masters are beginning to return. I meet them at intervals. They ask me what I have been doing. I mention Simeon Solomon and G. B. S. Some of them look vacant and smile in a blissful ignorance of either name. Others, illuminated by a kind of twilight knowledge, look shocked, blush, and go away. And these are the people who have the charge of my unconscious tender youth, and who bid me read Pater! . . . There are two classes of Rugby schoolmaster; those who insult Beauty by ignoring it, and those who insult Beauty by praising it.

To guard against the noxious influence of politics I shut myself up for an hour each evening, put a green shade over the light, and chant The Sphinx[2] in a jewelled monotone.

Thus I contrive to keep the *mens insana in corpore sano* which is all the English decadent may hope for.

Yours radically
Rupert Brooke

[1] A Headmasters' Conference held at Rugby.   [2] By Oscar Wilde.

To Frederic Keeling   *24 Bilton Road, Rugby*
                                   20–23 September 1910
                                        (Age 23)

Dear Ben,

I've several times started to write you a notable and rhetorical letter. But my life has been too jerky to admit of much connected thought lately. So the letter always fizzled away and was not. I'm sorry I didn't write sooner. But I wanted to be able to write down a great attack on your pessimism, in abundant reasoned language. And such a thing takes time and thought. Also, I may agree with you. What is pessimism? Why do you say you're becoming a pessimist? What does it mean? He may (I say to myself) mean that he thinks that the Universe is bad as a whole, or that it's bad just now, or that, more locally and importantly, things aren't going to get any better in our time and our country, no matter how much we preach Socialism and clean hearts at them. Is it the last two? Are you telling us that the world is, after all, bad and, what's more, horrible, without enough seeds of good in it? I, writing poetry and reading books and living at Grantchester all day, feel rather doubtful and ignorant about 'The world' – about England and men, and what they're like. Still, I see some, besides the University gang. I see all these queer provincials in this town, upper and middle and lower class. And God knows they're sterile enough. But I feel a placid healthy Physician about it all. (Only I don't know what drugs to recommend.) This is because I've such an overflowing (if intermittent) flood of anti-pessimism in me. I'm using the word now in what is, I expect, its most important sense, of a feeling rather than a reasoned belief. The horror is not *believing* the Universe is bad – or even believing the world won't improve – on a reasoned and cool examination of all facts, tendencies and values, so much as in a sort of general *feeling* that there isn't potentiality for good in the world and that anyhow it's a fairly dreary business, an absence of much appreciation and hope and a somehow paralysed will for good. As this is a feeling it *may* be caused by reason and experience, or more often by loneliness or soul-measles or indigestion or age or anything else. And it can equally be cured by other things than reason: by energy or weather or good people, as well as by a wider ethical grasp, at least so I've found in the rather slight temporary fits of depression I've had in exile and otherwise lately – or even in an enormous period of Youthful Tragedy with which I started at Cambridge. I have a remedy. It's a dangerous one, but I think very good on the whole; though it may lead to a sterile but ecstatic content, or even to the asylum. In practice I find it doesn't – or hasn't yet – made me inefficient.

I am addressing an Adult School on Sunday. I have started a group for studying the Minority Report here. I am going to Cambridge in a week to oversee, with the light of pure reason, the powerful energies of those who are setting forth the new Fabian Rooms; and later, to put the rising generations, Fabians and otherwise, on the way of Light, all next term. The remedy is mysticism, or Life, I'm not sure which. Do not leap or turn pale at the word Mysticism. I do not mean any religious thing, or any form of belief. I still burn and torture Christians daily. It is merely the *feeling* – or a kindred one – which underlay the mysticism of the wicked Mystics. Only I refuse to be cheated by the *feeling* into any kind of *belief*. *They* were convinced by it that the world was very good or that the Universe was one or that God existed. I don't any more believe the world to be good. Only I do get rid of the despair that it isn't, and I certainly seem to see additional possibilities of its getting better. It consists in just looking at people and things as themselves – neither as useful nor moral nor ugly nor anything else, but just as being. At least that's a philosophical description of it. What happens is that I suddenly feel the extraordinary value and importance of everybody I meet, and almost everything I see. In *things* I am moved in this way especially by some things; but in people by almost all people. That is, when the mood is on me. I roam about places – yesterday I did it even in Birmingham! – and sit in trains and see the essential glory and beauty of all the people I meet. I can watch a dirty middle-aged tradesman in a railway-carriage for hours, and love every dirty greasy sulky wrinkle in his weak chin and every button on his spotted unclean waistcoat. I know their states of mind are bad. But I'm so much occupied with their being there at all, that I don't have time to think of that. I tell you that a Birmingham goaty tariff-reform fifth-rate business-man is splendid and immortal and desirable. It's the same about the things of ordinary life. Half an hour's roaming about a street or village or railway station shows so much beauty that it is impossible to be anything but wild with suppressed exhilaration. And it's not only beauty, and beautiful things. In a flicker of sunlight on a blank wall, or a reach of muddy pavement, or smoke from an engine at night there's a sudden significance and importance and inspiration that makes the breath stop with a gulp of certainty and happiness. It's not that the wall or the smoke seem important for anything, or suddenly reveal any general statement, or are rationally seen to be good and beautiful in themselves – only that *for you* they're perfect and unique. It's like being in love with a person. One doesn't (now-a-days, and if one's clean-minded) think the person better or more beautiful or larger than the truth. Only one is extraordinarily excited that the person, exactly as he is, uniquely and splendidly just exists. It is a feeling, not a belief. Only it is a feeling that has amazing results. I suppose my occupation is being in love with the Universe – or (for it is an important difference) with certain spots and moments of it. I wish to God I could express myself. I have a vague notion that this is all very incoherent. But the upshot of it is that one's too happy to *feel* pessimistic; and too much impressed by the immense value and potentialities of *everything* to *believe* in pessimism, for the following reason, and in the following sense.

Every action, one knows (as a good Determinist), has an eternal effect. And every action, therefore, which leads on the whole to good, is '*frightfully*' important. For the good mystic knows how jolly 'good' is. It is not a question of either getting to Utopia in the year 2,000, or not. There'll be so much good then, and so much evil. And we can affect it. There – from the purely rational point of view – is the beginning and end of the whole matter. It oughtn't to make any difference to our efforts whether the good in 2000 A.D. will be a lot greater than it is now, or a little greater, or less. In any case, the amount of good we can cause by doing something, or can sub-tract by not doing it, remains about the same. And that is all that ought to matter. Lately, when I've been reading up the Elizabethans, and one or two other periods, I've been amazed more than ever at the way things change. Even in talking to my Uncle of 70 about the Victorians, it comes out astoundingly. The whole machinery of life, and the minds of every class and kind of man, change beyond recog-nition every generation. I don't know that 'Progress' is certain. All I know is that change is. These solid, solemn, provincials, and old maids, and business men, and all the immovable system of things I see round me will vanish like smoke. All this present overwhelming reality will be as dead and odd and fantastic as crinolines or 'a dish of *tay*'. Something will be in its place, inevitably. And what that something will be, depends on me. With such superb work to do, and with the wild adventure of it all, and with the other minutes (too many of them) given to the enchantment of being even for a moment alive in a world of real matter (not that imitation, gilt stuff, one gets in Heaven) and actual people – I have no time now to be a pessimist.

I don't know why I have scribbled down these thin insane vapourings. I don't suppose you're still as desperate as you were when you wrote in June. When are you coming to Cambridge? I am going to Germany for the Spring Term. But if you can get over next term, are you coming out to stay at Grantchester? I lead a lovely and dim and rustic life there and have divine food. Hugh [Dalton] is going to be in London, and Gerald [Shove] is old as the hills and withered as a spider, and I am the oldest Fabian left (except Tram,[1] who is senile) and I dodder about and smile with toothless gums on all the gay young sparks of the Fabian Society, to whom I am more than a father. So you might tell me if you are going to shake off for a day or a month the ghastly coils of British Family Life and of Modern Industry that you are wound in, and come to see the bovine existence of a farmer.

In the name of God and the Republic
Rupert

[1] V. H. Mottram.

To Frances Cornford   *Pension Bellevue, etc.* [*Munich*]
(only for a week more)
c. 10–15 February 1911

The worst of solitude – or the best – is, that one begins poking at one's own soul, examining it, cutting the soft and rotten parts away. And where's one to stop? Have you ever had, at lunch or dinner, an over-ripe pear or apple, and, determined to make the best of it, gone on slicing off the squashy bits? You may imagine me, in München, at a German lunch with Life, discussing hard, and cutting away at the bad parts of the dessert. 'Oh!' says Life, courteous as ever, 'I'm sure you've got a bad Soul there. Please don't go on with it! Leave it, and take another! I'm so sorry!' But, knowing I've taken the last, and polite anyhow, 'Oh no, *please!*' I say, scraping away, 'it's really all right. It's only a little gone, here and there – on the outside. . . . There's plenty that's quite good. I'm quite enjoying it.

You always have such delightful Souls! . . .' And after a minute, when there's a circle of messy brown round my plate, and in the centre a rather woebegone brown-white thin shapeless scrap, the centre of the thing, Life breaks in again, seeing my plight, 'Oh, but you can't touch any of that! It's bad right through! I'm sure Something must have Got Into it! Let me ring for another! There is sure to be some in the Larder. . . .' But it won't do, you know. So I rather ruefully reply 'Ye-e-s, I'm afraid it *is* impossible. But I won't have another, thanks. I don't really want one at all. I only took it out of mere greed . . . and to have something to do. Thank you, I've had quite enough. Such excellent meat and pudding! I've done splendidly. . . . But to go on with our conversation. About Literature – you were saying, I think . . . ?' and so the incident's at an end.

Dear! dear! it's very trying being ever so exalted one day & ever so desperate the next – this self-knowledge (*why* did that old fool class it with Self-reverence and Self-control? They're rarely seen together)! But so one lives in Munich.

And then your letter came! So many thanks. It made me shake with joy to know that Cambridge and England (as I know it) was all as fine as ever. That Jacques & Ka should be sitting in a *café* looking just like themselves – oh God! what an incredible lovely superb world! I fairly howled my triumph down the ways of this splendid city 'Oh! you fat muddy-faced grey jolly Germans who despise me because I don't know your rotten language. Oh! the people I know – and you don't! Oh! you poor things!' And they all growl at me because they don't know why I glory over them. But, of course, part of the splendour is that – if one only knew it – they, too – these Germans – are all sitting in *cafés* and looking just like themselves. That knowledge sets me often dreaming in a vague, clerical, world-mystic, spirit over my solitary coffee in one of the innumerable *cafés* here in which I spend my days. I find myself smiling a dim gentle poetic paternal Jehovah-like smile – over the ultimate excellence of humanity – at people of, obviously, the most frightful lives and reputations at other tables; who come presently sidling towards me. My mysticism vanishes and, in immense terror, I fly suddenly into the street. . . . Oh, but they're a kindly people. Every night I sit in a *café* near here, after the opera, and read the day-old *Times* (!) and drink – prepare to hear the depths of debauchery into which the young are led in these wicked foreign cities! – HOT MILK, a large glassful. Last night I spilt the whole of the hot milk over myself, while I was trying to negotiate the Literary Supplement. You've no idea how much of me a large glass of hot milk can cover. I was entirely white, except for my scarlet face. All the people in the café crowded round & dabbed me with dirty pocket-handkerchiefs. A kindly people. Nor did I give in. I ordered more hot milk and finished my supplement, damp but International.

Oh! no! Cambridge isn't very dim and distant, nor [E.J.] Dent a pink shade. I somehow manage, these days, to be aware of two places at once. I used to find it wasn't worth while; and to think that the great thing was to let go completely of a thing when you've done with it, and turn wholly and freshly to the next. 'Being able to take and to let go and to take, and knowing when to take and when to let go, and knowing that life's this – is the only way to happiness' is the burden of the Marschallin in *The Rosenkavalier* (the rage of Germany just now!). There's some truth in it. But sometimes, now, I find I can weave two existences together and enjoy both, and be aware of the unique things of each. It's true that as I write, there's an attitude of Jacques' or a slow laugh of Ka's or a moon at Grantchester or a speech of Dickinson's, that I'd love, and that I'm missing. But there'll be other such, no doubt, in May and June – and what if I'd not met the lovable Mr Leuba (and so differently lovable from an *English* unsuccessful journalist!) or the fascinating Miss Van Something or Other of Paris, or the interesting & wicked de Ravelli, or Dr Wolfskell who is shy and repeats Swinburne in large quantities with a villainous German accent, but otherwise knows no English, or that bearded man in the *café*, or the great Hegedin or Professor Sametsen? And what if I'd not seen Bozetti as Octavian, and Steinhals as Hans Sachs & Craft as Salome, and Steindruck as John Gabriel Borkman and the El Greco crucifixion & the Forain drawings & the good Diez's fantasies[?]

Eh, but I have grown clerical & solemn & moral. That is because I've been seeing so much Ibsen lately. I apologize. They do Ibsen here a lot – not so well as I'd been led to expect. The acting is, all round, nothing like as good as the English acting. Still, they do Ibsen: that's the great thing. I'm old-fashioned enough to admire that man vastly. I've seen five or six of his plays in four weeks. They always leave me prostrate. But if the Cambridge Stage Society want a stage-manager for Ibsen, they'll know where to come!

No. I've not yet been proposed to by young ladies in plaid blouses, not even one at a time. Still, your warning has made me tread cautiously. As a matter of fact I know only one or two such. Most of the people I see are working at some sensible thing like writing, music or painting, and are free and comradely. I made one or two incursions into German & Anglo-German Philistia, & came hurriedly forth. I'm damnably sorry for the plaid blouses (who *do* exist there and who are, at present, so much better than their mothers). I saw two stifling and crying. But I'm not going back to rescue them.

But in ordinary, & nicer ways I meet a lot of jolly people. It's true, a lot, I think – what you say about friends: but, oh dear people! it *is* fun going away and making thousands of acquaintances. I never talk or read a word of German. But I enjoy life hugely. There's Miss Grove, now: who has such a queer view of Cambridge & so hates it. (But what of the good part she *knows*, she likes.) She turns out, on cross-examination, *not* to be an illegitimate daughter of Mrs [J.G.] Fraser's, only a daughter by an earlier, & French, husband. Fancy being introduced to her in Munich! We swop Cambridge scandal. Then there's dear Professor Semon & his nice wife. 'There is one person in Cambridge I correspond with', said he at tea, 'do you know Pr-r-rofessor Doctor Fr-r-rancis Darrrwin?' I thought for a long time, & then it slowly dawned on me that I did. He produced a letter from your father to prove that he lied not.

I finish this tourist's effusion at 2 o'the morning, sitting up in bed, with my army blanket round me. My feet, infinitely disconnected, & southward, inform me that tonight it is freezing again. The bed is covered with Elizabethan & German books I may or may not read ere I sleep. In the distance glimmers the gaunt white menacing Ibsenite stove that casts a gloom over my life. The Algerian dancing-master next door is, for once, quiet. I rather think the Dragon overhead (the Dragon = that monstrous livid faced screeching pouchy creature of infinite age & horror who screams opposite me at dinner and talks with great crags of food projecting from her mouth: a decayed Countess, they say) is snoring. I have this evening been to *The Wild Duck*. It is not as good, I rather thought, as most. *Do* read 'John Gabriel Borkman'!

I'm glad about Vaughan-Williams: & that the play's going on.[1] I've not got far enough really to appreciate the difficulties, I think. I spend my time on lyrics – there's nothing new complete enough to send yet, though. Have you wholly left such things for your long flights? My labour is wasted: for though I've been inspired a lot lately, it's poor stuff; & moreover Dent[2] is now wanting me to leave out 'some too outspoken' poems! I am taking a Dignified line.

Oh, I sometimes make up a picture of Conduit Head, with Jacques in a corner & Gwen on other cushions and Justin on his back & Ka on a footstool & Francis smoking & Frances in the chair to the right (facing the fire). . . . It stands out against the marble of the *Luitpold Café* & then fades. . . . But say it's true!

All love to both. Even with an enormous stomach & a beard in Munich.

Yours
Rupert

[1] F.C.'s *Death and the Princess*.
[2] The publisher. The plan that he should publish Brooke's *Poems* fell through.

To Frank Sidgwick

The Old Vicarage
Grantchester
Wednesday, 20 September 1911

Dear Sidgwick,[1]

Is the objection to 'Lust' only that it's bad as poetry, or also that it's shocking as morals? I can't see that it's any worse as poetry than the rest of the book (except one or two poems). Technically it's not much, I admit; but any fool can write a technically good sonnet. And I hoped that the newness of the idea might counterbalance that.

If it's thought to be improper, it must be sadly misunderstood. Its meaning is quite 'proper' and so moral as to be almost untrue. If the title's too startling *Libido* or *'Ἐπιθυμία* could be substituted; tho' I'm afraid that would only make it more obscure.

My own feeling is that to remove it would be to overbalance the book still more in the direction of unimportant prettiness. There's plenty of that sort of wash in the other pages for the readers who like it. They needn't read the parts which are new and serious. About a lot of the book I occasionally feel like Ophelia, that I've turned 'Thought and affliction, passion, hell itself . . . to favour and to prettiness'. So I'm extra keen about the places where I think that thought and passion are, however clumsily, *not* so transmuted. This was one of them. It seemed to have qualities of reality & novelty that made up for the clumsiness. The expression is only good in places. But the idea seemed to me important and moving. I know a lot of people who like my earlier work better than my present. They will barely notice this sonnet. There are others who prefer my present stuff. I've shown the sonnet to some of them. They thought it good (by my standards, whatever they may be!). And they weren't, I assure you – though they were of all ages and kinds – shocked.

I should like it to stand, as a representative in the book of abortive poetry against literary verse; & because I can't see any aesthetic ground against it which would not damn ¾ of the rest of the book too, or any moral ground at all. If your reader has misunderstood the sonnet I will explain it to him. If you really think it finally ruins the chances of the book, I suppose it ought to go. If you think it will only decrease the sales, we could make some additional agreement about the number sold within the year, or something. If it's too near the beginning, it can be buried.

Yours

Rupert Brooke

I should like to know if the acknowledgement at the beginning is all right.

I can come to London (preferably Thursdays or Saturdays) if there's anything that needs discussion.

<hr/>

[1] Of Sidgwick and Jackson, publishers of the *Poems*.

To Katharine Cox   [*Rugby*]

[*March 1912*]

Noon: Friday

Nothing today. Do I deduce that you were tired last night? Ka! It raineth. Jacques is not yet here: he comes at 2.15, I hear. Silence, as Mr Ivanov so wonderfully says, is more than Words. So, though you hear nothing, think of me loving you a good deal during the week-end.

It's so hard to write just now: for I'm all the while occupied in soothing a new inmate, who was pretty disconsolate till she met me. A Cat. She arrived last night. Tell James. She kisses the end of my chin as I write. She kisses less well than you. I read a story about a woman who knew 127 different ways of kissing. I suppose you don't know of a book about it or anything?

The Ranee was so excited about Disestablishment last night, that she forgot you. And this morning, so far, she's lain pretty low.

I sit in here like a weather-beaten mariner, thinking of the stormy sea. Do you know it's less than three weeks since we were at Starnberg? The things – the adventures, Ka, we've been through together! It's quite certain no other two people in the world could have done it. I'm so old and proud and strong.

I forgot to tell you, I went to tea with Froylein on Tuesday and we talked Germany, and she was very keen on the *Rosenkavalier* and I was suddenly ferocious and talked of Nietzsche.

An Interlude. The Ranee entered from the rain, screaming 'Here's Mrs Bullock'. So I winked and put my tongue out; and the Ranee, as Mrs Bullock entered behind her, jigged and grimaced and shouted, in a stage whisper, 'You'd better go upstairs'. So here I am, upstairs. We don't like Mrs Bullock. But the Ranee's sorry for her, and helps her.

The Ranee, I'm glad to say, has given up the lost-child craze. At one time she used to wander about the streets accosting all small, lonely, tearful children. With infinite patience she used to discover they came from the other end of the town. Determinedly the Ranee would grip the lost baby, and march it back two miles to its hovel. Sometimes she'd meet an upper-class acquaintance bound in the same direction. 'Mr (or Mrs) Bradby's going in your direction. How fortunate!' the Ranee then roars to the amazed baby. Then to the sky, 'It *says* it lives in Paradise Court, and its name is Wilkins.' She would press the dirty small hand into the clean large one; and rush in the direction of the next small lonely creature: leaving a hot-faced wrathful young master or master's wife, and a hot-faced frightened baby to tread their joint paths in silence. But generally she followed it out to the end, scolded and made friends with the Mother, and adopted the whole family.

Thanks for St John's Wood. You seem to expect *me* to expect the whole family to be in mourning, tears, and insomnia. No. It's not done, or thought of, in those circles. I'm sorry Noel's looking ill.

I cease. It will be very nice when you come. *Do* behave, though. Will you remember *not* to call me 'Dearest'? Think it. I think it continually. I'm very well; and loving you very much; and quite happy, and only thinking that these days are going by, wasted a little, when one's well and twenty-four, and you're in London.

Go on resting – and loving. You are very splendid.

Rupert

To Cathleen Nesbitt   *Gray's Inn*
Saturday afternoon
[8 March 1913]

I adore you.

I was in a stupor all yesterday; partly because of my tiredness, and partly because of your face.

I'm gradually getting normaler again.

Why do you look like that? Have you any idea what you look like? I didn't know that human beings could look like that. It's as far beyond beauty as beauty is beyond ugliness.

I'd say you were beautiful if the word weren't a million times too feeble.

Hell!

But it's very amazing.

It makes me nearly imbecile when I'm talking with you – I apologize for my imbecility: it's your fault. You shouldn't look like that.

It really makes life very much worth while. My God!

I adore you.

Rupert

To Katharine Cox   *America* [*New York*]
June
[Postmark: 25 June 1913]

Oh, child!

I've kept thinking how to write in such a way as would be best for you. But I won't try to. There are disadvantages in telling the truth. But between us it is still the best.

My dear, I've been worrying so about writing. And almost every night as I crossed I dreamt about you. And you always seemed in pain. I hope to God nothing extra is wrong.

Being alone, I incline to get mad ideas. But also I'm getting to see all the past more steadily. So I'll try to stick to that, and minimize the former. And I'll try to put my feelings and ideas as clearly and honestly as I can before you. Forgive them if they hurt (I don't think they especially will): and forgive them where they're bad.

Well Ka, there are, as far as I can see, three purposes that drive me in what I do to or about you: (1) to be myself as little as possible worried or spoilt by uselessly keeping wounds open; (2) to see to it that you're able to keep clean and guarded against evil; (3) to see that you get clear and as happy as maybe, as soon as possible, and have the best and swiftest chance of realizing the loveliness and greatness of you.

I needn't go into the feelings on which these purposes are based. You know them.

The first I know is selfish, and whenever I'm conscious of it, I minimize it. I know what I owe to you and me (this is all very academically written). And I know that however we buy peace or anything else, you pay most.

I've tried for the second and third, as far as I could do anything. I thought I could secure both by not seeing you, and yet being in touch, writing.

I liked it too, my dear. It remains that we know each other better than anybody else. It was nice, writing and understanding.

But it has come upon me that it won't do. To realize the third purpose, I've got to leave the second out of my control. I've got to leave it to you.

You *must* get right clear of me, cease to love me, love and marry somebody – and somebody worthy of you.

Oh my dear, let's try together to put things right. It's so hard to know what to do – one's so stupid and blind and blundering.

What I feel about you is this – I'm not arguing if it's true, I just state it as it comes to my heart – 'Ka is more precious than anything. She has marvellous goodness and greatness in her. She has things so lovely it hurts to name them. She is greater and better, potentially, than any woman I know: and more woman. She is very blind, and infinitely easy to lead astray. Her goodness makes her a prey. She needs looking after more than anybody else in the world. She's a lovely child.'

And with that in my heart I have to leave you. It's very difficult. Oh Ka, you don't know how difficult it is! So have pity on me. And forgive my breaking out like this.

I have your promises and your experience, and the love of your friends for you to comfort me. No one could ever draw friends to them as you can. If it comes to this responsibility question, my dear – you've a great deal of responsibility.

And now – though I'm a bit hysterical – I've a clearer view. And what you wrote gave me strength. You give strength. You said, I mean, that we're free to go – but only to clean people. Oh, it's true, child. I feel it now. It comes of my seeing something of what I owe you.

Oh God, I'm such a coward. I funk writing to you. Because it makes me concentrate on thinking about you. And that gives me pain – thinking about you. I haven't touched this letter for days and days.

There's nothing to say, but what I've said. It's only that. You're not getting better. I don't know how I can make you get better. I'm helpless. I can only leave you altogether. I do not do you any good or help you by being in touch with you. And I harm you by keeping myself too alive in your heart. The only good I do is by keeping you sensible and straight with advice – oh, take that from other people, and that's all I want.

Dear child, dearest Ka, whom I've loved and known, you must get well and happy, and live the great life you can. It's the only thing I care for. Oh, child, I know I've done you great wrong. What could I do? It was so difficult. You had driven me mad.

I'm sorry for the wrong. It's the one thing in the world I'm sorry for: though I've done a lot of evil things.

I can't bear it that it is I have hurt you.

But you'll grow, and be the fine Ka. – In the end I know you, that you can't be broken or spoilt, I do know you.

What is there? Unless in the two weeks' mail that's waiting for me somewhere, or in reply to this, there's something from you that needs reply, I shan't write again. In a few years we'll meet. Till then – we can dodge each other. If we meet – we're big enough to manage that. The creatures who watch won't get much change out of us. If I irritate you or you want me out of the way – tell somebody, or me. But it won't happen. And if you see writings of mine – don't ever feel they're about you, and be hurt. I only write about suggested things and imagined you know.

There's one thing. Do you mind? I want to break the rule and give you a thing. A statuette of a mother and a child. It's now kept for me by Eddie. A tiny thing. He knows you're going to send him an address to send it you at. So when you're in England, will you send him the address?

I give it you; because you'll be the greatest mother in the world. And I'll not be anything but sad, till I've heard you're happy, and with a child of your own.

Let it stand: not for what we did: but for what we learnt.

I thought at one time I'd only learnt bad from you: now I know that before and after and over it all I learnt good – all that I have.

I've got to leave you. But if ever it happens you're in ultimate need of help – it may – you know I'll come, at any time and from any place, if you want it.

I'm very happy and well, travelling. And in the end I'll get back and work. Don't think of me.

Please, Ka, be good and happy: and stick to and be helped by your friends. That's the last thing I ask.

This is so bad a letter: and I wanted to make everything clear. Do believe. See what I've tried to write.

Preaching and everything aside, let's just be Ka and Rupert for a minute: and say good-bye so. I'll be loyal to the things we've learnt together: and you be loyal. And life'll be good.

Dear love, good bye
Rupert

To Edmund Gosse   McDonald's Hotel, Suva, Fiji
[Picture of a sailing boat full   *19 November 1913*
of Fijians – palm trees, etc.]
Dear Edmund Gosse,

Forgive this gaudy tropical notepaper. It's all I can find. I've just got into this place, from Samoa. I said to myself 'Fiji is obviously the wildest place I can get to round here. The name, and pictures of the inhabitants, prove it.' And lo! a large English town, with two banks, several churches, dental surgeons, a large gaol, auctioneers, bookmakers, two newspapers, and all the other appurtenances of civilization! But I fancy I'll be able to get some little boat and go off to some smaller wilder islands. This place and the country round have been stocked with Hindus, to work the plantations. Fifty thousand of them. For the Fijian has that curious quality, inexplicable and abhorrent to the white man, that he will not work for other men, as long as he has enough to live on without. And in this magic part of the world, so long as he is left with a few patches of land of his own, he can do this. He has only to shin up a coco-nut tree, and pull out a root, and there's food for the next week. Perplexing country! At home everything is so simple, and choice is swift, for the sensible man. There is only the choice between writing a good sonnet and making a million pounds. Who could hesitate? But *here* the choice is between writing a sonnet and climbing a straight hundred-foot coco-nut palm, or diving forty feet from a rock into pellucid blue-green water. Which is the better, there? One's European literary soul begins to be haunted by strange doubts and shaken with fundamental fantastic misgivings. I think I shall return home.

But if I *do* return, I know I shall be wanting, every now and then, to slip away to the South Seas once more. The attraction's queer. It's not really Romance. At least, I associate with Romance, something of veiled ladies, and moonlit serenades, and narrow Venetian or Oriental streets. Something just perceptibly feverish. But this is quite another world. It's getting back to one's childhood, somehow: but not to the real childhood, rather to the childhood that never was, but is portrayed by a kindly sentimental memory; a time of infinite freedom, no responsibility, perpetual play in the open air, unceasing sunshine, never-tiring limbs, and a place where time is not, and supper takes place at breakfast-time and breakfast in the afternoon, & life consists of expeditions by moonlight and diving naked into waterfalls and racing over white sands beneath feathery brooding palm-trees.

Oh, it's horribly true, what you wrote, that one only finds in the South Seas what one brings there. Perhaps I could have found Romance if I'd brought it. Yet I do not think one could help but find *less* trouble than one brings. The idea of the South Seas as a place of passion and a Mohammedan's paradise is but a sailor's yarn. It is nothing near so disturbing. It is rather the opposite of alcohol, according to the Porter's definition, for it promotes performance but takes away desire. Yet I can even understand Stevenson finding – as you put it – the Shorter Catechism there. One keeps realizing, however unwillingly, responsibility. I noticed in myself and in the other white people in Samoa, a trait I have remarked in schoolmasters and in the 'agents' who are appointed in Canada to live with, and look after, the Indians. You know that sort of slightly irritated tolerance, and lack of *ir*responsibility, that mark the pedagogue? One feels that one's a White Man* – ludicrously. I kept thinking I was in the Sixth at Rugby, again. These dear good people, with their laughter and friendliness and crowns of flowers – one feels that one *must* protect them. If one was having an evening

---

* Vide R. Kipling *passim.*

out with Falstaff and Bardolph themselves, and a small delightful
child came up with 'Please I'm lost and want to get home', wouldn't
one have to leave good fellowship and spend the evening in mean
streets tracking its abode? That's, I fancy, how the white man feels
in these forgotten – and dissolving – pieces of heaven, the South
Seas. And that perhaps is what Stevenson felt. I don't know enough
about him. His memory is sweet there, in Samoa; especially among
the natives. The white men – mostly traders – who remain from his
time – have – for such people – very warm recollections of his personality, but – with a touch of pathos – avow themselves unable to
see any merit in his work. Such stuff as the *Wrong Box* they frankly
can't understand a grown man writing. I went up the steep hill
above Vailima, where the grave is. It's a high and lovely spot. I took
a Samoan of about 20 to guide me. He was much impressed by
Stevenson's fame. 'That fellow' he said 'I think every fellow in
world know him.' Then he looked puzzled. 'But my father say', he
went on, 'Stevenson no big man – small man.' That a slight man of
medium height should be so famous, puzzled him altogether. If he
had been seven feet high, now! Fame is a curious thing.

I go round to Tahiti soon, and so back, to the bustle of the States.
Then gradually nearer home. Many thanks for your last letter. It's
nice to know that England, in spite of everything one reads in the
papers, still stands! A Merry Christmas! My best greetings to the
whole household –

Yours ever
Rupert Brooke

Oh, *do* forgive the envelope![1] My own – in this awful climate –
are all fast stuck, tho' never filled, like an English churchman's
mind. And I'm reduced to these fantastic affairs.

[1] It has the same picture on it as the paper.

To Jacques Raverat   *Suva, Fiji*
                                            1 December 1913

My dear,

This'll get you next year, won't it? Fancy us all having waded
through as far as 1914! – perhaps we shan't though, even yet.

I wander, seeking peace, and ensuing it. Several times I've nearly
found it: once, lately, in a Samoan village. But I had to come away
from there in a hurry, to catch a boat: and forgot to pack it. But I'll

have it yet. Fragments I have found, on various hills or by certain seas. It would be wonderful to find it.

*

Oh, I shall return. The South Seas are Paradise. But I prefer England. I shall return when I'm certain. I'm nearly certain now. I'd once thought it necessary to marry. I *approve* of marriage for the world. I think you're all quite right. So don't be alarmed. But not for me. I'm too old. The Point of marriage is Peace – to work in. But can't one get it otherwise? Why, certainly, when one's old. And so I will. I know what things are good: friendship and work and conversation. These I shall have. How one can fill life, if one's energetic, and knows how to dig! I have thought of a thousand things to do, in books and poems and plays and theatres and societies and housebuilding and dinner-parties when I get Home. Ho, but we shall have fun. Now we have so painfully achieved middle-age, shall we not reap the fruits of that achievement, my dyspeptic friend? By God! yes. Will you come and walk with me in Spain next summer? And will you join me on the Poet's Round, a walk I've planned? – One starts from Charing X, in a south-easterly direction, and calls on De la Mare at Anerley, on S.W. and find Davies at Sevenoaks, a day's march to Belloc at Kingsland, then up to Wibson[1] on the borders of Gloucestershire, back by (Stratford), Rugby, and the Chilterns, where Masefield and Chesterton dwell. Wouldn't it give one a queer idea of England!

Three months in a year I'm going to live with you and Gwen, three with Dudley and Anne [Ward], three with the Ranee, and three alone. A perfect life. I almost catch the next boat to 'Frisco at the thought of it.

There is nothing in the world like friendship. And there is no man who has had such friends as I, so many, so fine, so various, so multiform, so prone to laughter, so strong in affection and so permanent, so trustworthy, so courteous, so stern with vices, and so blind to faults or folly, of such swiftness of mind and strength of body, so polypist* and yet benevolent, and so apt both to make jokes and to understand them. Also, their faces are beautiful, and I love them. I repeat a very long list of their names, every night before I sleep. Friendship is always exciting and yet always safe. There is no lust in it, and therefore no poison. It is cleaner than love, and

* = of many faiths, *not* bespattered by a parrot, O Greekless!

older; for children and very old people have friends, but they do not love. It gives more and takes less, it is fine in the enjoying, and without pain when absent, and it leaves only good memories. In love all laughter ends with an ache, but laughter is the very garland on the head of friendship. I will not love, and I will not be loved. But I will have friends round me continually, all the days of my life, and in whatever lands I may be. So we shall laugh and eat and sing and go great journeys in boats and on foot and write plays and perform them and pass innumerable laws taking their money from the rich.

I err. I praise too extravagantly, conveying an impression that friendship always gives peace. And even at the moment I [feel] a hunger too rending for complete peace, to see all your faces again, and to eat food with you.

No homesick exile I, though. God, no! I've my time and emotions filled to overflowing with wandering through the strange and savage mountains of this land, or sitting and watching the varied population of the streets, Indians imported for labour cringing by in yellow and pink silks and muslins, and Fijians swinging along half naked with bun-faces and heads of hair just like Francis[Cornford]'s and the women with a gait like – oh, like no one you've ever seen in your misty tight-laced feminist lands.

But I'll not tell you of Abroad. Come and see it yourself. I do but write to tell you that I love you both very much, and that I live, and that any moment I may turn up and demand to stay with you for a year, so lay a place for me, and have a bottle or two of stout in.

Oh, I forgot – I've got to have rooms and live in King's for a term or two or three. I'll make 'em sit up. I'm going to get up lectures by Impossible People on all Subjects outside the Curriculum. Wibson and I are going to lecture on 'Poetry', W. H. Davies on 'Fleas', Harry Lauder on – Whatever he likes, and you and Gwen on 'Art'. I'm going to turn that damned hole into a Place of Education. Oh, and Eddie on 'Manners'. When you go through London, see that man – although Gwen's so bloody supercilious about him. It's eccentric, I admit, to conceal a good heart beneath good manners, but forgivable, surely. And he'd love to see you. He's really so nice, and deserves well. I fear lest you children get cut off too far from the world, without me to look after you.

Farewell, farewell, my dears. Won't 1914 be fun!

Talofa – with love
Rupert

Tell me, sometime, that you've seen Ka once or twice, and that she's well.

¹ His name for the poet, Wilfred Wilson Gibson.

To Violet Asquith   *Nearly half-way*
                                through December [1913]
          Somewhere in the mountains of Fiji.

Dear Miss Asquith,

Forgive this paper. Its limpness is because it has been in terrific thunderstorms, and through most of the rivers in Fiji, in the last few days. Its marks of dirt are because small naked brown babies *will* crawl up and handle it. And any blood-stains will be mine. The point is, will they. . . . It's absurd, I know. It's twenty years since they've eaten anybody, in this part of Fiji, and far more since they've done what I particularly and unreasonably detest – fastened the victim down, cut pieces off him one by one, and cooked and eaten them before his eyes. To witness one's own transubstantiation into a naked black man, that seems the last indignity. Consideration of the thoughts that pour through the mind of the ever-diminishing remnant of a man, as it sees its last limbs cooking, moves me deeply. I have been meditating a sonnet, as I sit here, surrounded by dusky faces and gleaming eyes:

'Dear, they have poached the eyes you loved so well.' It'd do well for No. 101 and last, in a modern sonnet-sequence, wouldn't it? I don't know how it would go on. The fourth line would have to be 'And all my turbulent lips are *maître-d'hotel*' – I don't know how to scan French, I fancy that limps. But *all* is very strong in the modern style.

The idea comes out in a slighter thing –

The limbs that erstwhile charmed your sight,
Are now a savage's delight;
The ear that heard your whispered vow
Is one of many *entrées* now;
Broiled are the arms in which you clung
And devilled is the angelic tongue; . . .
And oh! my anguish as I see
A Black Man gnaw your favourite knee!
Of the two eyes that were your ruin,
One now observes the other stewing.

My lips (the inconstancy of man!)
Are yours no more. The legs that ran
Each dewy morn their love to wake,
Are now a steak, are now a steak! . . .

Oh, dear! I suppose it ought to end on the Higher Note, the
Wider Outlook. Poetry has to, they tell me. You may caress details
all the main part of the poem, but at last you have to open the window
– turn to God, or Earth, or Eternity, or any of the Grand Old
Endings. It gives Uplift, as we Americans say. And that's so
essential. (Did you ever notice how the Browning family's poems
all refer suddenly to God in the last line. It's laughable if you read
through them in that way. 'What if that friend happened to be –
God?', 'What comes next – Is it God?', 'And with God be the rest',
'And if God choose, I shall but love thee better after Death' – etc.
etc. I forget the mall, now. It shows what the Victorians were.)
So must I soar –

O love, o loveliest and best,
Natives this *body* may digest,
Whole, and still yours, my *soul* shall dwell,
Uneaten, safe, incoctible.

It's too dull. I shall go out and wander through the forest paths by
the grey moonlight. Fiji in moonlight is like nothing else in this life
or the next. It is all dim colours and all scents. And here, where it's
high up, the most fantastically shaped mountains in the world tower
up all around, and little silver clouds and wisps of mist run bleating
up and down the valleys and hill-sides like lambs looking for their
mother. There's only one thing on earth as beautiful: & that's
Samoa by night. That's utterly different, merely Heaven, sheer
loveliness. You lie on a mat in a cool Samoan hut and look out on
the white sand under the high palms, and a gentle sea, & the black
line of the reef a mile out & moonlight over everything, floods and
floods of it, not sticky, like Honolulu moonlight, not to be eaten
with a spoon, but flat and abundant, such that you could slice thin
golden-white shavings off it, as off cheese . . . and among it all are the
loveliest people in the world, moving and running and dancing like
gods and goddesses, very quietly and mysteriously, and utterly
content. It is sheer beauty, so pure that it's difficult to breathe in it
– like living in a Keats world, only it's less syrupy. Endymion without sugar. Completely unconnected with this world.

There is a poem:

I know an Island,
Where the long scented holy nights pass slow,
And there, 'twixt lowland and highland,
The white stream falls into a pool I know,
Deep, hidden with ferns and flowers, soft as dreaming,
Where the brown laughing dancing bathers go.

It ends, after many pages,

I know an Island,
Where the slow fragrant-breathing nights creep past,
And there, 'twixt lowland and highland,
A deep, fern-shrouded murmurous water glimmers;
There I'll come back at last,
And find my friends, the flower-crowned laughing swimmers,
And . . .

I forget. And I've not written the middle part. And it's very bad, like all true poems. I love England; and all the people in it; but oh, how can one know of heaven on earth and not come back to it? I'm afraid I shall slip away from that slithery murky place you're (I suppose) in now, and return. Ridiculous.

I continue in a hot noon, under an orange tree. We rose at dawn and walked many miles and swam seven large rivers and picked and ate many oranges and pine-apples and drank coco-nuts. Now the two 'boys' who carry my luggage are asleep in the shade. They're Fijians of twenty-three or so who know a few words of English. One of them is the finest made man I've ever seen: like a Greek statue come to life: strong as ten horses. To see him strip and swim a half-flooded river is an immortal sight. Last night we stayed in the house of a mountain chief who has spasmodic fierce yearnings after civilization. When these grow strong he sends a runner down to the coast to buy any illustrated papers he can find. He knows no English, but he pastes his favourite pictures up round the wall and muses over them. I lectured on them – fragments of the *Sketch* and *Sphere* for several years – to a half-naked reverent audience last night (through my interpreters of course). The Prince of Wales, looking like an Oxford Undergraduate, elbows two ladies who display 1911 spring fashions. A golf champion in a most contorted position, occupies a central place. He is regarded, I fancy, as a rather potent and violent deity. To his left is 'Miss Viola Tree, as Eurydice', to his right Mrs Granville Barker as Jocasta (or whatever the lady was called), looking infinitely Mycenaean. I explained about incest, shortly, and Mrs B. rose tremendously in Fijian estimation. Why do people like their gods to be so eccentric, always? I fancy I left an impression that she was Mr H. H. Hilton's (is that right? you're a golfer) mother and wife. It is so hard to explain our civilization to simple people. Anyhow, I disturbed their theogony, and elevated Lillah [McCarthy] to the top place. How Eurydice came in puzzled them and me. I fancy they regard her as a holy ghostess, in some sort.

It's very perplexing. These people – Samoans and Fijians – are so much nicer, and so *much* better-mannered than oneself. They are stronger, beautifuller, kindlier, more hospitable and courteous, greater lovers of beauty, and even wittier, than average Europeans. And they are – under our influence – a dying race. We gradually fill their lands with plantations and Indian coolies. The Hawaians, up in the 'Sandwich Islands', have almost altogether gone, and their arts and music with them, and their islands are a replica of America. A cheerful thought, that all these places are to become indistinguishable from Denver and Birmingham and Stuttgart, and the people of dress and behaviour precisely like Herr Schmidt, and Mr Robinson and Hiram O. Guggenheim. And now they're so . . . it's impossible to describe how far nearer the Kingdom of Heaven – or the Garden of Eden – these good naked laughing people are than oneself or one's friends. But I forgot. You are an anti-socialist, and I mustn't say a word against our modern industrial system. I beg your pardon.

I go down to the coast to catch a boat to New Zealand, where I shall post this. Thence to Tahiti, to hunt for lost Gauguins. Then back to barbarism in America. God knows when I shall get home. In the spring, I hope. Is England still there? Forgive this endless scrawl. Don't read it. You'll be far too busy. It gives me pleasure to write it.

I suppose you're rushing from lunch party to lunch party, and dance to dance, and opera to political platform. Won't you come and learn how to make a hibiscus wreath for your hair, and sail a canoe, and swim two minutes under water catching turtles, and dive forty feet into a waterfall, and climb a coco-nut palm? It's more worth while.

Yours from Polynesia
Rupert Brooke

To Violet Asquith   *Hood Battalion*
                                          2nd Naval Brigade
Four days out.   [*8 March 1915*]

All day we've been just out of sight of land, thirty or forty miles away – out of sight, but in smell. There was something earthly in the air, and warm – like the consciousness of a presence in the dark – the wind had something Andalusian in it. It wasn't that wall of scent and invisible blossom and essential spring that knocks you flat, quite suddenly, as you've come round some unseen corner in the atmosphere, fifty miles out from a South Sea Island. But it *was* the good smell of land – and of Spain, too! And Spain I've never seen, and never shall see, maybe. All day I sat and strained my eyes to see, over the horizon, orange groves and Moorish buildings and dark-eyed beauties and guitars and fountains and a golden darkness. But the curve of the world lay between us. Do you know Jan [Masefield]'s favourite story – told very melodiously with deep voiced reverence – about Columbus? Columbus wrote a diary (which Jan reads) and described the coast of America (before Johnny Dodge's day) as he found it – *the* divinest place in the world. 'It was only like the Paradise of the Saints of God' – and then he remembered there was *one* place equal to it, the place where he was born, and goes on – 'or like the gardens of Andalusia in the spring.'

Another day; off Africa.

My dear, I don't know when, after Malta, I shall be able to get a letter through. We're in the dreamiest, most utter, most trustful, ignorance of what's to come. Some even say it'll all be over before we get there. I hope not: and certainly think not. Impossible. I rather figure us scrapping forlornly in some corner of the Troad for years and years. Everyone will forget all about us. We shan't even be told when peace is declared. . . .

Africa looks too glorious for words. I shall go there the minute the war's over – no, the minute our two-millions' plunge into luxury and revelry is over – and spend months there. The mountains look fascinatingly old and wrinkled and ponderous and elephantine: and lovely white mosques and walls and houses, all shining sunward, are laid along their feet. The sea and sky are all the colours of a peacock or a rainbow or a puddle of tar. I sit in a busy vacancy and review my life and the condition of my platoon. And occasionally I dip into a book on the early heresies.

One's so entirely 'surrounded by the horizon of the day', even –
perhaps more – in this odd little respite from war. I've not the
strength of mind to withdraw myself from the current, and think.
Perhaps I never have, even in peace. I'm a hand-to-mouth liver.
God help me.

*

Do not care much what happens to me or what I do. When I give
thought to it at all, I hate people – people I like – to care for me.
I'm selfish. And nothing but harm ever seems to have come of it,
in the past.

I don't know. In some moods that thought seems wrong.
Generally right. I don't know the truth about that – or about anything. But somewhere, I think, there's bad luck about me.

There's a very bright sun, and a lot of comedy in the world; so
perhaps there's some point in my not getting shot. But Also there's
point in my getting shot. Anyway, you're very good to me.

The Staff-Captain is going to seal up the mail bag. Good-bye.

Rupert

To Cathleen Nesbitt   *Off Gallipoli*
(to be opened on his death)   *18 March [1915]*
O my dear,

Life is a very good thing. Thank God I met you. Be happy and
be good. You have been good to me.

Goodbye, dearest child –

Rupert

4
Travel

Brooke wrote to Edward Marsh from Canada:

> For weeks I have not seen or touched a town so old as myself. Horrible! Horrible! They gather round me and say, 'In 1901 Calgary had 139 inhabitants, now it has 75,000': and so forth. I reply, 'My village is also growing. At the time of Julius Caesar it was a bare 300. Domesday Book gives it 347 and it is now close on 390.' Which is ill-mannered of me.

In retelling this story for the *Westminster Gazette*, Brooke modified it (the figures are less precise, the tone is less assertive); but the Englishman's aloofness from a 'world too new' is apparent in *Letters from America*. The first of them provoked a protest from an American: Mr Brooke's concept of American character was 'Dickensian'; he should study Henry James's *The American*. And it was James himself who longed to take him by the hand and 'show him finer lights – eyes of but meaner range, after all, being adequate to the gape at the vertical business blocks and the lurid sky-clamour for more dollars'.

As a lengthy preface to the posthumous collection of these articles, Henry James wrote, shortly before his own death, a remarkable tribute to his friend. In this, the last of his published writings, one senses the 'phantom with weighted motion' of Pound's *Canto VII*:

> *Grave incessu*, drinking the tone of things,
> And the old voice lifts itself weaving an endless sentence.

He strove to express what (to use his favourite word) he thought of as the 'felicity' of his subject. While feeling 'in a manner [Brooke's] sensibility wasted', 'we must leave him to himself and to youth's facility of wonder'.

It is moreover his sign, as it is that of the poetic turn of
mind in general, that we seem to catch him alike in
anticipations or divinations, and in lapses and freshnesses, of
experience that surprise us. He makes various reflections, some
of them all perceptive and ingenious – as about the faces, the
men's in particular, seen in the streets, the public
conveyances and elsewhere; though falling a little short, in
his friendly wondering way, of that bewildered apprehension
of monotony of type, of modelling lost in the desert, which
we might have expected of him . . .

A Canadian correspondent to the *Westminster* made a similar
point (albeit less finely) in attributing to the articles 'both the
merits and defects of the artistic method of writing'. The criticism
could hardly have surprised their author who, in a letter from
'Noo York' to Cathleen Nesbitt, provides (incidentally) a comment
upon James:

Today I have wandered in cars and on foot, noting details
and throwing off hurried, vast, entirely satisfactory generalizations. If I meet a man with a twisted lip, down it goes
'Americans have twisted lips'. In the end I shall shake them
up in a bag, paste them on sheets of paper, and send them
to the *Westminster* at two guineas a column. Such is my
trade.

For good and ill, the articles seem closer in style to modern
journalism than to that of Brooke's own day. What is most remarkable – remembering that they were written often hastily for a week-
end paper in 1913 – is that they should have retained such freshness.
As Marsh observed in an editorial note, Brooke 'would probably
not have republished them in their present form, as he intended to
write a longer book on his travels'. But they are interesting, none
the less: historically, topographically, and not least as expressions
of their author's personality. I have excerpted passages from all
but two of the *Westminster* articles (the exceptions are 'Ontario' and
'The Prairies'), and also from an article on Samoa which appeared
first in the *New Statesman*. Two of the articles, the first of three on
New York ('Arrival') and that on Niagara Falls, are given in full.

Arrival

However sedulously he may have avoided a preparatory reading of those 'impressions' of America which our hurried and observant Great continually record for the instruction of both nations, the pilgrim who is crossing the Atlantic for the first time cannot approach Sandy Hook Bar with so completely blank a mind as he would wish. So, at least, I found. It is not so much that the recent American invasion of London music-halls has bitten into one's brain a very definite taste of a jerking, vital, *bizarre* 'rag-time' civilisation. But the various and vivid comments of friends to whom the news of a traveller's departure is broken excite and predispose the imagination. That so many people who have been there should have such different and decided opinions about it! It must be at least remarkable. I felt the thrill of an explorer before I started. 'A country without conversation,' said a philosopher. 'The big land has a big heart,' wrote a kindly scholar; and, by the same post, from another critic, 'that land of crushing hospitality!' 'It's Hell, but it's fine,' an artist told me. 'El Cuspidorado,' remarked an Oxford man, brilliantly. But one wiser than all the rest wrote: 'Think gently of the Americans. They are so very young; and so very anxious to appear grown-up; and so very lovable.' This was more generous than the unvarying comment of ordinary English friends when they heard of my purpose, 'My God!' And it was more precise than those nineteen several Americans, to each of whom I said, 'I am going to visit America,' and each of whom replied, after long reflection, 'Wal! it's a great country!'

Travelling by the ordinary routes, you meet the American people a week before you meet America. And my excitement to discover what, precisely, this nation was *at*, was inflamed rather than damped by the attitude of a charming American youth who crossed by the same boat. That simplicity that is not far down in any American was very beautifully on the delightful surface with him. The second day out he sidled shyly up to me. 'Of what nationality *are* you?' he asked. His face showed bewilderment when he heard. 'I thought all Englishmen had moustaches,' he said. I told him of the infinite variety, within the homogeneity, of our race. He did not listen, but settled down near me with the eager kindliness of a child. 'You know,' he said, 'you'll never understand America. No, Sir. No Englishman can understand America. I've been in London. In your Houses of Parliament there is one door for peers to go in at, and one for ordinary people. Did I laugh some when I saw that? You bet your, America's not like that. In America one man's just as good as another. You'll never understand America.' I was all humility. His theme and his friendliness fired him. He rose with a splendour which, I had to confess to myself, England could never have given to him. 'Would you like to hear me re-cite to you the Declaration of Independence?' he asked. And he did.

So it was with a fairly blank mind, and yet a hope of under-standing, or at least of seeing, something very remarkably fresh that I woke to hear we were in harbour, and tumbled out on deck at six of a fine summer morning to view a new world. New York Harbour is loveliest at night perhaps. On the Staten Island ferry boat you slip out from the darkness right under the immense sky-scrapers. As they recede they form into a mass together, heaping up one behind another, fire-lined and majestic, sentinel over the black, gold-streaked waters. Their cliff-like boldness is the greater, because to either side sweep in the East River and the Hudson River, leaving this piled promontory between. To the right hangs the great stretch of the Brooklyn Suspension Bridge, its slight curve very purely outlined with light; over it luminous trams, like shuttles of fire, are thrown across and across, continually weaving the stuff of human existence. From further off all these lights dwindle to a radiant semicircle that gazes out over the expanse with a quiet, mysterious expectancy. Far away seaward you may see the low golden glare of Coney Island.

But there was beauty in the view that morning, also, half an hour after sunrise. New York, always the cleanest and least smoky of cities, lay asleep in a queer, pearly, hourless light. A thin mist softened the further outlines. The water was opalescent under a silver sky, cool and dim, very slightly ruffled by the sweet wind that followed us in from the sea. A few streamers of smoke flew above the city, oblique and parallel, pennants of our civilisation. The space of water is great, and so the vast buildings do not tower above one as they do from the street. Scale is lost, and they might be any size. The impression is, rather, of long, low buildings stretching down to the water's edge on every side, and innumerable low black wharves and jetties and piers. And at one point, the lower end of the island on which the city proper stands, rose that higher clump of the great buildings, the Singer, the Woolworth, and the

rest. Their strength, almost severity, of line and the lightness of
their colour gave a kind of classical feeling, classical, and yet not of
Europe. It had the air, this block of masonry, of edifices built to
satisfy some faith, for more than immediate ends. Only, the faith
was unfamiliar. But if these buildings embodied its nature, it is cold
and hard and light, like the steel that is their heart. The first sight
of these strange fanes has queer resemblances to the first sight of that
lonely and secret group by Pisa's walls. It came upon me, at that
moment, that they could not have been dreamed and made without
some nobility. Perhaps the hour lent them sanctity. For I have often
noticed since that in the early morning, and again for a little about
sunset, the sky-scrapers are no longer merely the means and local
convenience for men to pursue their purposes, but acquire that
characteristic of the great buildings of the world, an existence and
meaning of their own.

Our boat moved up the harbour and along the Hudson River
with a superb and courteous stateliness. Round her snorted and
scuttled and puffed the multitudinous strange denizens of the
harbour. Tugs, steamers, queer-shaped ferry-boats, long rafts carrying great lines of trucks from railway to railway, dredgers, motor-
boats, even a sailing-boat or two; for the day's work was beginning.
Among them, with that majesty that only a liner entering a harbour
has, she went, progressed, had her moving – English contains no
word for such a motion – '*incessu patuit dea.*' A goddess entering
fairyland, I thought; for the huddled beauty of these buildings and
the still, silver expanse of the water seemed unreal. Then I looked
down at the water immediately beneath me, and knew that New
York was a real city. All kinds of refuse went floating by: bits of
wood, straw from barges, bottles, boxes, paper, occasionally a dead
cat or dog, hideously bladder-like, its four paws stiff and indignant
towards heaven.

This analysis of fairyland turned me towards the statue of
Liberty, already passed and growing distant. It is one of those
things you have long wanted to see and haven't expected to admire,
which, seen, give you a double thrill, that they're at last *there*, and
that they're better than your hopes. For Liberty stands nobly.
Americans, always shy about their country, have learnt from the
ridicule which Europeans, on mixed æsthetic and moral grounds,
pour on this statue, to dismiss it with an apologetic laugh. Yet it
is fine – until you get near enough to see its clumsiness. I admired

the great gesture of it. A hand fell on my shoulder, and a voice said, 'Look hard at that, young man! That's the first time you've seen Liberty – and it will be the last till you turn your back on this country again.' It was an American fellow-passenger, one of the tall, thin type of American, with pale blue eyes of an idealistic, disappointed expression, and an Indian profile. The other half of America, personated by a small, bumptious, eager, brown-faced man, with a cigar raking at an irritating angle from the corner of his mouth, joined in with, 'Wal! I should smile, I guess this is the Land of Freedom, anyway.' The tall man swung round: 'Freedom! do you call it a free land, where – ' He gave instances of the power of the dollar. The other man kept up the argument by spitting and by asseveration. As the busy little tugs, with rugs on their noses, butted the great liner into her narrow dock, the pessimist launched his last shafts. The short man denied nothing. He drew the cigar from his lips, shot it back with a popping noise into the round hole cigars had worn at the corner of his mouth, and said, 'Anyway, it's some country.' I was introduced to America.

New York

In five things America excels modern England – fish, architecture, jokes, drinks, and children's clothes. There may be others. Of these I am certain. The jokes and drinks, which curiously resemble each other, are the best. There is a cheerful violence about them; they take their respective kingdoms by storm. All the lesser things one has heard turn out to be delightfully true. The first hour in America proves them. People here talk with an American accent; their teeth are inlaid with gold; the mouths of car-conductors move slowly, slowly, with an oblique oval motion, for they are chewing; pavements are 'sidewalks.' It is all true. . . . But there were other things one expected, though in no precise form. What, for instance, would it be like, the feeling of whatever democracy America has secured?

I landed, rather forlorn, that first morning, on the immense covered wharf where the Customs mysteries were to be celebrated. The place was dominated by a large, dirty, vociferous man, coatless, in a black shirt and black apron. His mouth and jaw were huge; he looked like a caricaturist's Roosevelt. 'Express Company' was written on his forehead; labels of a thousand colours, printed slips, pencils and pieces of string, hung from his pockets and his hands, were held behind his ears and in his mouth. I laid my situation and my incompetence before him, and learnt right where to go and right when to go there. Then he flung a vast, dingy arm round my shoulders, and bellowed, 'We'll have your baggage right along to your hotel in two hours.' It was a lie, but kindly. That grimy and generous embrace left me startled, but an initiate into Democracy.

The other evening I went a lonely ramble, to try to detect the essence of New York. A wary eavesdropper can always surprise the secret of a city, through chance scraps of conversation, or by spying from a window, or by coming suddenly round corners. I started on a 'car.' American tram-cars are open all along the side and can be entered at any point in it. The side is divided by vertical bars. It looks like a cage with the horizontal lines taken out. Between these vertical bars you squeeze into the seat. If the seat opposite you is full, you swing yourself along the bars by your hands till you find room. The Americans become terrifyingly expert at this. I have seen them, fat, middle-aged business men, scampering up and down the face of the cars by means of their hands, swinging themselves over and round and above each other, like nothing in the world so much as the monkeys at the Zoo. It is a people informed with vital energy. I believe that this exercise, and the habit of drinking a lot of water between meals, are the chief causes of their good health.

The Broadway car runs mostly along the backbone of the queer island on which this city stands. So the innumerable parallel streets that cross it curve down and away; and at this time street after street to the west reveals, and seems to drop into, a mysterious evening sky, full of dull reds and yellows, amber and pale green, and a few pink flecks, and in the midst, sometimes, the flushed, smoke-veiled face of the sun. Then greyness, broken by these patches of misty colour, settles into the lower channels of the New York streets; while the upper heights of the sky-scrapers, clear of the roofs, are still lit on the sunward side with a mellow glow, curiously serene. . . .

The American by race walks better than we; more freely, with a taking swing, and almost with grace. How much of this is due to living in a democracy, and how much to wearing no braces, it is very difficult to determine. But certainly it is the land of belts, and therefore of more loosely moving bodies. . . .

They have not yet thought of discarding collars; but they are unashamedly shirt-sleeved. Any sculptor, seeking to figure this Republic in stone, must carve, in future, a young man in shirt-sleeves, open-faced, pleasant, and rather vulgar, straw hat on the back of his head, his trousers full and sloppy, his coat over his arm. The motto written beneath will be, of course, 'This is some country.' . . .

Fifth Avenue is handsome, the handsomest street imaginable. It is what the streets of German cities try to be. The buildings are large, square, 'imposing,' built with the solidity of opulence. The street, as a whole, has a character and an air of achievement. 'Whatever else may be doubted or denied, American civilization has produced this.' One feels rich and safe as one walks. Back in Broadway, New York dropped her mask, and began to betray herself once again. A little crowd, expressionless, intent, and volatile, before a small shop, drew me. In the shop-window was a young man, pleasant-faced, a little conscious, and a little bored, dressed very lightly in what might have been a runner's costume. He was bowing, twisting, and posturing in a slow rhythm. From time to time he would put a large card on a little stand in the corner. The cards bore various legends. He would display a card that said, 'THIS UNDERWEAR DOES NOT IMPEDE THE MOVEMENT OF THE BODY IN ANY DIRECTION.' Then he moved his body in every direction, from position to position, probable or improbable, and was not impeded. With a terrible dumb patience he turned the next card: 'IT GIVES WITH THE BODY IN VIOLENT EXERCISING.' The young man leapt suddenly, lunged, smote imaginary balls, belaboured invisible opponents, ran with immense speed but no progress, was thrown to earth by the Prince of the Air, kicked, struggled, then bounded to his feet again. But all this without a word. 'IT ENABLES YOU TO KEEP COOL WHILE EXERCISING.' The young man exercised, and yet was cool. He did this, I discovered later, for many hours a day.

Not daring to imagine his state of mind, I hurried off through Union Square. One of the many daily fire-alarms had gone; the traffic was drawn to one side, and several fire-engines came, with clanging of bells and shouting, through the space, gleaming with brass, splendid in their purpose. Before the thrill in the heart had time to die, or the traffic to close up, swung through an immense open motor-car driven by a young mechanic. It was luxuriously appointed, and had the air of a private car being returned from repairing. The man in it had an almost Swinburnian mane of red hair, blowing back in the wind, catching the last lights of day. He was clad, as such people often are in this country these hot days, only in a suit of yellow overalls, so that his arms and shoulders and neck and chest were bare. He was big, well-made, and strong, and he drove the car, not wildly, but a little too fast, leaning back rather insolently conscious of power. In private life, no doubt, a very ordinary youth, interested only in baseball scores; but in this brief passage he seemed like a Greek god, in a fantastically modern, yet not unworthy way emblemed and incarnate, or like the spirit of Henley's 'Song of Speed.' So I found a better image of America for my sculptor than the shirt-sleeved young man.

*   *   *

It all confirms the impression that grows on the visitor to America that Business has developed insensibly into a Religion, in more than the light, metaphorical sense of the words. It has its ritual and theology, its high places and its jargon, as well as its priests and martyrs. One of its more mystical manifestations is in advertisement. America has a childlike faith in advertising. They advertise here, everywhere, and in all ways. They shout your most private and sacred wants at you. Nothing is untouched. Every day I pass a wall, some five hundred square feet of which a gentleman has taken to declare that he is 'out' to break the Undertakers' Trust. Half the advertisement is a coloured photograph of himself. The rest is, 'See what I give you for 75 dols.!' and a list of what he does give. He gives everything that the most morbid taphologist could suggest, beginning with 'splendidly carved full-size oak casket, with black ivory handles. Four draped Flambeaux . . .' and going on to funereal ingenuities that would have overwhelmed Mausolus, and make death impossible for a refined man.

*   *   *

Cities, like cats, will reveal themselves at night. There comes an hour of evening when lower Broadway, the business end of the town, is deserted. And if, having felt yourself immersed in men and the frenzy of cities all day, you stand out in the street in this sudden hush, you will hear, like a strange questioning voice from another world, the melancholy boom of a foghorn, and realise that not half a mile away are the waters of the sea, and some great liner making its slow way out to the Atlantic. After that, the lights come out up-town,

and the New York of theatres and vaudevilles and restaurants
begins to roar and flare. The merciless lights throw a mask of un-
radiant glare on the human beings in the streets, making each face
hard, set, wolfish, terribly blue. The chorus of voices becomes
shriller. The buildings tower away into obscurity, looking strangely
theatrical, because lit from below. And beyond them soars the
purple roof of the night. A stranger of another race, loitering here,
might cast his eyes up, in a vague wonder what powers, kind or
maleficent, controlled or observed this whirlpool. He would find
only this unresponsive canopy of black, unpierced even, if the seeker
stood near a centre of lights, by any star. But while he looks, away
up in the sky, out of the gulfs of night, spring two vast fiery tooth-
brushes, erect, leaning towards each other, and hanging on to the
bristles of them a little Devil, little but gigantic, who kicks and
wriggles and glares. After a few moments the Devil, baffled by the
firmness of the bristles, stops, hangs still, rolls his eyes, moon-large,
and, in a fury of disappointment, goes out, leaving only the night,
blacker and a little bewildered, and the unconscious throngs of
ant-like human beings. Turning with terrified relief from this
exhibition of diabolic impotence, the stranger finds a divine hand
writing slowly across the opposite quarter of the heavens its igneous
message of warning to the nations, 'Wear —— Underwear for
Youths and Men-Boys.' And close by this message came forth a
youth and a man-boy, flaming and immortal, clad in celestial
underwear, box a short round, vanish, reappear for another round,
and again disappear. Night after night they wage this combat.
What gods they are who fight endlessly and indecisively over New
York is not for our knowledge; whether it be Thor and Odin, or
Zeus and Cronos, or Michael and Lucifer, or Ormuzd and Ahriman,
or Good-as-a-means and Good-as-an-end. The ways of our lords
were ever riddling and obscure. To the right a celestial bottle,
stretching from the horizon to the zenith, appears, is uncorked,
and scatters the worlds with the foam of what ambrosial liquor may
have been within. Beyond, a Spanish goddess, some minor deity in
the Dionysian theogony, dances continually, rapt and mysterious,
to the music of the spheres, her head in Cassiopeia and her twinkling
feet among the Pleiades. And near her, Orion, archer no longer,
releases himself from his strained posture to drive a sidereal golf-
ball out of sight through the meadows of Paradise; then poses,
addresses, and drives again.

O Nineveh, are these thy gods,
Thine also, mighty Nineveh?

Why this theophany, or how the gods have got out to perform their various 'stunts' on the *flammantia mœnia mundi*, is not asked by their incurious devotees. Through Broadway the dingily glittering tide spreads itself over the sands of 'amusement.' Theatres and 'movies' are aglare. Cars shriek down the street; the Elevated train clangs and curves perilously overhead; newsboys wail the baseball news; wits cry their obscure challenges to one another, 'I should worry!' or 'She's some Daisy!' or 'Good-night, Nurse!' In houses off the streets around children are being born, lovers are kissing, people are dying. Above, in the midst of those coruscating divinities, sits one older and greater than any. Most colossal of all, it flashes momently out, a woman's head, all flame against the darkness. It is beautiful, passionless, in its simplicity and conventional representation queerly like an archaic Greek or early Egyptian figure. Queen of the night behind, and of the gods around, and of the city below – here, if at all, you think, may one find the answer to the riddle. Her ostensible message, burning in the firmament beside her, is that we should buy pepsin chewing-gum. But there is more, not to be given in words, ineffable. Suddenly, when she has surveyed mankind, she closes her left eye. Three times she winks, and then vanishes. No ordinary winks these, but portentous, terrifyingly steady, obliterating a great tract of the sky. Hour by hour she does this, night by night, year by year. That enigmatic obscuration of light, that answer that is no answer, is, perhaps, the first thing in this world that a child born near here will see, and the last that a dying man will have to take for a message to the curious dead. She is immortal. Men have worshipped her as Isis and as Ashtaroth, as Venus, as Cybele, Mother of the Gods, and as Mary. There is a statue of her by the steps of the British Museum. Here, above the fantastic civilisation she observes, she has no name. She is older than the sky-scrapers amongst which she sits; and one, certainly, of her eyelids is a trifle weary. And the only answer to our cries, the only comment upon our cities, is that divine stare, the wink, once, twice, thrice. And then darkness.

Baseball at Harvard

. . . Baseball is a good game to watch, and in outline easy to understand, as it is merely glorified rounders. A cricketer is fascinated by their rapidity and skill in catching and throwing. There is excitement in the game, but little beauty except in the long-limbed 'pitcher,' whose duty it is to hurl the ball rather further than the length of a cricket-pitch, as bewilderingly as possible. In his efforts to combine speed, mystery, and curve, he gets into attitudes of a very novel and fantastic, but quite obvious, beauty. M. Nijinsky would find them repay study.

One queer feature of this sport is that unoccupied members of the batting side, fielders, and even spectators, are accustomed to join in vocally. You have the spectacle of the representatives of the universities endeavouring to frustrate or unnerve their opponents, at moments of excitement, by cries of derision and mockery, or heartening their own supporters and performers with exclamations of 'Now, Joe!' or 'He's got them!' or 'He's the boy!' At the crises in the fortunes of the game, the spectators take a collective and important part. The Athletic Committee appoints a 'cheer-leader' for the occasion. Every five or ten minutes this gentleman, a big, fine figure in white, springs out from his seat at the foot of the stands, addresses the multitude through a megaphone with a 'One! Two! Three!' hurls it aside, and, with a wild flinging and swinging of his body and arms, conducts ten thousand voices in the Harvard yell. That over, the game proceeds, and the cheer-leader sits quietly waiting for the next moment of peril or triumph. I shall not easily forget that figure, bright in the sunshine, conducting with his whole body, passionate, possessed by a demon, bounding in the frenzy of his inspiration from side to side, contorted, rhythmic, ecstatic.

Montreal

Determined to be in all ways the complete tourist, I took a rough preliminary survey of Montreal in an 'observation-car.' It was a large motor-wagonette, from which everything in Montreal could be seen in two hours. We were a most fortuitous band of twenty, who had elected so to see it. Our guide addressed us from the front through a small megaphone, telling us what everything was, what we were to be interested in, what to overlook, what to admire. He seemed the exact type of a spiritual pastor and master, shepherding his stolid and perplexed flock on a regulated path through the dust and clatter of the world. And the great hollow device out of which our instruction proceeded was so perfectly a blind mouth. I had never understood *Lycidas* before. We were sheepish enough, and fairly hungry. However, we were excellently fed. 'On the right, ladies and gentlemen, is the Bank of Montreal; on the left the Presbyterian Church of St Andrew's; on the right, again, the well-designed residence of Sir Blank Blank; further on, on the same side, the Art Museum. . . .' The outcome of it all was a vague general impression that Montreal consists of banks and churches. The people of this city spend much of their time in laying up their riches in this world or the next. . . .

Quebec and the Saguenay

Is there any city in the world that stands so nobly as Quebec? The citadel crowns a headland, three hundred feet high, that juts boldly out into the St Lawrence. Up to it, up the side of the hill, clambers the city, houses and steeples and huts, piled one on the other. It has the individuality and the pride of a city where great things have happened, and over which many years have passed. Quebec is as refreshing and as definite after the other cities of this continent as an immortal among a crowd of stockbrokers. She has, indeed, the radiance and repose of an immortal; but she wears her immortality youthfully. When you get among the streets of Quebec, the mediæval, precipitous, narrow, winding, and perplexed streets you begin to realise her charm. . . .

The American Jew and I took a *calèche*, a little two-wheeled local carriage, driven by a lively Frenchman with a factitious passion for death-spots and churches. . . .

We rattled up and down the steep streets, out among tidy fields, and back into the noisily sedate city again. We saw where Wolfe fell, where Montcalm fell, where Montgomery fell. Children played where the tides of war had ebbed and flowed. . . .

But Quebec is too real a city to be 'seen' in such a manner. And a better way of spending a few days, or years, is to sit on Dufferin

Terrace, with the old Lower Town sheer beneath you, and the river beyond it, and the citadel to the right, a little above, and the Isle of Orleans and the French villages away down-stream to your left. Hour by hour the colours change, and sunlight follows shadow, and mist rises, and smoke drifts across. And through the veil of the shifting of lights and hues there remains visible the majesty of the most glorious river in the world.

* * *

It was almost full night when we left the twenty-mile width of the St Lawrence, and turned up a gloomy inlet. By reason of the night and of comparison with the river from which we had come, this stream appeared unnaturally narrow. Darkness hid all detail, and we were only aware of vast cliffs, sometimes dense with trees, sometimes bare faces of sullen rock. They shut us in, oppressively, but without heat. There are no banks to this river, for the most part; only these walls, rising sheer from the water to the height of two thousand feet, going down sheer beneath it, or rather by the side of it, to many times that depth. The water was of some colour blacker than black. . . . The whole scene seemed some Stygian imagination of Dante. As we drew further and further into that lightless land, little twists and curls of vapour wriggled over the black river-surface. Our homeless, irrelevant, tiny steamer seemed to hang between two abysms. One became suddenly aware of the miles of dark water beneath. I found that under a prolonged gaze the face of the river began to writhe and eddy, as if from some horrible suppressed emotion. It seemed likely that something might appear. I reflected that if the river failed us, all hope was gone; and that anyhow this region was the abode of devils.

By daylight some of the horror goes, but the impression of ancientness and desolation remains. The gloomy flood is entirely shut in by the rock or the tangled pine and birch forests of these great cliffs, except in one or two places, where a chine and a beach have given lodging to lonely villages. One of these is at the end of a long bay, called Ha-Ha Bay. The local guide-book, an early example of the school of fantastic realism so popular among our younger novelists, says that this name arose from the 'laughing ejaculations' of the early French explorers, who had mistaken this lengthy blind-alley for the main stream. 'Ha! Ha!' they said. So like an early explorer.

Niagara Falls

Samuel Butler has a lot to answer for. But for him, a modern traveller could spend his time peacefully admiring the scenery instead of feeling himself bound to dog the simple and grotesque of the world for the sake of their too-human comments. It is his fault if a peasant's *naïveté* has come to outweigh the beauty of rivers, and the remarks of clergymen are more than mountains. It is very restful to give up all effort at observing human nature and drawing social and political deductions from trifles, and to let oneself relapse into wide-mouthed worship of the wonders of nature. And this is very easy at Niagara. Niagara means nothing. It is not leading anywhere. It does not result from anything. It throws no light on the effects of Protection, nor on the Facility for Divorce in America, nor on Corruption in Public Life, nor on Canadian character, nor even on the Navy Bill. It is merely a great deal of water falling over some cliffs. But it is very remarkably that. The human race, apt as a child to destroy what it admires, has done its best to surround the Falls with every distraction, incongruity, and vulgarity. Hotels, power-houses, bridges, trams, picture post-cards, sham legends, stalls, booths, rifle-galleries, and side-shows frame them about. And there are Touts. Niagara is the central home and breeding-place for all the touts of earth. There are touts insinuating, and touts raucous, greasy touts, brazen touts, and upper-class, refined, gentlemanly, take-you-by-the-arm touts; touts who intimidate and touts who wheedle; professionals, amateurs, and *dilettanti*, male and female; touts who would photograph you with your arm round a young lady against a faked background of the sublimest cataract, touts who would bully you into cars, char-à-bancs, elevators, or tunnels, or deceive you into a carriage and pair, touts who would sell you picture post-cards, moccasins, sham Indian bead-work, blankets, tee-pees, and crockery; and touts, finally, who have no apparent object in the world, but just purely, simply, merely, incessantly, indefatigably, and ineffugibly – to tout. And in the midst of all this, overwhelming it all, are the Falls. He who sees them instantly forgets humanity. They are not very high, but they are over-powering. They are divided by an island into two parts, the Canadian and the American.

Half a mile or so above the Falls, on either side, the water of the great stream begins to run more swiftly and in confusion. It descends with ever-growing speed. It begins chattering and leaping, breaking

into a thousand ripples, throwing up joyful fingers of spray. Sometimes it is divided by islands and rocks, sometimes the eye can see
nothing but a waste of laughing, springing, foamy waves, turning,
crossing, even seeming to stand for an instant erect, but always
borne impetuously forward like a crowd of triumphant feasters. Sit
close down by it, and you see a fragment of the torrent against the
sky, mottled, steely, and foaming, leaping onward in far-flung
criss-cross strands of water. Perpetually the eye is on the point of
descrying a pattern in this weaving, and perpetually it is cheated by
change. In one place part of the flood plunges over a ledge a few
feet high and a quarter of a mile or so long, in a uniform and stable
curve. It gives an impression of almost military concerted movement, grown suddenly out of confusion. But it is swiftly lost again
in the multitudinous tossing merriment. Here and there a rock
close to the surface is marked by a white wave that faces backwards
and seems to be rushing madly up-stream, but is really stationary
in the headlong charge. But for these signs of reluctance, the waters
seem to fling themselves on with some foreknowledge of their fate,
in an ever wilder frenzy. But it is no Maeterlinckian prescience.
They prove, rather, that Greek belief that the great crashes are
preceded by a louder merriment and a wilder gaiety. Leaping in the
sunlight, careless, entwining, clamorously joyful, the waves riot on
towards the verge.

But there they change. As they turn to the sheer descent, the
white and blue and slate-colour, in the heart of the Canadian Falls
at least, blend and deepen to a rich, wonderful, luminous green.
On the edge of disaster the river seems to gather herself, to pause,
to lift a head noble in ruin, and then, with a slow grandeur, to
plunge into the eternal thunder and white chaos below. Where the
stream runs shallower it is a kind of violet colour, but both violet
and green fray and frill to white as they fall. The mass of water,
striking some ever-hidden base of rock, leaps up the whole two
hundred feet again in pinnacles and domes of spray. The spray
falls back into the lower river once more; all but a little that fines
to foam and white mist, which drifts in layers along the air, graining
it, and wanders out on the wind over the trees and gardens and
houses, and so vanishes.

The manager of one of the great power-stations on the banks of
the river above the Falls told me that the centre of the riverbed at
the Canadian Falls is deep and of a saucer shape. So it may be

possible to fill this up to a uniform depth, and divert a lot of water for the power-houses. And this, he said, would supply the need for more power, which will certainly soon arise, without taking away from the beauty of Niagara. This is a handsome concession of the utilitarians to ordinary sight-seers. Yet, I doubt if we shall be satisfied. The real secret of the beauty and terror of the Falls is not their height or width, but the feeling of colossal power and of unintelligible disaster caused by the plunge of that vast body of water. If that were taken away, there would be little visible change; but the heart would be gone.

The American Falls do not inspire this feeling in the same way as the Canadian. It is because they are less in volume, and because the water does not fall so much into one place. By comparison their beauty is almost delicate and fragile. They are extraordinarily level, one long curtain of lacework and woven foam. Seen from opposite, when the sun is on them, they are blindingly white, and the clouds of spray show dark against them. With both Falls the colour of the water is the ever-altering wonder. Greens and blues, purples and whites, melt into one another, fade, and come again, and change with the changing sun. Sometimes they are as richly diaphanous as a precious stone, and glow from within with a deep, inexplicable light. Sometimes the white intricacies of dropping foam become opaque and creamy. And always there are the rainbows. If you come suddenly upon the Falls from above, a great double rainbow, very vivid, spanning the extent of spray from top to bottom, is the first thing you see. If you wander along the cliff opposite, a bow springs into being in the American Falls, accompanies you courteously on your walk, dwindles and dies as the mist ends, and awakens again as you reach the Canadian tumult. And the bold traveller who attempts the trip under the American Falls sees, when he dare open his eyes to anything, tiny baby rainbows, some four or five yards in span, leaping from rock to rock among the foam, and gambolling beside him, barely out of hand's reach, as he goes. One I saw in that place was a complete circle, such as I have never seen before, and so near that I could put my foot on it. It is a terrifying journey, beneath and behind the Falls. The senses are battered and bewildered by the thunder of the water and the assault of wind and spray; or rather, the sound is not of falling water, but merely of falling; a noise of unspecified ruin. So, if you are close behind the endless clamour, the sight cannot recognise liquid in the

masses that hurl past. You are dimly and pitifully aware that sheets
of light and darkness are falling in great curves in front of you. Dull
omnipresent foam washes the face. Farther away, in the roar and
hissing, clouds of spray seem literally to slide down some invisible
plane of air.

Beyond the foot of the Falls the river is like a slipping floor of
marble, green with veins of dirty white, made by the scum that was
foam. It slides very quietly and slowly down for a mile or two,
sullenly exhausted. Then it turns to a dull sage green, and hurries
more swiftly, smooth and ominous. As the walls of the ravine close
in, trouble stirs, and the waters boil and eddy. These are the lower
rapids, a sight more terrifying than the Falls, because less intelligible.
Close in its bands of rock the river surges tumultuously forward,
writhing and leaping as if inspired by a demon. It is pressed by the
straits into a visibly convex form. Great planes of water slide past.
Sometimes it is thrown up into a pinnacle of foam higher than a
house, or leaps with incredible speed from the crest of one vast wave
to another, along the shining curve between, like the spring of a
wild beast. Its motion continually suggests muscular action. The
power manifest in these rapids moves one with a different sense of
awe and terror from that of the Falls. Here the inhuman life and
strength are spontaneous, active, almost resolute; masculine vigour
compared with the passive gigantic power, female, helpless and overwhelming, of the Falls. A place of fear.

One is drawn back, strangely, to a contemplation of the Falls,
at every hour, and especially by night, when the cloud of spray
becomes an immense visible ghost, straining and wavering high
above the river, white and pathetic and translucent. The Victorian
lies very close below the surface in every man. There one can sit
and let great cloudy thoughts of destiny and the passage of empires
drift through the mind; for such dreams are at home by Niagara.
I could not get out of my mind the thought of a friend, who said
that the rainbows over the Falls were like the arts and beauty and
goodness, with regard to the stream of life – caused by it, thrown
upon its spray, but unable to stay or direct or affect it, and ceasing
when it ceased. In all comparisons that rise in the heart, the river,
with its multitudinous waves and its single current, likens itself to a
life, whether of an individual or of a community. A man's life is of
many flashing moments, and yet one stream; a nation's flows
through all its citizens, and yet is more than they. In such places,

one is aware, with an almost insupportable and yet comforting certitude, that both men and nations are hurried onwards to their ruin or ending as inevitably as this dark flood. Some go down to it unreluctant, and meet it, like the river, not without nobility. And as incessant, as inevitable, and as unavailing as the spray that hangs over the Falls, is the white cloud of human crying. . . . With some such thoughts does the platitudinous heart win from the confusion and thunder of Niagara a peace that the quietest plains or most stable hills can never give.

To Winnipeg

As we drew out into the cold magnificence of Lake Superior, the receding woody shores were occasionally spotted with picnickers or campers, who rushed down the beach in various deshabille, waving towels, handkerchiefs, or garments. We were as friendly. The human race seemed a jolly bunch, and the world a fine, pleasant, open-air affair – 'some world,' in fact. A man in a red shirt and a bronzed girl with flowing hair slid past in a canoe. We whistled, sang, and cried 'Snooky-ookums!' and other words of occult meaning, which imputed love to them, and foolishness. They replied suitably, grinned, and were gone. A little old lady in black, in the chair next mine, kept a small telescope glued to her eye, hour after hour. Whenever she distinguished life on any shore we passed, she waved a tiny handkerchief. Diligently she did this, and with grave face, never visible to the objects of her devotion, I suppose, but certainly very happy; the most persistent lover of humanity I have ever seen. . . .

*   *   *

An Indian, taciturn and Mongolian, led us on next day, by boat and on foot, to the lonely log-house we aimed at. It stood on high rocks, above a lake six miles by two. There was an Indian somewhere, by a river three miles west, and a trapper to the east, and a family encamped on an island in the lake. Else nobody.

It is that feeling of fresh loneliness that impresses itself before any detail of the wild. The soul – or the personality – seems to have indefinite room to expand. There is no one else within reach, there never has been anyone; no one else is *thinking* of the lakes and hills you see before you. They have no tradition, no names even; they are only pools of water and lumps of earth, some day, perhaps, to be clothed with loves and memories and the comings and goings of men, but now dumbly waiting their Wordsworth or their Acropolis to give them individuality, and a soul. In such country as this there is a rarefied clean sweetness. The air is unbreathed, and the earth untrodden. All things share this childlike loveliness, the grey whispering reeds, the pure blue of the sky, the birches and thin fir-trees that make up these forests, even the brisk touch of the clear water as you dive.

That last sensation, indeed, and none of sight or hearing, has impressed itself as the token of Canada, the land. Every swimmer knows it. It is not languorous, like bathing in a warm Southern sea; nor grateful, like a river in a hot climate; nor strange, as the ocean always is; nor startling, like very cold water. But it touches the body continually with freshness, and it seems to be charged with a subtle and unexhausted energy. It is colourless, faintly stinging, hard and grey, like the rocks around, full of vitality, and sweet. It has the tint and sensation of a pale dawn before the sun is up. Such is the wild of Canada. It awaits the sun, the end for which Heaven made it, the blessing of civilisation. Some day it will be sold in large portions, and the timber given to a friend of ——'s, and cut down and made into paper, on which shall be printed the praise of prosperity; and the land itself shall be divided into town-lots and sold, and sub-divided and sold again, and boomed and resold, and boosted and distributed to fishy young men who will vend it in distant parts of the country . . .

But at present there are only the wrinkled, grey-blue lake, sliding ever sideways, and the grey rocks, and the cliffs and hills, covered with birch-trees, and the fresh wind among the birches, and quiet, and that unseizable virginity. Dawn is always a lost pearly glow in the ashen skies, and sunset a multitude of softly-tinted mists sliding before a remotely golden West. They follow one another with an infinite loneliness. And there is a far and solitary beach of dark, golden sand, close by a deserted Indian camp, where, if you drift quietly round the corner in a canoe, you may see a bear stumbling along, or a great caribou, or a little red deer coming down to the water to drink, treading the wild edge of lake and forest with a light, secret, and melancholy grace.

The Indians

When I was in the East, I got to know a man who had spent many years of his life living among the Indians. He showed me his photographs. He explained one, of an old woman. He said, 'They told me there was an old woman in the camp called Laughing Earth. When I heard the name, I just said, "Take me to her!" She wouldn't be photographed. She kept turning her back to me. I just picked up a clod and plugged it at her, and said, "Turn round, Laughing Earth!" She turned half round, and grinned. She *was* a game old bird! I joshed all the boys here Laughing Earth was my girl – till they saw her photo!'

There stands Laughing Earth, in brightly-coloured petticoat and blouse, her grey hair blowing about her. Her back is towards you, but her face is turned, and scarcely hidden by a hand that is raised with all the coyness of seventy years. Laughter shines from the infinitely lined, round, brown cheeks, and from the mouth, and from the dancing eyes, and floods and spills over from each of the innumerable wrinkles. Laughing Earth – there is endless vitality in that laughter. The hand and face and the old body laugh. No skinny, intellectual mirth, affecting but the lips! It was the merriment of an apple bobbing on the bough, or a brown stream running over rocks, or any other gay creature of earth. And with all was a great dignity, invulnerable to clods, and a kindly and noble beauty. By the light of that laughter much becomes clear – the right place of man upon earth, the entire suitability in life of very brightly-coloured petticoats, and the fact that old age is only a different kind of a merriment from youth, and a wiser.

And by that light the fragments of this pathetic race become more comprehensible, and, perhaps less pathetic. . . . The happiest, whether Indian or half-breed, are those who live beyond the ever-advancing edges of cultivation and order, and force a livelihood from nature by hunting and fishing. Go anywhere into the wild, and you will find in little clearings, by lake or river, a dilapidated hut with a family of these solitaries, friendly with the pioneers or trappers around, ready to act as guide on hunt or trail. The Government, extraordinarily painstaking and well-intentioned, has established Indian schools, and trains some of them to take their places in the civilisation we have built. Not the best Indians these, say lovers of the race. I have met them, as clerks or stenographers, only distinguishable from their neighbours by a darker skin and a sweeter voice and manner. And in a generation or two, I suppose, the strain mingles and is lost. So we finish with kindness what our fathers began with war.

The Government, and others, have scientifically studied the history and characteristics of the Indians, and written them down in books, lest it be forgotten that human beings could be so extraordinary. They were a wandering race, it appears, of many tribes and, even, languages. Not apt to arts or crafts, they had, and have, an unrefined delight in bright colours. They enjoyed a 'Nature-Worship,' believed rather dimly in a presiding Power, and very definitely in certain ethical and moral rules. One of their incomprehensible customs was that at certain intervals the tribe divided itself into two factitious divisions, each headed by various chiefs, and gambled furiously for many days, one party against the other. They were pugnacious, and in their uncivilised way fought frequent wars. They were remarkably loyal to each other, and treacherous to the foe; brave, and very stoical. 'Monogamy was very prevalent.' It is remarked that husbands and wives were very fond of each other, and the great body of scientific opinion favours the theory that mothers were much attached to their children. Most tribes were very healthy, and some fine-looking. Such were the remarkable people who hunted, fought, feasted, and lived here until the light came, and all was changed. Other qualities they had even more remarkable to a European, such as utter honesty, and complete devotion to the truth among themselves. Civilisation, disease, alcohol, and vice have reduced them to a few scattered communities and some stragglers, and a legend, the admiration of boyhood. Boys they were, pugnacious, hunters, loyal and cruel, older than the merrier children of the South Seas, younger and simpler than the weedy, furtive, acquisitive youth who may figure our age and type. 'We must be a Morally Higher race than the Indians,' said an earnest American businessman to me in Saskatoon, 'because we have Survived them. The Great Darwin has proved it.' . . .

. . . What will happen? Shall we preserve these few bands of them, untouched, to succeed us, ultimately, when the grasp of our 'civilisation' weakens, and our transient anarchy in these wilder lands recedes once more before the older anarchy of Nature? Or will they be entirely swallowed by that ugliness of shops and trousers with which we enchain the earth, and become a memory and less than a memory? They are that already. The Indians have passed. They left no arts, no tradition, no buildings or roads or laws; only a story or two, and a few names, strange and beautiful. The ghosts of the old chiefs must surely chuckle when they note that the name by which Canada has called her capital and the centre of her political life, Ottawa, is an Indian name which signifies 'buying and selling.' And the wanderer in this land will always be remarking an unexplained fragrance about the place-names, as from some flower which has withered, and which he does not know.

The Rockies

... For nearly two hundred miles the train pants through the homeless grandeur of the Rockies and the Selkirks. Four or five hotels, a few huts or tents, and a rare mining-camp – that is all the habitation in many thousands of square miles. Little even of that is visible from the train. That is one of the chief differences between the effect of the Rockies and that of the Alps. There, you are always in sight of a civilisation which has nestled for ages at the feet of those high places. They stand, enrobed with worship, and grander by contrast with the lives of men. These unmemoried heights are inhuman – or rather, irrelevant to humanity. No recorded Hannibal has struggled across them; their shadow lies on no remembered literature. They acknowledge claims neither of the soul nor of the body of man. He is a stranger, neither Nature's enemy nor her child. She is there alone, scarcely a unity in the heaped confusion of these crags, almost without grandeur among the chaos of earth.

... The Observation-Car is a great invention of the new world. At the end of the train is a compartment with large windows, and a little platform behind it, roofed over, but exposed otherwise to the air. On this platform are sixteen little perches, for which you fight with Americans. Victorious, you crouch on one, and watch the ever-receding panorama behind the train. It is an admirable way of viewing scenery. But a day of being perpetually drawn backwards at a great pace through some of the grandest mountains in the world has a queer effect. Like life, it leaves you with a dizzy irritation. For, as in life, you never see the glories till they are past, and then they vanish with incredible rapidity. And if you crane to see the dwindling further peaks, you miss the new splendours.

* * *

... I was advised by various people to 'stop off' at Banff and at Lake Louise, in the Rockies. I did so. They are supposed to be equally the beauty-spots of the mountains. How perplexing it is that advisers are always so kindly and willing to help, and always so undiscriminating. It is equally disastrous to be a sceptic and to be credulous. Banff is an ordinary little tourist-resort in mountainous country, with hills and a stream and snow-peaks beyond. Beautiful enough, and invigorating. But Lake Louise – Lake Louise is of another world. Imagine a little round lake 6000 feet up, a mile across, closed in by great cliffs of brown rock, round the shoulders of which are thrown mantles of close dark pine. At one end the lake is fed by a vast glacier, and its milky tumbling stream; and the glacier climbs to snowfields of one of the highest and loveliest peaks in the Rockies, which keeps perpetual guard over the scene. To this place you go up three or four miles from the railway. There is the hotel at one end of the lake, facing the glacier; else no sign of humanity. From the windows you may watch the water and the peaks all day, and never see the same view twice. . . .

... If you climb any of the ridges or peaks around, there are discovered other valleys and heights and ranges, wild and desert, stretching endlessly away. As day draws to an end the shadows on the snow turn bluer, the crying of innumerable waters hushes, and the immense, bare ramparts of westward-facing rock that guard the great valley win a rich, golden-brown radiance. Long after the sun has set they seem to give forth the splendour of the day, and the tranquillity of their centuries, in undiminished fulness. They have that other-worldly serenity which a perfect old age possesses. And as with a perfect old age, so here, the colour and the light ebb so gradually out of things that you could swear nothing of the radiance and glory gone up to the very moment before the dark.

It was on such a height, and at some such hour as this, that I sat and considered the nature of the country in this continent. There was perceptible, even here, though less urgent than elsewhere, the strangeness I had noticed in woods by the St Lawrence, and on the banks of the Delaware (where are red-haired girls who sing at dawn), and in British Columbia, and afterwards among the brown hills and colossal trees of California, but especially by that lonely golden beach in Manitoba, where the high-stepping little brown deer run down to drink, and the wild geese through the evening go flying and crying. It is an empty land. To love the country here – mountains are worshipped, not loved – is like embracing a wraith. A European can find nothing to satisfy the hunger of his heart. The air is too thin to breathe. He requires haunted woods, and the friendly presence of ghosts. The immaterial soil of England is heavy and fertile with the decaying stuff of past seasons and generations. Here is the floor of a new wood, yet uncumbered by one year's autumn fall. We Europeans find the Orient stale and too luxuriantly fetid by reason of the multitude of bygone lives and thoughts, oppressive with the crowded presence of the dead, both men and gods. So, I imagine, a Canadian would feel our woods and fields heavy with the past and the invisible, and suffer claustrophobia in an English countryside beneath the dreadful pressure of immortals. For his own forests and wild places are windswept and empty. That is their charm, and their terror. . . .

. . . The maple and the birch conceal no dryads, and Pan has never been heard amongst these reed-beds. Look as long as you like upon a cataract of the New World, you shall not see a white arm in the foam. A godless place. And the dead do not return. That is why there is nothing lurking in the heart of the shadows, and no human mystery in the colours, and neither the same joy nor the kind of peace in dawn and sunset that older lands know. How far away seem those grassy, moonlit places in England that have been Roman camps or roads, where there is always serenity, and the spirit of a purpose at rest, and the sunlight flashes upon more than flint! Here one is perpetually a first-comer. The land is virginal, the wind cleaner than elsewhere, and every lake new-born, and each day is the first day. The flowers are less conscious than English flowers, the breezes have nothing to remember, and everything to promise. There walk, as yet, no ghosts of lovers in Canadian lanes. This is the essence of the grey freshness and brisk melancholy of this land. And for all the charm of those qualities it is also the secret of a European's discontent. For it is possible, at a pinch, to do without gods. But one misses the dead.

The South Seas

The South Sea Islands have an invincible glamour. Any bar in
'Frisco or Sydney will give you tales of seamen who slipped ashore
in Samoa or Tahiti or the Marquesas for a month's holiday, five,
ten, or twenty years ago. Their wives and families await them yet.
They are compound, these islands, of all legendary heavens. They
are Calypso's and Prospero's isle, and the Hesperides, and Paradise,
and every timeless and untroubled spot. Such tales have been made
of them by men who have been there, and gone away, and have been
haunted by the smell of the bush and the lagoons, and faint thunder
on the distant reef, and the colours of sky and sea and coral, and the
beauty and grace of the islanders. And the queer thing is that it's
all, almost tiresomely, true. In the South Seas the Creator seems to
have laid Himself out to show what He *can* do. Imagine an island
with the most perfect climate in the world, tropical, yet almost
always cooled by a breeze from the sea. No malaria or other fevers.
No dangerous beasts, snakes, or insects. Fish for the catching, and
fruits for the plucking. And an earth and sky and sea of immortal
loveliness. What more could civilisation give? Umbrellas? Rope?
Gladstone bags? ... Any one of the vast leaves of the banana is
more waterproof than the most expensive woven stuff. And from
the first tree you can tear off a long strip of fibre that holds better
than any rope. And thirty seconds' work on a great palm-leaf
produces a basket-bag which will carry incredible weights all day,
and can be thrown away in the evening. A world of conveniences.
And the things which civilisation has left behind or missed by the
way are there, too, among the Polynesians: beauty and courtesy
and mirth. I think there is no gift of mind or body that the wise
value which these people lack. A man I met in some other islands,
who had travelled much all over the world, said to me 'I have found
no man, in or out of Europe, with the good manners and dignity
of the Samoan, with the possible exception of the Irish peasant.'
A people among whom an Italian would be uncouth, and a high-
caste Hindu vulgar, and Karsavina would seem clumsy, and Helen
of Troy a frump.

*   *   *

I wish I were there again. It is a country and a life, that bind the
heart. . . . In the South Seas, if you live the South Sea life, the

intellect soon lapses into quiescence. The body becomes more active, the senses and perceptions more lordly and acute. It is a life of swimming and climbing and resting after exertion. The skin seems to grow more sensitive to light and air, and the feel of water and the earth and leaves. Hour after hour one may float in the warm lagoons, conscious in the whole body, of every shred and current of the multitudinous water, or diving under in a vain attempt to catch the radiant butterfly-coloured fish that flit in and out of the thousand windows of their gorgeous coral palaces. Or go up, one of a singing flower-garlanded crowd, to a shaded pool of a river in the bush, cool from the mountains. The blossom-hung darkness is streaked with the bodies that fling themselves, head or feet first, from the cliffs around the water, and the haunted forest-silence is broken by laughter. It is part of the charm of these people that, while they are not so foolish as to 'think,' their intelligence is incredibly lively and subtle, their sense of humour and their intuitions of other people's feelings are very keen and living. They have built up, in the long centuries of their civilisation, a delicate and noble complexity of behaviour and of personal relationships. A white man living with them soon feels his mind as deplorably dull as his skin is pale and unhealthy among those glorious golden-brown bodies. But even he soon learns to *be* his body (and so his true mind), instead of using it as a stupid convenience for his personality, a moment's umbrella against this world. He is perpetually and intensely aware of the subtleties of taste in food, of every tint and line of the incomparable glories of those dawns and evenings, of each shade of intercourse in fishing or swimming or dancing with the best companions in the world. That alone is life; all else is death. And after dark, the black palms against a tropic night, the smell of the wind, the tangible moonlight like a white, dry, translucent mist, the lights in the huts, the murmur and laughter of passing figures, the passionate, queer thrill of the rhythm of some hidden dance – all this will seem to him, inexplicably and almost unbearably, a scene his heart has known long ago, and forgotten, and yet always looked for.

5
Politics

Brooke's paper 'Democracy and the Arts' was delivered to the Cambridge University Fabian Society in the spring or summer of 1910, his year of Presidency. Three years earlier, in *The Cambridge Review*, he had reported a lecture by Granville Barker to the C.U.F.S.:

> The charm of Mr. Barker's voice and manner would render the most conventional absurdities plausible. And his ideas are far from conventional or absurd. His lecture was principally a plea for the recognition of the Drama as a state service. The chief article of Mr. Barker's faith was 'look after the economics, and the art will come of itself'.

Brooke's vision was to go further than Barker's plea for the starting of repertory theatres in the provinces, and the concern expressed in his far-sighted paper extends beyond the art of drama.

The paper was first published in 1946, when, as its editor truly commented, the subject had 'suddenly become topical, more topical than when it was written, with the dawning of the Socialist State in England of which Brooke was one of the Minor Prophets'. Addressing himself to Hugh Dalton, Geoffrey Keynes concluded:

> Perhaps Brooke's word will remind the present Chancellor of the Exchequer (who may, indeed, never have forgotten) that once he too believed in the importance of the Arts in the national life, and he may be encouraged to assign to his object the funds that could do so much, if applied in the right way, to encourage the artists and to foster appreciation of their arts.

If Brooke's voice has carried some slight influence in the years which have followed, his words could even now be heeded.

Typical of Brooke's earlier and – as Dalton would have said – 'woollier' socialism is the review of a book by his uncle, C. C. Cotterill, *Human Justice for Those at the Bottom from Those at the Top*. Thanking his uncle for the book, he regretted the selfish approach to socialism of some of his Cambridge contemporaries, and asked: 'Must every cause lose part of its ideal, as it becomes successful?' One cannot help wondering whether, if he had lived, he might not have agreed with that mad priest of Kent, the subject of Morris's finest prose romance, who recognized, on waking from his dream, that 'Men fight and lose the battle, and the thing that they fought for comes about in spite of their defeat, and when it comes turns out not to be what they meant'.

Review of *Human Justice for Those at the Bottom from Those at the Top* by C. C. Cotterill

The author of this book is one who has realized very keenly the pitiable condition of the very poor in England today, and the shocking contrasts of society as it exists at present. These cannot long continue. But as the regeneration of society will probably be slow, it is intolerable that those at the very bottom should have to wait. He puts forward a plan by which the very richest should instantly and voluntarily come to the help of the very poorest in the land, since both chiefly owe their condition to the same cause, our modern commercial system. The success of this plan would not only remove an enormous blot on our civilisation, but give a splendid example of national feeling for future work, and inaugurate by love and goodwill that social change that must otherwise come about by ill-feeling and hatred. The author bases his appeal on the goodness of human nature, still so splendid and lovable in natures tarnished by the infinite meanness of 'the vulgarest warfare ever urged' – our modern commercial life, and on the real worth of the characters of those at the top. He discusses the various obstacles, wealth and the commercial system, party politics, and the education and lack of imagination of the upper classes, with sincerity and an absence of prejudice in either direction. Finally, he insists on the right spirit, on unity of action, and on personal service as necessary for success. The whole book is filled by a splendid atmosphere of faith and idealism; besides its large practical value. It is primarily directed only to those at the top, and we hope it may achieve its purpose. But it is of the greatest interest to a much larger audience. For it displays a plan which will appeal to all men of all creeds and parties, and a spirit of love and an earnest faith in human goodness that are too rare in many of our modern reformers.

(*The Cambridge Review*, 28 May 1908)

Democracy and the Arts

I am not going to rhapsodize about the Spirit of Democracy as dawning in the operas of Wagner or the anarchic prose of Whitman or Carpenter. 'Brotherhood' will not be heard of in this paper. Neither comrade nor cumrade shall be mentioned by me. I would detain you this side of the millennium. What I want to discuss, to ask one or two questions about, is the effect that a democratic form of society – *our* democratic form of society – has, and will have, on the production of pictures, music and literature; and how we are to control that effect. I nearly wrote a paper on 'The Artist under Socialism', but I didn't for two reasons. One was that the phrase 'under Socialism' regrettably tends to drop the pink gauze of unreality over the whole issue. The other was that I wanted not to scare off any good people, who, though Progressive, Democratic, Socialistic and the rest, can't bring themselves to be so absolutely sure as to call themselves *Socialists*, [or to believe] that the pearl-button industry really *ought* to be taken over by the State – at any rate just *yet*.

I use the word 'Democracy'. It seems to me that this century is going to witness a struggle between Democracy and Plutocracy. Democracy is the ordering of the national life according to the national will. Its probable and desirable increase in the near future entails a great growth in collective control, in various ways, of every side of the life of the nation, and organizing – or wilfully not organizing – it to attain the collectively-willed good. It is not the time now to spread into how this growth of Democracy will insist on a great liberty and security and independence for each man. I feel sure that in this general question most people, in theory anyhow, will agree with me. And in the end it is one of the few questions that matter. I am one of those who care for the *result* of actions. If anybody tells me that an absolute hereditary monarchy based on slave labour, or an agricultural oligarchy of Plato's φύλακες, is the ideal state which *he* will always advocate, I can only take him up to a high place, and say, 'My dear creature, up North there are twenty millions who want Democracy; down South there are twenty millions who want Plutocracy. Are you coming North with me?' And the same to any Democrat who tries to differ with me about, say, the exact relations between Local and National Government fifty years on.

This democratization of our land, then, which we so greatly desire (and which will require, I believe, so much Collectivism), will reduce the number of those who live on money they do not earn most or all their lives. Observe the situation, and remember it's a real one, not one in a book. (1) Art is important. (2) The people who produce art at present are, if you look into it, nearly always dependent on unearned income. (3) We are going to diminish and extinguish the number of those dependent on unearned income. We shall also reduce the number of those rich enough to act the patron to artists, and change in a thousand other ways the circumstances of the arts and of the artists.

We must, then, acknowledge that there may be something in the objections of the average anti-democrat, the refined vague upper-class person, that we are making the arts impossible. The literature of the future will be blue-books, its art framed plans of garden cities. The anti-democrat himself is generally easy enough to answer. The decay of Culture, he wails, the neglect of Art, the absence of fine literature – points to the halfpenny papers, shudders at the grimy Philistines. You ask him how often *he* goes to the National Gallery, how lately *he* has read the six best plays of Shakespeare. . . . But the fact remains. Very little attention is paid, as we change the structure of Society, to the claims of the Arts. Artists have lived, in the past and present, on inherited capital or on the patronage of rich men or corporations. How are *we* going to arrange for them? I sympathize – slightly – with those who airily cry, with Whistler, 'Art? Oh, Art – *happens!*' But that won't do. It never would, or should, have done. Now least of all. For while everything has, in a way, 'happened' hitherto, *now* we are trying this tremendous experiment of Democracy, of taking our own fate into our own hands, controlling the future, shaping Life to our will. Now most

of all when we are, however roughly, trying to foresee and provide for everything, we must provide for Art. It is permissible
to take what flowers you find best in a wood. A garden requires
planning.

I've indicated what I mean by Democracy. I suppose the Arts
don't need definition. Both these things will become clearer in the
course of the paper. We want to see how we can produce as large
and appreciative a public as possible; a state of things where the
fineness (not the refinedness) of Art will enter deeply into many
men's lives, and as many good works of art as possible. It is this
last thing I am most concerned with, dealing with the producers
and production, not the questions of distribution or consumption.

But it may be useful to discuss what we mean by Art a little
further. The air is full of sentimentalities and false notions about it,
and should be cleared. A good many people – especially democratic
people – will say the question of Art and Artists has already been
answered, and point to William Morris and the Arts and Crafts.
This is very dangerous. There are several perils connected with that
sort of thing. No answer to the question of Artists has come from
these sources; not even a realization of the question. I want to
disavow almost altogether what Mr. H. G. Wells once called
Hampstead-and-Hammered-Copper Socialism (that was before he
went to live at Hampstead). For one thing you must separate the
questions of Art and of Crafts. *Crafts* I won't discuss now, beyond
suggesting that you can't get a revival of Crafts by any movement
consisting of people making a piece of unpolished furniture a year
and living on dividends, and of bookbinding by unoccupied young
ladies. It must come, if at all, through the Trades Unions. And
anyhow, don't mix up Art and Crafts. It is so easy to do so, and so
tempting to slide from the keen edge of Art into the byways, the
pursuits that don't disturb, the paths that lead to antiquarianism
and hobbies, bibliography, love of seventeenth-century prose which
is quaint, beautiful handwriting. These things are excellent, but not
to the point. Revive handicrafts as much as you can for the sake of
the Craftsman. Art is a different matter. We want *King Lear* and
'The Polish Rider' for what we get out of them, not the pleasure
it gives Shakespeare and Rembrandt to make them. Morris, or at
least the Morrisite, approaches the matter from a wrong side. It is
no good going back to the Middle Ages and the great communal
art of the Cathedrals and the folksongs. If you can revive communal

art, well and good. But it is a small thing. We have done much better since. Individuals have made tunes and poems as good as those we are told came from the people. Burns, perhaps, has done so. And you won't find any band of mediæval rustics in an inn inspired to troll out *Paradise Lost* or a Beethoven Concerto between the bouts of mead.

We live in our own age (a very intelligent and vital one) and we must throw ourselves in with all its arts and schools of art, music, and literature. Tapestries are both unhealthy and ugly. Let romaunt and clavicithern moulder together.

But there arises from *dicta* of Morris a belief that too many hold – that art is an easy thing, a πάρεργον. Morris said, I believe, that all poetry ought to be of the kind a man can make up while he is working at a loom. Much of his own was. That may be why a lot of it is so dull. 'Easy writing', someone said, 'makes damned hard reading'. Not so did Shakespeare or Balzac write or Beethoven compose. It is an infamous heresy of his, and it extends to other arts besides poetry, though it is about poetry most people hold it. It leads to this too common idea that the various artists of the future will be able to do ordinary work for so many hours a day, and pursue their arts in their leisure time. You don't find artists advocating that: only some of the ordinary cultured public. It is a thing we can't allow. It means the death of the Arts, a civilization of amiable amateurs, of intermittent Alexandrians. We have too much of this system already – it is no fault of the individual – the Civil Service poets, the stockbroker who does water-colours in the evenings, the music-master who has the holidays to compose in. Better, almost, a literature of blue-books than a literature of belles-lettres.

There is another wrong notion of art that falsifies the opinions of many on this subject. Let us beware of those who talk of 'the art of the people', or of 'expressing the soul of the Community'. The Community hasn't got a soul; you can't voice the soul of the Community any more than you can blow its nose. The conditions of Democracy may profoundly alter the outlook of many artists, and partly their style and subject matter. But the *main* business of art has been, is, and, one must assume, will be an individual and unique affair. 'I saw – *I* saw', the artist says, 'a tree against the sky, or a blank wall in the sunlight, and it was so thrilling, so arresting, so particularly itself, that – well really, I *must* show you! . . . There!'

Or the writer explains, 'Just so and just so it happened, or might happen, and thus the heart shook, and thus ...' And suddenly, deliciously, with them you see and feel.

Art is not a criticism of Life. There *is* a side of it that makes problems clear, throws light on the complexity of modern life, assists one to understand. It is a function much dwelt on nowadays. A section of modern drama is praised for explaining religion, or the relation of the sexes, or of Capital and Labour. It is incidental. Discussion is merely one of the means, not the end, of literary art. You are in the midst of insoluble problems of temperance reform and education and organization. The artist, as artist, is not concerned. He leads you away by the hand and, Mamillius-like, begins his tale: 'There was a man – dwelt by a churchyard' – it is purely irrelevant.

But how important these intimate irrelevances are! I hold the view most fervently. If not this paper would be found inexcusable – quite inexcusable. Yet I must apologize to those who hold it a waste of time to consider anything for the moment but material social reform. With all my soul I'm with them. I feel deeply with Morris when he cries out about 'filling up this terrible gap between riches and poverty'. Doubtless many things will go to filling it up, and if Art must be one of those things, let it go. (What business have we with Art at all unless we can share it?) I am not afraid but that Art will rise from the Dead, whatever else lies there. And if it were a choice between keeping the Arts and establishing a high National Minimum, I would not hesitate a moment. I hate the *dilettante* and unimaginative hypocrisy that would. But things don't happen that way. We have forsworn Revolution for a jog-trot along Social Reform, and there is plenty of time to take things with us on the way – Art above all. The tradition of art-work and artists is worth keeping – the sort of tradition, I mean, that links Milton and Keats and Francis Thompson. It is a jumping ground, not a clog. The heritage is valuable. Art, if it cannot make men much better as means, can make them very good as ends. To most people it can give something. To some it can give the highest and supremest part of their lives. It multiplies the value of the life we are trying to organize to have. Not only for the moments when we hear or read or see the Arts do we prize them, though these would be hard to know the full worth of. But when the tree or the wall or the situation meets us in real life, they find profounder hosts. In the transience and hurry Art opens out every way on to the Eternal Ends.

Democracy and the Arts! This paper, like all good papers, has given its first half to saying what it's going to be about. Like all good papers it had better give most of its second half to saying why it is about it.

Partly because, as I have said, we are on the way to extinguish artists by destroying the systems which enabled them to live. Only the most fanatical and the most immediately popular could survive – by no means the best types. But in any case other systems have been irregular and bad – most of all the present one. We can do something far better. Also, we *must* realize that in a thousand ways new conditions and vast possibilities are round us and ahead. The circumstances of modern life offer new temptations and new dangers to the artist. Enormous potential art publics grow slowly before our eyes. And both they and the artist are increasingly helpless before the blind amoral profit-hunger of the commercial. We must not be unprepared for the effects these dark multitudes will have on the Arts.

The question of the Public of the future requires consideration, though it is not the central point of this paper. We want it large and varied. A culture sustained by an infinitesimal group of the infinitely elect will not be possible or desirable. Though, indeed, there are, and increasingly will be, many groups each thinking itself to be such: and a good thing too, so long as the conditions of modern life keep the groups from getting too isolated and stagnant. We need not complain if the Public only means a mass of little publics. It would be a good thing if the whole artistic public of England twenty years hence would delight in Gauguin. We shall be content if half a million worship the Impressionists, and half a million adore the Post-Impressionists. It may be one of the conditions of life. It is especially one of the things we must fearlessly accustom ourselves to, the growth of diverse circles and publics, to whom local or special kinds of poets and painters will appeal. From such artists the greater, and more widely reaching, will roughly emerge, spreading to other circles, more distant ears and eyes. It used to be, in a general way, true to say of a great author – of Dryden or Johnson or Pope – that all England read them – all England that read any literature. That time has utterly gone – it is not realized how irrevocably that time has gone. There are twenty millions who read in England today, millions of them reading literature. The numbers of a potential literary public increase enormously year by year. No one man, except one or two classics, can touch more than a fraction. This change in the old conditions, this breaking up of unity, this multitude of opening minds, may bring perplexity and apparent confusion of standards; but also (I say it soberly) the chance of vast, unimaginable, unceasing additions to the glory of the literature of England.

There are two other points, points on which many go wrong when they contemplate the present and future publics for the Arts. There is the mistake of the man who says, 'When Everyman has reached a decent amount of leisure and education, the whole community will foster and patronize and delight in the Arts'. An inspection of the class that has had leisure and education does not justify this opinion. It may be objected that public school education is not good. That is true. But it will be a long time before you can ensure the whole nation getting a considerably better education than the modern public school and university one. And even then I do not suppose more than a small part of the nation will ever be much interested in the Arts, though it is easy to imagine a state of things coming to pass where perhaps most people will pretend to be. But such things are beyond our vista. The first generation of universal education has not given us a nation of art-lovers. Nor will the second, nor the third. We must face the problem on the assumption that public demand isn't going to settle much of it for us for a long while yet.

And then there's the idea that the lower classes, the people who are entering into the circle of the educated, are coarsely devoid of taste, likely to swamp – swamping – the whole of culture in undistinguished, raucous, stumpy arts that know no tradition. If the washy, dull, dead upper-class brains this idea haunts were its only home we could leave it. But it lurks in the Victorian shadows and dusty corners of finer types of mind. Ideas in other parts of this paper may help to kill it, I hope. I would say one or two things about it here. In the first place, it is not relevant that the newly encivilized and educated classes should not be able to leap at once to the superb heights to which we have toiled through so many generations. It is the future – their future fineness – we work for. It is only natural that the taste of the lower classes should be at present infinitely worse than ours. The amazing thing is that it is probably rather better. It is true many Trades Unionists do not read Milton. Nor do many University men. But take the best of each. Compare the literary criticism of the *Labour Leader* with that of the *Saturday Review*. It is, I assure you, enormously better, enormously readier to recognize good new literature. Think of the working-class support of Miss Horniman's Repertory Theatre in Manchester. Compare the fate of the progeny of middle- and upper-class intellectualism, Mr. Frohman's Repertory Theatre, and the Vedrenne-Barker company, and Mr. Herbert Trench's dream. Compare the style of the *Cambridge History of English Literature* with that of Mr. Arnold Bennett's handbook on the subject. They are separated – how can I express the difference? – more widely than Hell and Heaven. The gulf that parts them is the greatest gulf there is, the one which divides the dead from the living. Put, finally – for we must stop this sometime – put the *Spectator* beside the *Clarion* for pure literary merit. I do not wish to decry the *Spectator*. In common with many other Socialists I have written in it. But – on the honour of an enthusiast for literature – the *Clarion* wins all the way. Those who have determined to make the State we live in, and are forming for the future, as fine as possible, must be very careful to oppose the force of primness in this matter. Unnecessarily to divide the traditions we have got from the new life of the time, to assist in divorcing good taste from popular literature, is to rob and weaken both. Those whose test of painting is perspective, whose test of literature is the absence of split infinitives, cry 'Vulgarity!' and 'Bad Grammar!' They are the epithets corpses fling at the quick, dead languages at living. Accept them and pass on. They do not matter. More, they are praise.

I have met a group of young poets in London. Some of them are in money extremely poor. They talk Cockney. And they write – some are good, others bad – as they talk. This is to say, their poems give fullest value when pronounced as they thought and felt them. They allow for *ow* being *aow*. Their love-poems begin (I invent) 'If yew wd come agin to me'. That is healthy. That way is life. In them is more hope – and more fulfilment – than in the old-world passion and mellifluous despair of any gentleman's or lady's poetry.

To sum up, the influence of Democracy on the Arts from this point of view – the Public – need not be bad. To show that it is good, and to make it better, it is most importantly our duty to welcome and aid all the new and wider movements that come with the growth of Democracy and the rise of new generations. I say new generations, for we are old-fashioned I find, in danger of being out of touch, we whose life is divided between university, a few similar people in London, and the country rectories that are our homes. And it is even more important when we see the idols we most worship attacked and crumbling, to acquiesce, to accept where we cannot understand, to endure the boots and accent of the unrefined in the sanctuary, for the sake of the new Gods that follow. It will be very difficult.

But the subject I am most concerned with now is, as I said at the beginning, that of the Artist himself, how we are to make certain of his turning up. It would be more amusing than profitable to go into the economic status of the Artist in past times, a study that has not been sufficiently worked out. At least notice that no past age can jeer at us and go unscathed. Take literature. To each generation of the last century we can reply with John Clare and James Thomson and Francis Thompson. Ask those of the great age of letters, the eighteenth century, what they did with Chatterton, who might have been the greatest of them all. Consider Michael Drayton, and a dozen more of the Elizabethans. The truth is that no system has worked well for long. With painters I believe the guild system did for a time. The State in Athens, founded, we are told, on popular good taste, out-rivalled the great courts of Syracuse and elsewhere. Our problems are different from theirs; our machinery cannot be so simple. Patronage is often loosely praised, held up to us as the golden age for artists. It is grossly over-estimated. Once or twice it has worked: Italy will witness. And the conception of musicians, poets and painters, healthy and wealthy, crowding round a prince of perfect taste, perfect appearance, and immense generosity, is delightful. But who will honestly hope our millionaires will fill their distinguished places? And it was an untrustworthy transient business. It only works with a small rich court of highly cultured people. Patronage, to be of great use, must endow the artist thoroughly. The ordinary system of incomplete endowment and jobbery and such things as payment for dedications, was a ramshackle affair. You see it at work in Elizabethan times, when most of the best writers lost all their shame (which doesn't much matter) and half their vitality (which does) in cadging and touting.

They were in continual poverty and debt, and driven to hackwork. Few dramatists could make as much as the equivalent of £200 a year. Jobbing was all right when it could be invoked and if it jobbed the man into a sinecure. Often, as with Spenser, it didn't. So we have lost half the *Faery Queen* (oh, *I* shouldn't care if we'd lost it all. It's the principle of the thing). It has been the same since. It is impossible to know how much more Milton and Marvell would have given us if they had had money enough to live on. If anything at all, the loss is enormous. If Dryden and Addison had not had to sell themselves to politics, our literature could only have gained.

Only in a few cases and in a few kinds of literature have writers been able to make a living. Even lately and with the most popular this is true. Tennyson did not make enough to live on till he was middle-aged. He had to put off his marriage eleven years. Tom Hood, a great writer, both comic and serious, was, artistically, ruined by the continuous flood of jokes he had to pour forth all his life. And, in the waste of the past centuries, you must not only count the cases of starvation or over-production, nor even the artistic potentialities sown here and there in the undistinguished mass of the people, which have perished unconscious in that blindest oblivion – the mute inglorious Miltons of the village and slum Beethovens – but also the many who have had the chance of an artist's career that would have produced good, and have not thought the risk worth while. Alfred Tennyson died, but was not born, the only poet in that family.

And nowadays: it is worth considering what we do, or rather what Fate does, now, to enable artists to produce works of art. It is terrifying, when you examine the matter, to find how many of them live on unearned, presumably inherited, capital. As there are comparatively few people who can do this, a million or two, and as we are going to reduce the number, it is an alarming outlook. The only creative artistic profession you have much chance of making a living at, fairly soon, is that of a dramatist. I suppose it is almost inconceivable that a creative musician can live by composing till he has passed thirty; few then. It is in the process of making a public that the modern artist has to have extraneous financial support or go under. (There are various ways of going under. Mr. Somerset Maugham and Mr. Hall Caine chose one way, the better. Rimbaud, who went East and was last heard of driving a caravan in Arabia,[1] another. Chatterton a third.) The painter's only hope is to paint the portraits of the extremely rich and extremely un-distinguished. It is not always open, nor always attractive, to him to take the revenge Sargent sometimes takes. In future, perhaps, we'll have our big painters painting the great, not the rich.

Poetry is even worse off than the other arts. Even Mr. Rudyard Kipling could not live on his poetry. Very few poets, perhaps one or two in five years, sell 1000 copies of a volume. If they do, and if they find a very generous publisher, and if they charge 5s. for their volume (an absurdly high price) they get £25! An experienced publisher's reader tells me no one in England makes £50 a year by poetry – except perhaps Mr. Kipling and Mr. A. Noyes. Fiction's far better: but you can't live by writing good fiction – so writers of good fiction inform me. Henry James can *now*, no doubt, at sixty. He could not if he were thirty.

What then, as we grow more democratic and more people have to work for their living, since the noblest work of all does not produce a livelihood, are we to do? To make a great creative artist is beyond the power of eugenist or schoolmaster. All we can hope to do is to spot them when they come, and enable them to realize their genius. We have laid down one axiom – the artist is to be free from other work. If you won't do that, at any rate let the other work be as disgusting as possible. An artist will do better art-work in intervals if his livelihood is got by cleaning sewers than if he takes up some more fascinating occupation, like teaching, or critical work. But if we're going to do away with the very clumsy and inefficient machinery of patrons (who don't work at all now) and inherited capital, we, the community, must endow the artist. This has often enough been put forward as a necessary part of some Utopian – probably strongly Collectivist – State, the sort of State the year 2050 may see. I submit that it is a thing that should be begun now. It should go on concurrently with taxation; be a financially minor, but actually important, part of the annual Budget. It is absurd to wait till the Death Duties have done their work, to begin remedying the bad effects of it. With scholarships, of course, a little is done this way; but very little and very clumsily and very unconsciously. This evening I want to suggest a few ideas about endowment. If people accept the general theory, a detailed plan

[1] Brooke is here at fault. Rimbaud, after travelling in Abyssinia, died in hospital at Marseilles.

would not be hard to elaborate. It is the sort of idea that must be accepted generally as commonsense, not a startling novelty, and must be part of the ordinary background of people's minds. Fix your eye firmly on what we want to do, to endow the great creative artists. Now it must obviously be endowment for ever. It is no use paying a man to learn the intricacies of musical composition for seven or eight years and then leaving him stranded. It is just the greatest who would suffer. Verdi might come out of it all right: not Wagner. Nor can we have anyone dictating to the artists how they must work, on pain of having their scholarships taken away. A system so brilliantly efficacious with undergraduates and schoolboys would not work in this case. Nor, of course, could questions of morality enter. And the endowment must not be removed if the artist becomes popular enough to earn a living without it. We don't want to prolong the present condition by which, if an artist strikes a vein which is popular, he is economically bound to continue in it for the rest of his life. By that, Shakespeare, being successful with histories, daren't proceed to *As You Like It*, or, having 'scored a success' in comedy, can't go on to *Hamlet*. No, the endowment must be unconditioned, even, I suggest, as regards production. We might perhaps insist on one picture, book, or piece of music in ten years. Nothing more stringent. The only debatable point seems to me to be the forbidding of other trades. We *might* forbid them to earn money by doing quite different work to any large extent. No doubt the Government will begin that way. I expect it's not worth doing, though. There are a lot of details, like the increase of endowment if the artist married. The Eugenics Society would see we got that.

The point where most people profess to find the greatest difficulty is in the machinery for selecting people for endowment. 'The State', they say, 'is always stupid about Art'. Also 'a Committee always compromises'. They talk of 'officialdom'. As every Socialist knows, these silly generalizations are always being flung in to cloak muddled thinking. To begin with, the State hasn't tried anything of this kind. It has only muddled feebly with Art here and there. To argue from that is like bringing up the bad management of occasional railways by individualist governments as an argument against the considered socialization of monopolies. In any case, State activity is not uniformly stupid. The Royal Academy perhaps is bad. The National Gallery is good. So, on the whole, is the Civil

List – as far as it goes. The chief faults in these two departments are those of meanness. We can remedy that if we want to.

As far as efficiency of endowment goes, any modern Cabinet Minister with a few hundred thousand a year to spend and the advice of a couple of literary journalists would be more successful, and infinitely less wasteful, than the present system of capital. But that is a low standard. And the one-man method is not the best. A committee is obvious. It is a system that fulfills its purpose very well, for example, in electing to college fellowships, especially where the number of fellowships is large. For notice, the ordinary objections to a committee on an æsthetic subject apply only when it is to choose some single object. A committee of artists met to select one from one thousand designs, say for a bridge across the Thames, will compromise and not choose the most beautiful. But if the Supreme and Omniscient Art Critic required them to pick the ten most beautiful, and gave them one hundred shots, they would probably succeed. And that is what we want. Take the endowment of pure creative literature. I conceive of a committee of, say, thirty. It could and should be constituted in many different ways, by nomination by the Crown, by, perhaps, the Universities, by various official and semi-official bodies such as the Society of Authors, and in other ways – the more irregular the better. You'd get a few stuffy people, no doubt; you'd also get a few creative artists, Thomas Hardy and Yeats, and critics like Professor Sir Walter Raleigh and Mr. Gosse. They would have outer circles of advisers and suggesters. It seems to me certain that, if such a Committee had to choose one hundred writers of poetry to endow, and voted on some system of proportional representation, in such a way that two or three, or even one, who was keen enough, could make certain of a candidate, they would sweep in almost every writer who could possibly turn out to be any good. Remember, it is people like these who have always been the first to recognize genius. Think how Tennyson or James Thomson or Yeats or Meredith were discovered. Think, from the other side, of the work Henley and Ben Jonson did.

It may be objected that we should waste a lot in endowing failures, ten of them perhaps for every one even moderate success. Certainly. It is an integral part of the scheme. The choice is between endowing twenty Tuppers to one Byron – and endowing neither; and the present system, which consists in endowing twenty thousand Tuppers and one Byron, *and* – for that might be worth while – very effectually disendowing and spoiling twenty million Tuppers – and who dare say how many Byrons among them?

Indeed, I'd have you notice that the kind of failures we endow are likely to be useful to our purpose. There is frequently among artists of all kinds generosity that seems extraordinary in a commercial age. The example of French painters is a notable one. And there are several cases today in literature, where good writers of some genius have been helped with money, advice and advertisement, most freely and solely for their genius' sake, by smaller writers of more fortunate lot – just the kind who would have been endowed on their early promise, and would not have accomplished anything great.

That is all to the good. For we must insist on the need for as many channels as possible through which the Arts may be subsidized. Each additional channel may mean fresh artists who would have escaped our notice otherwise; and each helps to provide for fresh, unexpected developments.

Besides the central State endowments it would be a good thing to have more local and special ones. If the numerous universities of Great Britain could be given money to endow creative artistic work, it would be excellent. At present they only endow critical work and knowledge. They would be able to do the other, too, quite admirably. Municipalities also might be encouraged to take steps in that direction. The more progressive of them are ready enough to be the first, driven by those motives of honourable rivalry which already have so finely influenced some of our great cities and districts. With the present growth of local pride, and of universities in large centres, and with the system of County Council scholarships, it should be easy to encourage local endowment of Art, with desirable results of variety and thoroughness. I can imagine Manchester and others being keen enough to get the credit of connexion with the next great painter or dramatist.

This local connexion may be increased and improved incidentally by a plan that has been suggested, by which the local or national authority endowing might receive, under conditions, a share in, or the whole of, the copyright of an endowed artist's work after his death. This applies only, apparently, to music and books. But the lines on which it may be extended to pictures can be seen if you consider the admirable proposal that a percentage of the *increase* in value of a picture should go to the artist or his heirs every time

it is sold. This copyright business may allay the fears of the parsi-
monious, for obviously the State would begin to *gain* by the endowment of Art in a generation. Still it is very important. The cost of
endowing Art in England is absurdly small. Suppose you give
artists an average of £500 a year – and I personally think *half* that
is all that is necessary. Endow for life two hundred musicians, two
hundred painters and sculptors, two hundred poets, and three
hundred other creative literary men, keeping one hundred endowments for special richness in one section or unclassified creative
artistic genius, you would spend half a million a year. Half a million!
I need not tell students of modern budgets what a drop that is. If
anyone wants to realize its insignificance let him consider modern
expenditure on armaments. Half a million to secure the Arts in
England! (I appeal to my friends the politicians in this Society to
see that this is done!) If there's any politician present there's his
chance!

Each Art has different conditions and demands different treatment.
I am afraid I have considered too much the conditions of Literature.
But the principles of endowment apply throughout in music and
painting. The system of scholarships from County Council and other
schools is good enough, but must be continually increased. We want
to drain the nation. More scholarships should come both through the
County Councils and at the various Academies and Colleges of
Music and Art, which, conditionally, could be State-aided. They
must be sufficient in amount and period. People should be able to
travel and study on them.

(If anyone wants to know how well, even now, such scholarships
can be applied, he can examine the L.C.C. Art scholarships. To be
sure they don't lead to dead Official Art, ask anyone at the Slade
School of Art, which is not generally thought to be over-academic.
He will tell you of the extraordinarily good scholars they get from
the L.C.C. You will learn of the Michael Angelo of the twentieth
century, as a youth is named who has been discovered in the back
streets of London, and can draw better than any upper-class rival.
It is the right process. I'm told by people at the Slade that the
holders of L.C.C. scholarships are some of the best people there.
And that they should be sent or be able to go to the Slade shows that
these municipal bodies wouldn't encourage only dead official art.)

I will not worry about more details. I only want to insist that endowment is the only thing for us to do, and is immediately necessary. In considering such a scheme certain requirements must be kept in mind as a guide. The artist must be able to devote himself to his work. He must be left to himself as much as possible. He should have, I think, an economic spur to production and popularity, the chance, that is, of greater wealth if his work catches on. And endowment should be of as various kinds as possible.

And besides all these more or less official forces at work, we must see that there are private ones. More and more as the public for the Arts grows wider shall we find private societies and groups in immense variety helping our work. This may take the form of endowment, group-patronage, an excellent thing, already less rare than is generally known. It requires a genuine and rather beautiful faith in an artist's work and future for large numbers of his friends to sacrifice something in order that he may be able to realize his fate unhindered. But more usually these societies will be bands of consumers, of purchasers, acting together to be more effective, combining to finance the production of new plays or music, or to buy pictures and statues. I do not refer to such bodies as the National Art Collections Fund or the Friends of the Fitzwilliam Museum. Their work is excellent. But it only indirectly affects the living artist. No activity of theirs would have saved Monticelli or Epstein or Van Gogh or Clare or Nerval from the hindrances and degradation of poverty. I mean rather an extension and multiplication of the Contemporary Art Society, which buys modern pictures before they have become old masters. It will be private bodies, formed in such ways, that will come to the rescue, perhaps, when the great event happens for which our prayers go up night and day, and a great writer or painter or composer appears, so monstrously blasphemous or indecent that the most hardened Municipality or University or member of the National Endowment Committee will have nothing to do with him.

There is, perhaps, one more aspect of Democracy and the Arts besides the Public and the Artist, which can be mentioned. It is one on which a whole book might throw light – two pages are useless. It is the question of what fools call the æsthetic aspirations of the community, and journalists call an atmosphere, and hard clear thinkers vow non-existent, and wise men know to be an attitude of mind. Is there anything more we can do about the artistic atmosphere in this Democracy? Is it possible to ensure that artist and critic will be living, eager about new productions and experiments, believing in their arts? What should our own attitude of mind be?

There is nothing, I suppose, to be *done*, except indirectly by smashing smugness and propriety, and encouraging enthusiasm rather than criticism in the world. All one can do is to turn out a great many artists and critics (real critics). This sort of thing is a matter of tradition largely. You get a whole lot of people, a class or a town or circle, falling naturally into the belief that Art is worth while and means a lot to them. They mostly lie. But they are necessary. Remember that, when a lot of idiots yearn to you about the Irish plays. *They* are the condition of J. M. Synge. Concerts, we hear, are hard enough to get up in Cambridge. If only those who cared for the music went they would be impossible. The Arts are built up on a crowd of prattlers, *dilettanti*, wits and pseudo-cultured. It is worth while.

But there is one thing we can do. To give vitality to the Arts it is necessary to direct a large proportion of our interest to contemporary art. The need for this is not fully recognized, especially in that half-cultivated class *we* belong to. There are two points about it I should like to mention. One is the obvious one that has already come out. It is our *duty* to be interested in contemporary art for the artist's sake, first that he may live, second that he may turn out better stuff. All your praise of Shakespeare will not turn him to his too neglected task of 'blotting' at any rate *some* lines: nor will Leonardo ever complete his head of Christ. But the living, them you can stir or warm and enable to work, and work at their best. Do you think this unnecessary, slightly insulting? Is anyone muttering, 'But we *are* modern and up-to-date. Nietzsche is our Bible. Van Gogh our idol. We drink in the lessons of Meredith and Ibsen and Swinburne and Tolstoy! ... Dostoieffsky and Tour-genieff. ...' They are dead, my friends, all dead. Beware, for the generations slip imperceptibly into one another, and it is so much easier to accept standards that are prepared for you. Beware of the dead.

But it is not only a question of duty to living artists – a sufficiently dreary appeal. So much sentimentality has been talked about the immortality of Art that it is a *heresy* that I now suggest to you. To open eyes the nature of Art forbids this immortality. If you write a poem on Tuesday it begins to die on Wednesday. Some take longer dying than others. That is all. Anyhow a few thousand years will finish off the Parthenon Marbles, and Shakespeare will not outlive half a dozen more civilizations. But time has a quicker, quieter way than that. Necessary to Art is the recipient, and he must change. No man alive can read Shakespeare quite as Shakespeare meant it. The subtle shades of words have changed. The Elizabethans' common words seem strange to us. And we can never recapture the fine thrill of surprise they had at words that were delightful fresh inventions of theirs – words like *prejudice*. There is something in almost all Art that only a contemporary can get – only one who shares with the artist the general feeling for ideas and thoughts and outlook of the time. *That* is the great reason for interest in the art of one's own time. Think of what we *do* feel and value. Take – I pick almost at random – Henry James's last volume of stories, and, most delightful in the most delightful of them,[1] the phrase, 'She just charmingly hunched her eyes at him'. Thirty years hence and for ever after, will they be able to get just what we get from that, in meaning and intonation, the caress of the adverb, the exact shade of comedy in the verb, the curve of the sentence?

There is much to be said. But it is late, and each can say it for himself, if only he'll do what people romantically never will do, for all my persuasion – only connect Art and Democracy. Upper-class young people who live on money they don't earn and dabble with painting or writing (I am one) are always, and so finely, a little too *temperamentvoll* to be interested in 'politics'. It's much easier and much splendider to assume that social organization or disorganization has no effect on people – on artists at least: to fly off with some splashing war-cry that 'Art will out', that 'The True Artist (wonderful abstraction!) is only Improved by Poverty'. The wonderful old-world romanticism of it all! The fineness, even, when it's done by poor people! It's only when it's carelessly flung out by people who *have* an assured unearned few hundreds a year, that the sentiment may ring a little discordant, taste a trifle unwholesome, something like Lord Rosebery's, to the over-sensitive palate. You feel that if the misty splendour of these artists turned perspicuous, it would for a second reveal them leaning after all against an ordinary wall, in an attitude that's exactly between the ever so

[1] 'A Round of Visits' in *The Finer Grain*, 1910.

slightly silly and the ever so slightly something worse. Like the lovers at the end of the modern poem:

Flamingly, flamingly good as ends,
Heart of my heart, are dividends.

And against them stand the politicians, who are only occupied with social and political changes: who also, less gloriously, leave Art to take care of itself. Now more than ever. 'Politics', I heard two old clergymen in Oxford say, on a tram last July, 'are no laughing matter nowadays'. Those who never found them a laughing matter will be full these days of vaster questions than endowing artists. Their hearts thrill with great cries – Home Rule – Insurance – Peace. In such a mood 'Democracy' is only a long word, a mouthful, a battle-cry, a sound that evokes tumultuous applause and right voting: or perhaps an emotional dim ideal. Regard it as a present process. The word should picture *us*, with our habits of feeling and thought, and, more particularly, thousands and millions of wakening minds everywhere. More than a million Trades Unionists, a million belonging to P.S.A. Brotherhoods, bodies with an outlook and importance we haven't dimly begun to grasp, the W.E.A., the Adult Schools – these and many more are spreading, further than ever our narrow conceits carry, fresh enthusiasms and loyalties and intellectual keenness. These, and we, and the traditions and institutions of the land, and the infinite entanglement of will and instinct and fate, individual and collective, are bound together weaving the future. It is possible and desirable to guard and aid the Arts as Democracy grows. But it must be by a conscious effort, by not being afraid of new things, by helping to build up an atmosphere and tradition of honour for the Arts, by living in the present as well as in the past, and especially, and more easily because more tangibly, by endowing artists, we can do this. Like the rest of the great adventure of Democracy it is a superb, an exhilarating chance. We, rotund and comfortable, are willy-nilly rolling out on the most amazing expedition. There's but one danger, one misconception more I would point out. Two years ago I heard a lecture on Social Reform and the Drama, delivered by a great living critic, a keen, able, solemn, whiskered, well-meaning man, Mr. William Archer. His theory was that Art depends for its subject-matter (*a*) on people having so much money and so much leisure as to be able to get into scrapes; (*b*) on social injustice and evil laws which lead to misery. Conclusion: successful social reform on democratic lines means the end of Art. He was, it is unnecessary to say, in earnest. It is a theory that has crept into too many minds. It is the ultimate disloyalty – not to Democracy, but to Art. We need not point out that all the poets and dramatists and half the painters have found their subject-matter in the past. Nor need we bring up those artists from Whitman to Meunier who have begun to invade the vast new provinces now opening to them. We shall – rather we *will* – find that the old unchanging ground for the artist stands fast, the emotions of the individual human heart. Imagination will only grow profounder, passions and terrors will come in stranger shapes. Tragedy and Comedy will not leave the world while two things stay in it, the last two that Civilization will cure us of, Death and Fools. In new shapes Hamlet and Othello and Macbeth will move among us, as they do today. Though we perfect the marriage laws it will still be possible to fall in love with the wrong person or with two people; and still painful. Still, while Democracy grows, down the ages we may have the figure of a critic, an elderly man, explaining to a group of young people that the stuff of Art is being ruled out of life, black-whiskered and perplexed and in earnest – slightly resembling Matthew Arnold, a recurrent figure of most excellent comic value.

6
Philosophy

The title of this chapter may seem bombastic: Brooke himself would have laughed at it, and would never have thought himself a philosopher. But his papers to the Apostles could be called – however vaguely and lightly – philosophical; it seems right to include an example of them, as they show a side of him which does not appear elsewhere; and 'A or B?' does not obviously belong under any other head.

The tone of his Apostles papers is suggested by such titles as 'Why not try the other leg?', and 'Are the playing of cards and the attendance at the theatre amusements inconsistent with the character of a clergyman?' One can hear, over half a century, the donnish and the undergraduate giggles. As one might expect, the papers have private allusions directed to the small circle of the society – in the paper I have chosen perhaps less so than in some others. And it is important to set it in its context. Brooke, in his third year as an undergraduate, is addressing the company to which I have referred. The manuscript shows signs of hasty composition; we may guess that he might have improvised and adapted it as he read. It is amusing, too, to try to cast these *Mikado* characters. The emotional Pitti-Sing is, of course, the author; but Katisha – could she be Strachey? And Pooh-Bah – does the interjection of 'Beethoven' hint at E. M. Forster? A period piece, in truth, but this is not its sole interest, nor should its lightness of touch lead one to dismiss lightly the thought. Together with the letter to F. H. Keeling (chapter 3) the paper shows how a sensitive, intelligent man of the time could respond to the limitations of Moore's *Principia Ethica*; and it looks forward to Sartre and Existentialism before even the works of Kierkegaard had become known in English.

'A or B?'

The air was singularly bland and encouraging. There was a confidential serenity in the equitable spring sun, the enamelled green surface of the lawn, and the five little round plum-coloured mats on which they squatted. They ate peaches filled with scented jellies, and sipped pale tea from inconceivably small cups; while the cherry-blossom fell slowly about them. They were attended by dumb naked boys, who ran to and from the pagoda in a constant stream bearing food or drink or toys and practising light lust with one another on the way; whose skin was of an uniform light puce colour, and their black thin eyes were set in faces that never stirred even under the most trying situations. Surrounded thus by all the comforts known to man, the five were going through their parts in the customary manner. 'It's an unjust world', the Mikado had just said, 'and virtue is triumphant only in theatrical performances.' With leisurely assurance they proceeded to the glee – but here an acute spectator might have noticed that there was at least a slight divergence from the established ritual. For Katisha was not there: and her place in the quintette was taken by Pish-Tush. Indolently the Mikado, Ko-Ko and Pooh-Bah led off.

> See how the Fates their gifts allot,
> For A is happy – B is not.
> Yet B is worthy, I dare say,
> Of more prosperity than A!

'*Is* B more worthy?' queried Pish-Tush and Pitti-Sing, doubtfully. The reply came firm and precise:

> I should say
> He's worth a great deal more than A.

Softly all joined in:

> Yet A is happy!
> Oh, so happy!
> Laughing, Ha! ha!
> Chaffing, Ha! ha!
> Nectar quaffing, Ha! ha! ha! ha!
> Ever joyous, ever gay,
> Happy, undeserving A!

In the second verse, Pooh-Bah, whose clear excited soprano had already outsoared the rest, took up the burden almost alone, the Mikado and Ko-Ko softly humming in a dilettante and academic agreement.

If I were Fortune – which I'm not –

(he announced with vast conviction)

B should enjoy A's happy lot,
And A should die in miserie –
That is, assuming I am B.

'But *should* A perish?' asked Pish-Tush and Pitti-Sing, drearily.

That should be
(of course assuming I am B)
B should be happy!
Oh, so happy!
Laughing, Ha! ha!
Chaffing, Ha! ha!
Nectar quaffing, Ha! ha! ha! ha!

The note of resigned fierceness died away, and Pooh-Bah, in an ecstatic return to bitter melancholy, sighed the rest:

But condemned to die is he,
Wretched, meritorious B!

There was a moment's wild silence, filled, as Pitti-Sing said to herself, with the thunder of dumb sobs. Katisha had crept in from the wings and had sorrowfully buried her face in a large blue handkerchief. There was an atmosphere of high B-ness about the place. Ko-Ko, cheerily vacuous yet dimly conscious, as usual, returned from joke hunting, and drying a polite tear, was about to pick up his cue, when Pitti-Sing sprang absurdly to her feet and screamed. 'I don't believe it,' she cried. 'I prefer A!' 'Yes,' said Ko-Ko, smoothly and readily, 'but do you think he was *right?*' 'By Gad,' said Pitti-Sing, '*Yes!*'

Katisha screamed with mirth. Pooh-Bah groaned. Pish-Tush looked alarmed; the Mikado cautious. Pitti-Sing continued. 'You see, you've brought me up to believe in Good being in *states of mind* and that sort of thing, or in organic unities or something – anyhow,

I mean, it all comes to the same in the end. Well, anyhow, I'll accept all that, you see; and I suppose one should aim at good. Also I've been told that we have an immediate perception, or something, of what good states of mind are; which can't be argued about. The latter part of the statement seems to me superficial and a lie; as I don't confine argument to logical reasoning. For instance I doubt if *I* could logically prove to poor old Katisha here (if, as is probable, she would deny it) that the predominant colour in the sky at sunset on an average evening is green. I could not logically prove it; nor, though she has seen a thousand sunsets, has she ever noticed it. But if I took her by the arm at 5.30 tomorrow and led her out and made her look, she would acknowledge it. One cannot prove what states of mind (taking, for the time, that notation) are good. But one can often point them out, show them as good, display them and they are seen to be good. This of course is the province of all Art – ' (There were signs of fury. The Mikado was enraged. Katisha and Pish-Tush growled, preliminarily.) 'Anyway, of some art,' went on Pitti-Sing, hastily, 'and many people in conversation, by art or personality, can do it. It's obvious. But, anyhow, we are, theoretically, often very well agreed as to what good states of mind are, vaguely. Enough to start on. "Certain personal relations and aesthetic emotions," we say, happily. "And various other states, undefined," we think. Anyhow, I was very well content. For my own ideas of good seemed *fairly* near to all yours; and they will always (I thought) tend to approximate. "How happy they must all be!" I thought. You being wise and clever, must know so well what good is. You had only to ensue it. But then I was perplexed for I couldn't understand why you asked and spoke and thought so oddly, and were, some of you, not extremely happy. And still I don't know how much our disagreement is because we differ, most of you and I, about what good is, and how much because you live unconsciously, like nearly everybody, an instinctive life that's very little affected by your theories.'

'I don't see,' said the Mikado and Ko-Ko, pronouncing each word exactly together, 'why you should take it for granted that the better one is, the happier,' 'Nor do I,' said the other three, hastily, for they, too, had been thinking hard.

'It's not necessary to what I want to say,' replied Pitti-Sing, 'but it seems to me likely. In the first place, human beings are so oddly constituted, with this thing they call a conscience, that they generally attain a large amount of happiness merely by satisfying their conscience and following the good, and, conversely, become quite miserable whenever, in disobedience to the voice within them, they pursue that which they know to be evil. That bit's by Plato; and quite true. Moreover, the states of mind we hold to be good seem to me to be generally happy ones: whether by coincidence or no does not matter. Good feelings towards persons indeed need not always be pleasant; but I should have thought that by all theories they should be, as a rule: – and to me it seems obvious that the very great majority of the quite good states of mind of people in love must be extremely happy. (Pardon the nauseating ugliness of this dialect,' she said in a parenthesis, 'I loathe it and speak it with difficulty. But it may aid me to be understood.) To know oneself to be deeply in love is most gladdening. To know that love returned may multiply the joy by a million. But the mere feeling a onesided love, unless it be mean and shallow, should make you sing for gladness the whole day. While as for the aesthetic emotions (which seem to include those felt before works of art and also those felt before natural beauty) they are always accompanied by pleasure. Even Pooh-Bah, with utmost effort and (I suspect) a large personal appeal to his own life, can but rarely feel actual pain with his aesthetic emotions.'

'King Lear –' began the Lord High Executioner.

'Beethoven –' began the Lord High Everything Else.

'Exceptions,' Pitti-Sing shouted – 'the exceptions I had already carefully explained, where, through your own conscious sentimental efforts, or effects separate from the *aesthetic* emotions, your mind is momentarily in a state rather of pain than pleasure. However, your collective lack of the incessant and almost infinite happiness I had, rightly or wrongly, expected to find in you, led me to consider the states of mind of each of you, and of myself.'

'With the possible exception of the last, my dear child,' said Katisha, 'you know nothing at all of the minds of any of us. You are the worst judge of character in Titipu.'

Pitti-Sing got very angry. 'It is you who are blind, and bad judges of character,' she screamed. Then everybody gobbled with rage. For in Japan this is one of the two insults that are unforgivable. You may tell a mandarin that he has no manners and no taste and no brains, that he knows nothing of Science or Art or Literature, that he cannot tell a tribrach from a triolet, nor Breughel from Borgognone, and he will often smile and be rather pleased. But tell him that he is a poor judge of character and he will gobble, and loathe you.

'I can prove I am not a bad judge,' Pitti-Sing continued, 'for my verdict about each of you agrees in the obvious things with the verdict of all the rest of you about that one: only, in the finer points I alone have sight. Anyhow, your states of mind seemed to me bad; bad, at least, as ends. For instance, you're all jolly warmhearted and enthusiastic and exclusive about seeking for truth, and partly, as you assert, for truth's sake. As a means, it is agreed, this is useful. But as an end? Is the state of mind of one seeking truth, therefore good? I do not think so, and Katisha at least agrees with me, as she has told me. At most, this is but a small part of good. But this point illustrates, I think, the tendency of some among us to regard themselves too much as means, too little as ends. I don't believe poor old Pish-Tush has ever thought of himself as an end. And yet when are ends to be, if not, in part, now? And where if not in us? Are they all to be in the dim future, to which Pish-Tush works; or mostly in other people as the half-Christian Katisha might seem to desire. I declare that we are better than anybody else, and should be ends ourselves. What magnificent ends we might be!'

'Are,' came a whisper.

'I do think we try to be; and very successfully,' said Pooh-Bah, majestically.

Pitti-Sing sighed. 'Perhaps you *do* think our states of mind good. But I feel we don't always try our best. There is limited good in observing human relationships, more, occasionally, in taking part in them. But to confine ourselves so much to observing or assisting and discussing that infinitely complex web of myth and elaborate induction with which Pooh-Bah like a little black spider covers Titipu and its inhabitants – that seems to me not to produce at all good states of mind, perhaps not to be able to, and certainly to be a most insignificant corner of the world of possibilities. But besides the pursuit of truth and personal relationships there is a whole possible world of good "states of mind" we too rarely approach. Laughter and the pursuit of amusing or interesting knowledge occupy the rest of our common time. Whether the comic spirit is good at all as an end is an enquiry of enormous interest that we must postpone to another occasion. At least neither of these occupations will be held to lead at all directly to very good states of mind. But think of the very many other extraordinarily exciting things! There is so much else besides people. Why should I find it impossible to conceive Katisha communing with Nature, or the Mikado ecstatically contemplating a rose? And yet, quite seriously, I believe that extremely good states of mind might follow from these simple acts. There are a thousand beauties and splendours here in Japan we let slip irrevocably past every day. Why do we cut ourselves off from so much experience? The world would be much bigger and finer for us if we went about with our eyes and ears open, if we plunge into Life, and did mad things for the joy of it and rushed all over Japan suddenly instead of decaying in Titipu. My instances are wild, but oh! observe the spirit of them: catch the meaning! Why should we neglect the beauty of the world because *poseurs* have pretended to love it? Because our neighbour Mr Bunthorne gazed at lilies, may not the Mikado? Because they are hypocrites in England, must we be pedants in Japan? We refuse to discuss Literature and Art, than which there is nothing that has a nobler effect on the mind, or opens wider horizons, because fools and liars have discussed them hatefully. Would you be ashamed of loving, because sentimentalists have loved sloppily? It is a confession of weakness to find discussion of a thing that should matter immensely, and produce ecstatic and splendid states of mind, dull. And it is not if we are willing to do this, but if we *want* to, that is important. If B was unhappy, he was a fool and probably wicked. C was the same, who thought he was happy, but was only smugly content. You must be consciously, madly happy, like A, deliriously pleased with the vast amount of splendid things. There is virtue in such happiness; in melancholy and content, none!' At this point Pitti-Sing, an emotional girl, burst into tears, and rushed into the pagoda. The rest sighed a little, and then hurried on with their daily task. For the sun had set, and the willows and cherry-trees were shivering a little. Ko-Ko took up his long-interrupted cue serenely. 'Well! a nice mess you've got us into . . .'

(Paper to the Apostles, 13 February 1909)

7
Criticism

Apart from the monograph on 'Puritanism in English Drama up to 1642' with which he won the Harness Prize, Brooke's only sustained work of criticism is his Fellowship dissertation, 'John Webster and the Elizabethan Drama'. In this, as in his journalistic criticism, he adopted a vigorous, sometimes jaunty style, which owed something to Walter Headlam (whose Cambridge lectures he much admired), and suggests, in that unfortunate phrase which Scott applied to Byron, 'the negligent ease of a man of quality'. Brooke had no patience with the prevailing critical pedantry. Reviewing the fifth volume of *The Cambridge History of English Literature*, he wrote characteristically:

> It is amazing that experts and professors of English literature, familiar with so many live and glowing styles, should write such uniform lustreless English, with all the faults of journalese – the flaccidity, the circumlocutions, the trite lifeless unmeaning metaphors, the interminable string of abstract substances – without its occasional brightness. They vary; but the tendency is towards this flat stuff, which blurs thought, slips along, forbids the mind to grasp or remember anything, is, in a word, dead. Professor Saintsbury's chapters among the rest stand out like a hippopotamus in an expanse of mud, clumsy and absurd, but alive.

And he concluded:

> There seem to be so many people who could write well about English Literature if they knew more about it; and so many who know – if they could but write!

Brooke shared with Headlam a concern for accuracy of scholarship, an aptitude for going straight to the point, and that rare combination of artistic perception and robust common-sense. Hassall calls *John Webster* 'one of the necessary books for a serious student'. Lest this judgment be dismissed as showing the partiality of a biographer, it can be supported by that of F. L. Lucas who, in the preface to his standard edition of Webster, acclaimed Brooke 'the best of Webster's critics'.

> *John Webster & the Elizabethan Drama* is indeed a very
> youthful book: that is why it is so good. Its author had not
> had time to amass the mountainous erudition which goes into
> much modern study of the Elizabethans: but another
> quality, rarer in commentators and even more essential here,
> he did possess – he was alive to the finger-tips.

Brooke wrote, as always, largely to please himself. In the vein of the 'unpleasant' poems, he eulogized Marston, who 'loved dirt for truth's sake; also for its own. Filth, horror, and wit were his legacy; it was a splendid one.' Not even Hazlitt, who likewise overrated him, gave Marston unqualified praise for his filth. But Brooke dwelt with peculiar relish on whatever might offend a weak stomach, forgetting, perhaps, that even Marston urged, 'Be not obsceane though wanton in thy rimes'. Such youthful excesses should not obscure the value of his judgments. Though the erudition might not have been mountainous, the sheaves of scribbled notes which survive among his manuscripts, together with the ten appendices (as long almost as the essay itself), are witness to the care and scholarship.

My first excerpt is from the opening chapter in which Brooke presents a general aesthetic. An awareness of linguistic pitfalls enables him, with remarkable percipience, to detect a chink in the philosophy of Moore and the Cambridge Realists. C. K. Ogden and I. A. Richards ask in *The Meaning of Meaning*:

> Why should there be only one subject of investigation
> which has been called Aesthetics? Why not several fields
> to be separately investigated, whether they are found to be
> connected or not? . . . What reason is there to suppose
> that one aesthetic doctrine can be framed to include all the
> valuable kinds of what is called Literature?

It is no small tribute that they find Brooke to be 'the only author who appears to have expressly admitted this difficulty and recognized its importance'.

The second excerpt, on Seneca's influence, is from the second chapter, 'Origins of Elizabethan Drama'; the third, largely on Kyd and Marlowe, and the fourth on the period 1600–1610, are from the third chapter, 'The Elizabethan Drama'. The fifth and longest excerpt is from the final chapter on 'Some Characteristics of Webster'. I have given here almost the whole of Brooke's discussion of Webster's use of notebooks because it throws such interesting light upon his own practice.

My excuse, similarly, for including two articles on John Donne from the journalistic criticism is their relevance to Brooke's own writing. Written as reviews of the Grierson edition for separate periodicals, the articles are surprisingly free of repetition. I have given each in full, as I have all but one of the remaining pieces, which have been chosen in part to suggest the range of Brooke's critical interest. The early piece on Clare is the latter half only of a short review of Arthur Symons's selection.

From a Review of *Poems by John Clare*

This strange creature had exquisitely delicate senses, an ear for poetic harmony, and a great love of the real country, which he described minutely with a quiet sincere beauty. His poetry has an immediacy of vision that sometimes recalls Blake. He had, as he says, a passionate love for all the aspects of life he knew, and he communicates it. His evasive charm may be increased by the few very beautiful odd provincial and archaic words or expressions he uses:

And the little chumbling mouse
Gnarls the dead weed for her house. . . .

or

And the breeze, with feather feet,
Crimping o'er the waters sweet . . .

The glossary, which is quite inadequate, only includes a few of his rusticisms.

At times he mixes in, quite sincerely, some of the common poetical stuff of the annuals of the day – musings on gravestones and the like; sometimes merely tacking it on as a conventional ornament, sometimes making it oddly real and his own. There is a quaint, bird-like note in his poems written in the asylum, that has led Mr Symons, and most recent reviewers, to prefer them to the work of his sane years. This very modern and sentimental judgment is not justified. Clare's best and most characteristic poetry is found in such poems as 'The Flitting' and 'The Progress of Rhyme'. He was a minor, but very true-born poet, and, like so few country poets, really 'of the soil'; though not an 'untutored songster', no 'sing-as-the-birds-sing' fraud, of course. For, with all his handicaps he had read widely, as every poet must have done, in the poetry of his predecessors. If his body and mind had been properly fed, if he had had a fair chance, the advantages of even Keats, what might he not have given us! At any rate the delicate and faint music that did come from the stunted brain and poor twisted nerves, is now, thanks to Mr Symons, within the reach of anyone who cares for poetry. There is no longer any excuse for being ignorant of Clare.

(*The Cambridge Review*, 11 March 1909)

Review of *Last Poems* by Meredith

In this very small volume have been collected some 'fragments' left by Meredith, some verses written for occasions, and a few miscellaneous poems. The best way to honour a great poet of so sternly truthful a heart as Meredith is to tell the truth; so it must not be pretended that these, with one or two exceptions, have any merit on their own account. Led astray by the common metaphors applied to old age, comparisons with the golden splendour of autumn or the serene mellow afterglow of sunset, people expect from poets of seventy or eighty, work that if it has lost some of the old fire has gained a new glory, a note of strength and peace, such as they claim to find in 'The Tempest'. They do not realise that death is a gradual process, that the poetic powers far more than the intellectual, fade with the physical. Those who have listened to Meredith's teaching of Youth and Earth would do wrong in yielding, even in this one case, to that pleasant blindness. Most of these poems deal with centenaries, with conscription, the Royal Family, Ireland, Imperialism, and so forth, and are without merit. The 'Voyage of the Ophir' is especially bad. The political opinions he would preach seem to have less loftiness of morality than of old. The two sonnets have something of the old humour; but most of the book brings up irresistibly the slightly uncomfortable thought, 'what would Dr Shrapnel have said to this?' Meredith's last gifts to the world at first sight seem to be less of a summing-up of his life's work, to have less of the nature of a conscious and solemn valediction, than those of many great poets. The terrible fate of all official poets and all who too strenuously have a doctrine to preach, has overtaken him. The feeling of dulness, perfunctoriness and repetition continually creeps in. The four fragments are truer Meredith, of one stuff with the whole characteristic body of his work. More than the rest of the book, however, they suffer from bad editing. The punctuation has been mis-managed in several places, though one wants all help possible in reading Meredith. There seems to have been an odd mistake, whether of Meredith's or of the editor's, in the second fragment:

A wilding little stubble flower,
The sickle scorned which cut for corn,
Such was our hope in that dark hour
When nought save uses held the street,
And daily pleasures, daily needs,
With barren vision, looked ahead.
And still the same result of seeds
Gave likeness twixt the live and dead.

The comma in the sixth line, of course, should be deleted. But every ear, at the end, must find the lack of rhyme in the second and fourth lines most uncomfortable, in this unusually smooth verse form. Is it not obvious – though it has not yet been noticed, as far as we know – that the last word in the now too cacophonous second line should be 'wheat', 'corn' having been written before the fourth line was thought out or having crept in by the influence of 'scorned'? It is to be hoped that the correction will be made, or noted, in future editions.

The five first poems seem to be the gleanings of Meredith's real poetry. They are barely less beautiful and inspiring than the work of his maturity. 'The Years had Worn' is delightful, a mingling of Meredith and Wordsworth. 'On Como' is among the best and most individual poems he ever wrote. It is marred by silly mis-punctuation on the second page. But the best is the little lyric 'Youth in Age'. It is most of all free from any suspicion of being the work of an old man trying to write as he did in his prime. Its glory is its own. Not Meredith at twenty or at forty could have written this. It is the cry of a poet and a lover of life in his old age. Those of the present generation to whom Meredith's Earth-poetry, with all its faults, has come with an appeal more poignant, and an inspiration in some ways more glorious, than any other literature or thought has given, will find in this the real and significant farewell of a guide whose directions, at length, were no 'vain words' but invaluably concerned with the 'wayfaring', who revealed Man's only and sufficient heaven – in Earth.

Youth in Age
 Once I was part of the music I heard
  On the boughs or sweet between earth and sky.
  For joy of the beating of wings on high
 My heart shot into the breast of the bird.

 I bear it now and I see it fly,
  And a life in wrinkles again is stirred,
  My heart shoots into the breast of the bird
 As it will for sheer love till the last long sigh.

     (*The Cambridge Review*, 18 November 1909)

The Post-Impressionist Exhibition at the Grafton Galleries

Two years ago, such English people as look at pictures were startled and shocked by an exhibition of 'Post-Impressionist' art in London. Names that have since grown familiar – Cézanne, Van Gogh, Gauguin – began to crop up in conversation and discussion. Some praised the novelties, some wondered, many laughed. In France, Germany, and Russia, of course, these pictures had been known for many years. We get things late in England. But by now the first shock, even with us, has worn off. And the 'Second Post-Impressionist Exhibition' in the Grafton Galleries, off Bond Street, finds a more critical, and less shockedly hostile public. It is almost unnecessary in *The Cambridge Magazine* to say that everybody who is interested in pictures must go to this exhibition. Most people of that kind who read this page will already have been. For those who have not been, and those who are not certain if they should go, I want in this article to suggest shortly what the 'new movement' in art is, what this exhibition is, and what its merits and faults are. And I must defend myself beforehand by saying that I am neither painter nor art-critic, but write as an ignorant and commonplace person, with a mild liking for good pictures.

In the first place, 'Post-Impressionist' is rather a silly name. It has the negative advantage of covering a great many different schools and tendencies – all, in fact, that come after the Impressionists. But if in the various currents of modern art there *is* one general stream – and there probably is – this name does not help to recognize it. In France, the modernists in art are usually known as *Les Fauves*, in Germany as *Die Wilden* or *Die Expressionisten*. *Expressionism* is, on the whole, the best name that has been found. It will probably spread. It recognizes what is, roughly, the main reason of this modern art – a very sensible one – namely, that the *chief* object of a good picture is to convey the expression of an emotion of the artist, and *not*, as most people have been supposing, his impression of something he sees. In other words, the goodness of a good picture does not consist in its resemblance to 'nature'. It is not true that the better a picture is, the more like reality it is. It is not true that the less like reality a picture is, the worse it is. Giotto is better than Andrea del Sarto. Passion before Perspective.

This is, of course, the merest common sense. But the feature of this new movement that has swept in most of the best artists of modern Europe, and has begun to touch England, is that it has begun to act on these common-sense truths. I have tried to give the simplest theoretical essence of the 'Expressionists'. Their theories are pushed much further in the most divergent directions. Some declare their object to be to portray 'the treeness of the tree'. Some talk only of 'design'. Some would bring reality to you through the brain, reducing it to geometrical shapes. And, of course, the general aesthetic tone of most of these new pictures (for there is one, in the same way as there is in Renaissance sculpture, or Elizabethan plays, or, I am told, Russian literature), which is the important thing and necessarily the justification of the whole movement, would take far more space to explain than there is room for here.

The present exhibition professes to represent the 'Post-Impressionists' of three countries – France, Russia, and England – and contains only the work of living artists, except for a few pictures by Cézanne. It is a pity that the committee could not have included works by, at any rate, Erbslöh, Jawlensky, and Kandinsky of Munich, Pechstein of Berlin, and Kokoschka of Vienna, who paint pictures at least as good and as interesting as most of those here. To dwell further on this would be ingratitude to the energy and love of art that have given us the chance of seeing such an exciting and lovely exhibition. But one grumble must be permitted, at the air of slight incompetency that hangs over the whole exhibition. When I last visited it, for instance, on November 5th, it had been open just a month. And still some of the best Russian pictures, referred to in the preface, were not hung. And look at the catalogue! For the immense sum of a shilling you get three little prefaces, a list of the pictures and owners, and an index, which occasionally gives the date and place of the artist's birth; sometimes, as with Mr. Gill, merely mentions the heartening fact that he *has* been born; and sometimes gives no information at all. A decent catalogue would have contained small reproductions of some of the better pictures, and, most certainly, the date of painting of each exhibit. The latter omission is particularly scandalous in the case of Picasso.

The three prefaces, by Mr. Clive Bell on 'The English Group', by Mr. Roger Fry on 'The French Group', and by M. von Anrep on 'The Russian Group', are worth reading. M. von Anrep gives information, the other two write mostly on theory. Mr. Fry is the more helpful. But the innocent spectator will do best if he approaches the pictures with as willing and unsuspicious a mind as possible. Modern art can make its own defence against anything except prejudice.

The collection is rather a hotch-potch. Some of the pictures ought rather to be in the Royal Academy, some in the New English Art Club, a few in the muck-heap. There are, for instance, some sickening soapy pictures by a M. van Dongen which would disgrace even the New English Art Club. I shall only touch briefly on some of the artists who, being both good and 'Post-Impressionist', are rightly in this show. To begin with there are the French, headed by Matisse. The great glory of this exhibition is that it gives us at length a chance of judging and appreciating Matisse. Some twenty pictures and nearly as many drawings. The pure bright and generally light colour, and the stern simplicity and unity of design, fascinate the beholder. Look at *Les Capucines*, *Les poissons rouges*, *Caucous sur le tapis bleu et rose*, and the great *La danse*. There are moments in the life of most of us when some sight suddenly takes on an inexplicable and overwhelming importance – a group of objects, a figure or two, a gesture, seem in their light and position and colour to be seen in naked reality, through some rent in the grotesque veil of accidental form and hue – for a passing minute. Matisse seems to move among such realities; but lightly and dispassionately. He is entirely, almost too purposefully, free from the emotions they bring. His world is clean, lovely and inhuman as a douche of cold water. He paints dancing; and it is the essential rhythm of dance that, with a careless precision, he gets. God, certainly, does not paint like Matisse; but it is probable that the archangels do.

Picasso, the other most famous modern master represented, is very different and distinctly inferior. His method opens – as far as one can judge at present – but a narrow field. It is he who extracts from the real object he paints a pattern of lines, angles, whorls, surfaces, curves, and shadings, which is unintelligible to the spectator who would connect it with the reality. You can see his progress in this logicalization of the real world, from pictures with an obvious relation to the object portrayed, to arrangements of lines which seem to have no connection at all with those human or material forms, the names of which supply their titles. The pictures he painted *during* this progress are unsuccessful. They tend to have an uncomfortable, unhelpful similarity with the real. But his journey has landed him in an absolute art which grows better as it disentangles itself from that unholy hybrid condition. Unfortunately Picasso seems not to care about colour. His paintings have a drab ugliness about them for this reason; and so his merits can best be seen in the two little drawings in the end gallery. 'Patterns', they are, if you like; but patterns, queerly, in three dimensions; lovely and self-sufficient and inexplicable as a fugue. They do not 'represent' anything. Why should they? But they express that slight, real, half-romantic pathos – almost verging on sentimentality – which pervades all Picasso's work. A 'minor' artist.

Several other good painters of the younger generation in France are well represented here. There are certainly a dozen to twenty pictures of exhilarating strength and beauty. One, perhaps the best picture in the exhibition, certainly the most excitingly beautiful, is by M. Simon Bussy; his only exhibit. A fortnight ago it was not hung. When it is it will be worth a trip to London to see that picture alone. But M. Bussy is a school to himself, and stands outside the ordinary modern movement. Cross and Signac, who are as good as most of these artists, are – perhaps justifiably – not represented here. But you find the gloomy passion of Derain, some admirable still-life by Herbin, and attractive, earnest work by Flandrin, Vlaminck, and Girieud – though the latter is not very well represented. L'Hote and Braque (when he is not following Picasso) have a lovely light way of treating landscape. It is, indeed, in landscape that these younger French painters achieve their greatest successes. They paint it with an individual simplifying inspiration that starts originally from Cézanne. There is, alas, only one picture by the extraordinary and gifted Rousseau.

The Russians in this exhibition have hitherto been unknown to England; almost, I should think, to Western Europe. They have almost no connection with the French, German and English 'Post-Impressionists'. In his preface, indeed, M. von Anrep especially disclaims Western influence. Their work is difficult to appreciate at first. It is heavy with soul, packed with religious romanticism. The first attitude an ignorant Western mind takes up towards it is one of suspicious awe. The pictures seem to vary between pomposity and real mysticism, and to be of a more 'literary' nature than the French and English exhibits. At first sight M. Stelletsky's seem the most convincing. Even his Byzantinism is affected by the desperate and gloomy heat of unquiet that tinges all these Russian pictures.

One turns to the English section with the most lively interest. Can we hold our own yet in modern art? The answer is 'No!' But it is certainly refreshing to see that 'advanced' English art has moved beyond the stage of a few years ago, when a simple recipe for producing a picture throbbing with 'lyrical beauty' was to depict a human figure (preferably female) with one or both arms uplifted in unusual attitudes. There is not much cohesion about the English Post-Impressionists – perhaps it is as well. A not inconsiderable section of them is not represented here. Of those that are, Mr. Stanley Spencer exhibits the most remarkable picture – especially remarkable as it was painted in his eighteenth year – *John Donne arriving in Heaven*. It has a passion of design and form sadly absent from many of the others; a crude and moving nobility. Mr. Wyndham Lewis is more or less alone in resembling Picasso in method. But he gives an angular geometrical representation of reality which has an unexpected amount of emotional appeal – of a different kind from Picasso's, stern and rather simple. His *Mother and Child*, and some of his black and white work, are powerful.

Messrs. Fry, Grant, and Etchells form more of a group. Mr. Fry has the advantage of knowing what a good picture is far better than the others. He aims at a pure, neither grandiose nor twisted, beauty; and achieves it with a delightful certainty. There are several pictures in this exhibition which may or may not be distinctly better than his, but few that are so certainly and definitely beautiful pictures as at least two by him. Mr. Grant and Mr. Etchells, being younger, are declared to show more 'promise'. Mr. Grant has painted better things, perhaps, than any he shows here. But several of these are lovely. He is always a trifle disappointing. One always feels there ought to be more body in his work, somehow. Even his best pictures here are rather thin. But there is beauty in *The Seated Woman*, an exquisite wit and invention in the delightful *The Queen of Sheba*, and a grave loveliness in *The Dancers*. His genius is an elusive and faithless sprite. He may do anything or nothing. Also, he is roaming at present between different styles and methods. What an eye for beauty! Why aren't his pictures better? But it's absurd to suppose they won't be when he has 'found himself'. Both he and Mr. Etchells are unfortunately fond of a spotty way of laying their paint on, which, as they employ it, seems to the inexpert eye not to advnatage them. Mr. Etchells' danger also lies in a lack of fervour; but he inclines to stolidity, Mr. Grant to prettiness. It is a pity Mr. Etchells is largely represented by landscape, as his portraits are better. His *The Dead Mole* has honesty and some power.

There is also a small amount of sculpture in the exhibition. Some by Matisse, which verges on the commonplace. It is a pity there is nothing by Lehmbruck; but it is a pleasure to find several things of Mr. Gill's. Mr. Gill is as certainly better than any Continental 'Post-Impressionist' sculptor, as the Continental 'Post-Impressionist' painters are better than ours. His genius is not represented by any of its greatest triumphs, except, perhaps, the *Garden Statue*. But there is enough here for even those unacquainted with his work to begin to suspect that he is the greatest living English artist, and one of the three or four great sculptors of the past hundred years.

(*The Cambridge Magazine*, 23 and 30 November 1912)

'Tchekoff's Plays'
Review of *Plays by Anton Tchekoff* translated
with an introduction by Marian Fell

Anton Tchekoff died in 1904, at the age of 44. His plays are known
by now in most civilized countries. They have begun to affect
European drama. This volume contains translations of three plays,
Ivanoff (early), *The Sea-Gull* (of his middle period), and *Uncle
Vanya* (late); also an early scrap, called *The Swan-Song*. Besides
this there is only one volume of translations from Tchekoff's plays
in English, Mr. George Calderon's, containing *The Sea-Gull* and
The Cherry Orchard. Mr. Calderon's translation is better than this
one, which is a little flat. But a good deal of the plays seems to come
through. Tchekoff is no violent innovator in dramatic craft. His
peculiarity, and his distinction, lie chiefly in the atmosphere he
throws over his plays, and the kind of people he liked to portray.
Still, he considerably relaxes the tightness of the rules of drama
that have obtained, at least in England and France, lately. There
are several soliloquies. It is an entertaining cynicism that in the
new version of Sardou's *Diplomacy*, 'brought up to date', which
has just been produced in London, all the soliloquies have been
carefully cut out; and in twenty years, when they're reviving Shaw
and Barker, they'll have to bring *them* up to date by as carefully
inserting these devices. One must be nimble, even to be old-
fashioned, these days. Tchekoff's own plays changed in character
very rapidly: but that was less, no doubt, owing to fashion, than
because he was finding the most perfect expression of his mood.
Ivanoff is rather dull, *The Sea-Gull* interesting but a little un-
satisfactory, *Uncle Vanya* much the best. The first two end with
suicides, the third just ends. Tchekoff was irresistibly drawn to the
rather faded and unsuccessful people in the world: people suffering
from nervous breakdown, an inimical critic might say. Mr. William
Archer has declared that if our legislation were good enough, all
drama would vanish. Certainly, if Tchekoff's characters were all
fed up to normal weight, the bottom would fall out of most of his
plays. A modern playwright has described his feelings when, late
back and tired from his work, in London, he slowly crawls up the
dim interminable stairs to his attic, and wonders if, when he opens
the door he won't horribly see, sitting in his easy-chair, reading a
book, and smoking, – himself. If he does, he knows he will have

to turn back down the long stairs and creep out into the street again, hopeless and homeless. He is a victim of modern nerves. The world is divided into those who would plunge in – and bedamned to 'themselves' –, and those who would crawl away, like the poet, leaving 'themselves' in possession: those whose bodily and instinctive selves over-ride the phantasies of their nervous imaginations, and those who give in to them. Most of Tchekoff's characters are of the second class; they would go downstairs again.

Still, there is beauty and the power of moving you in these plays. And that is all that matters. A queerly appealing atmosphere clings round them; a grey silvery mistiness, a charm of silences and hazy distances and causeless melancholy, such as you particularly find on a late afternoon in February in Cambridge. In *Uncle Vanya* this becomes poignantly beautiful. The play deals with the ordinary Tchekoffian collection of discontented or unsuccessful lives. A loves B: B loves C: C loves D . . . the old story. A doctor and a professor's wife are, more or less, in love with one another; not enough, though, to do anything. They merely part. Most of the characters drift away in the end; their problems unsolved, – unstated, even. Very like life. The old nurse's soothing of the love-lorn and perplexed girl can stand as the motto of it all. 'It's all right, my baby. When the geese have cackled, they will be still again. First they cackle, and then they stop.'

Tchekoff's characters talk aimlessly. Their remarks often lead nowhere. He uses them to create an atmosphere, not to forward the plot. His people start topics, and do not pursue them. They talk about one thing, while they think about another – just like real men and women. They talk about their own subjects, and do not listen. Every dialogue, like dialogues in actuality, is two alternating monologues. And they cry, men and women, continually, like the Old Greeks and Romans.

Lebedieff: What are you crying about?

Shabelski: Nothing in particular. I was just crying.

That might come in any act of any of these plays. It does come in *Ivanoff*, as a matter of fact. In England middle-aged men don't behave like that in the presence of other middle-aged men. It is difficult for our more deeply emotional race to understand it. The Russians, like the Romans, seem to be children. Tchekoff is a pathetic, as Dostoieffsky is an hysterical, child. And Tchekoff's world is one of tired children, who hurt each other, but not very much, because they're not very strong.

(*The Cambridge Magazine*, 26 April 1913)

Two Reviews of *The Poems of John Donne*, edited by H. J. C. Grierson

I

One of the most remarkable of the English pictures in the recent Post-Impressionist exhibition depicts *John Donne arriving in Heaven.* 'I don't know who John Donne is,' a sturdy member of the public was lately heard to remark in front of it, 'but he seems to be getting there.' Unconsciously, he summed up Donne's recent history. Of all the great English poets, his name is least known beyond 'literary' circles; but he is certainly 'getting there'. If one has entered, any time these last years, a railway carriage, and found some studious vagabond deep in a little blue book, it generally turns out to be Mr. Chambers's invaluable edition in the Muses' Library. And now Professor Grierson and the Delegates of the Clarendon Press have given us, clothed in the most attractive garb possible, a perfect text of the poems, and an immense body of elucidatory comment.

Such service is merited. It proceeds, perhaps, from our modern clearer perception of the true nature of that Elizabethan literature of which Donne was a chief glory. The writers, principally the dramatists, of that great period between 1580 and 1640 have been treated without discrimination. From Lamb and Swinburne, who revered almost all as gods, they have passed into the hands of scholars, who find each equally a subject for annotation and conjecture. At length we are beginning to discern their degrees and kinds, and to note the limits and nature of the short period when the Elizabethans found their highest expression – a period whose spirit is almost completely the spirit of Donne. For the drama, the crown of the time, was at its best for little more than a decade. Between, roughly, 1598 and 1613, all the dramatists were doing their best work. The spirit of power came upon them startlingly. Outside that period there are only the isolated magnificence of Marlowe and the Indian summer of Ford. Within it came the best work of Shakespeare, the Tragedies, and the only good work of Webster, Jonson, Chapman, and Beaumont. Even Middleton, Dekker, and Fletcher were fired above themselves. The history of this efflorescence is perfectly clear and entirely surprising. The 'eighties and 'nineties were given over to the blood-and-thunder melodrama, the infinitely dreary history-play, and then the unimportant sweetness of the romantic comedy. Shakespeare's genius touched the second of these types with excitement, and the third with a clear prettiness; but, in general, the nonage of the Elizabethan drama was marked by all the dullness and sentimentality of youth. But as the century died, patriotism and sugar lost their savour; and, rather suddenly, a new taste came in. The soul woke in Elizabethan plays and poetry, and the usual trouble ensued. That extraordinary gloomy unknown genius, Marston, who profoundly impressed his contemporaries, set the fashion in drama. He dished up the old blood-and-thunder play with new condiments, intellectual passion, satire, dirt, bitterness, and wit. Ben Jonson's additions to the *Spanish Tragedy*, and such late comedies of Shakespeare as *Measure for Measure*, have the same flavour. Marston invented the witty, malcontent, bitter-tongued, tragic hero, with his grave-yard meditations on mortality. In the general furbishing-up of the melodramas of the 'eighties, one old revenge-play fell to Shakespeare's lot. He perfected the hero of Marstonian lines, and the character – a Prince of Denmark – has since achieved some fame. Being a decade of tragedy, the only one in our history, this was also an age of farce. Ben Jonson's farces of 'humours' had a short glory, till they, too, with tragedies, were swallowed up in the sickly-sweet tragi-comedies and romances with which Fletcher drowned truth and passion. Webster, always a slightly old-fashioned figure, who brings up the rear with his two great tragedies of 1611–1613, already out of date, seems the last of Earth gazing out over a sea of saccharine.

One must understand this period, his background, to understand Donne. The soul of its art was the soul of his. Webster repeatedly steals from his published poems. His wit was essentially of that curious kind the austere Chapman somewhere praises:

Your wit is of the true Pierian spring,
That can make anything of anything.

Hamlet, with his bitter flashes, his humour, his metaphysical inquisitiveness, and his passion, continually has the very accent of the secular Donne; but that he is an avenger, not a lover. To Ophelia he must have been Donne himself. Indeed, Donne, the bulk of whose good poetry seems to have been written between 1595 and 1613, heralded, and in some part led, this age, when English literature climbed and balanced briefly on the difficult pinnacle of sincerity. Poetry is always a few years ahead of drama. But Donne applied the same spirit the dramatists applied to the whole world, almost solely to love. He is, for width and depth, incomparably the greatest love-poet in English. Every pain or pleasure contained in or relevant to that emotion come under his notice. He can praise in lines where all the music of verse of the last three centuries seems to ring together:

> So may thy mighty, amazing beauty move
> Envy in all women, and in all men, love!

or harp on that external perplexity of human relationships:

> What hate can hurt our bodies like our love?

He belonged to an age when men were not afraid to mate their intellects with their emotions. In his own words, he 'loved to be subtle to plague himself'. He would startle the soul from her lair with unthinkable paradoxes, and pursue her, with laughter and tears, along all the difficult coasts between sense and madness. At one moment he knows the most unworldly ecstasy of the communion of two souls:

> And whilst our souls negotiate there,
>   We like sepulchral statues lay!
> All day the same our postures were,
>   And we said nothing, all the day.

At another he contemplates the consummation of human love within the black, bright walls of a flea. He compares his lady to a primrose, an angel, the number five, Mary Magdalen, a ginger-bread figure, Newfoundland, the stationary leg of a compass, God. And one can never doubt his sincerity.

One of the minor merits of this edition is that it puts within our reach the two great portraits of this extraordinary man, surely the most fascinating of all portraits of English poets – the one of an eighteen-year-old countenance, sensual, witty, passionate, informed by an inward fire of intellect; the other, made shortly before death, facing eternity with an incredible, ferocious mirth. But Mr. Grierson's chief claim to our praise is his text. He has spent several years over it, collating and arranging the many manuscripts. Never was work better worth doing. A careful examination of the text reveals practically no errors, whether of judgement or carelessness, and innumerable convincing restorations and emendations. There is scarcely a poem where he has not repeatedly amended Mr. Chambers's text. His services are threefold. He has used the manuscripts to improve on all the printed editions, notably in three important instances in Donne's greatest poem, *The Ecstasy*. He has corrected or defended readings by means of a thorough knowledge of Donne's prose works, and of the scholastic thought which permeated his mind. And he has that characteristic of a good editor – he prefers the harder reading, and justifies it. There is also a mass of commentary, chiefly useful again where it elucidates Donne's queer mental processes from scholastic theology and from his sermons. Here there are one or two lapses and signs of hurry. For instance, he might explain 'boored' (*Progress of the Soul*, XXVII). And he promises a note on a new punctuation in the third letter to the Countess of Bedford, but never gives it. These are specks. A more general fault is the slight lack of lucidity in that part of Volume II given up to an account of the manuscripts and editions and the text. He describes too much, and tabulates too little. It scarcely detracts from the value of his laborious researches. He is equally patient and clear-headed on the canon of Donne's poems; a trifle too sceptical, if anything. But he makes out only too good a case for giving the lovely lyric, *Absence*, to John Hoskyns. The one portion of these two volumes that is not entirely necessary is the fifty pages of introduction on 'The Poetry of Donne'. To have had the main facts of his life put down would have been more useful; or even more detailed and technical observations on his metre and style. Mr. Grierson points out elsewhere how the superb *Sappho to Philænis* has influenced Swinburne's *Anactoria*. As a matter of fact, it is even closer to *Erotion*. Donne's metrical power is marvellous, and Swinburne learnt only some of his lessons. His passionate colloquialism of style has influenced even later poetry.

Mr. Grierson's general remarks about the 'philosophy of Donne's love-poetry' are not sufficiently illuminating. Moreover, he is reprehensibly out of sympathy with some sides of that many-coloured character. He misses the point of that superb and extraordinary satiric poem, *The Progress of the Soul*; he undervalues *The Second Anniversary*, one of the greatest long poems in English. Worst of all, he is prudish about Donne; a serious handicap in an editor or critic of the Elizabethans. It is so easy to distinguish between obscenity and non-obscenity; so hard and so much more important to distinguish between cleanness and dirtiness. But, on the whole, this edition is one of those triumphs of industry, clear thinking, and literary knowledge, which occur only a few times in a generation, and establish the nobility of scholarship. To obtain a perfect text of the obscure Donne was one of the chief needs of literature. Our gratitude and praise go out together to Mr. Grierson; to the Clarendon Press, too. Two volumes can complete this joint achievement – the extension of the edition to include Donne's prose works, and the issue of the text alone of the poems in a cheap, small volume. Donne's glory is ever increasing. He was the one English love-poet who was not afraid to acknowledge that he was composed of body, soul, and mind; and who faithfully recorded all the pitched battles, alarms, treaties, sieges, and fanfares of that extraordinary triangular warfare.

(*The Nation*, 15 February 1913)

2

Praise is the prerogative of the good. And those who are wise as well as good spend all their waking hours, it is well known, in laudation. In general they praise beauty, the sun, colour, virtue, and the rest of the doxology; in the intervals more particular things: Charing Cross Bridge by night, the dancing of Miss Ethel Levey, the Lucretian hexameter, the beer at an inn in Royston I will not advertise, the sausages at another inn above Princes Risborough, and the Clarendon Press editions of the English poets. But the beer and the sausages will change, and Miss Levey one day will die, and Charing Cross Bridge will fall; so the Clarendon Press books will be the only thing our evil generation may show to the cursory eyes of posterity, to prove it was not wholly bad. They are lovely things, these books; beautiful in arrangement, size, and type; filled with good stuff to read; and prepared with the exact amount of scholarship that shall escape pedantry and yet rise far above dilettantism. These two volumes of Donne crown the series. To open them is to make even a scholar love poetry, even a poet adore scholarship. Mr. Grierson's services to the text cannot be over-praised. Any fool can write criticism, but it takes a man who understands poetry really to restore a faulty text to perfection. Other editors of Donne will come, who will perhaps be able to show more clearly the two or more different original versions of some of the poems. That is all they will find to do. The commentary is a little less complete than the work on the text, but almost equally rich a gift. Donne is the one poet who demands a commentary, not for allusions, but, sometimes, for his entire train of thought. And in the same way he is the one poet who requires a perfect text, for (it is a minor merit) all his lines always *mean* something. Both text and commentary are prepared for us by Mr. Grierson, with a result which must have demanded an extraordinary amount of work, and a rarely patient and unlapsing judgement. Mr. Grierson is very good in the one point where nearly all modern English literary scholarship is mad and bad enough to shock the most imbecile lawyer: in knowledge of the laws of evidence. Mr. Grierson has both our praise and our gratitude Donne was labelled, by Johnson, a 'metaphysical' poet; and the term has been repeated ever since, to the great confusion of critics. Mr. Grierson attempts to believe that it means erudite, and that erudition is one of the remarkable and eponymous characteristics of Donne's poetry. It rested on erudition, no doubt, as Mr. Grierson has valuably shown; but it was not so especially erudite – not so erudite as the writings of Ben Jonson, a far less 'metaphysical' poet. But the continual use of this phrase may have aimed vaguely at a most important feature there is in Donne's poetry. He is the most *intellectual* poet in English; and his intellectualism had, even, sometimes, a tendency to the abstract. But to be an intellectual poet does not mean that one writes about intellectual things. The pageant of the outer world of matter and the mid-region world of the passions came to Donne through the brain. The whole composition of the man was made up of brain, soul, and heart in a different proportion from the ordinary prescription. This does not mean that he felt less keenly than others; but when passion shook him, and his being ached for utterance, to relieve the stress, expression came through the intellect. Under the storm of emotion, it is common to seek for relief by twisting some strong stuff. Donne, as Coleridge said, turns intellectual pokers into love-knots. An ordinary poet, whose feelings find far stronger expression than a common man's, but an expression according to the same prescription, praises his mistress with some common idea, intensely felt:

Oh, thou art fairer than the evening air,
Clad in the beauty of a thousand stars!

Donne, equally moved and equally sincere, would compare her to a
perfectly equilateral triangle, or to the solar system. His intellect
must find satisfaction. If a normal poet – it is not very probable – in
thinking of his mistress being ill with a fever, had had suggested to
him the simile of these fevers soon passing and dying away in her,
just as shooting stars consume and vanish in the vastness and purity
of the sky, he would have tried to bring the force of his thought
home by sharpening and beautifying the imagined vision. He might
have approached it on the lines of:

> Through the serene wide dark of you
> They trail their transient gold, and die.

Donne feels only the idea. He does not try to visualize it. He never
visualizes, or suggests that he has any pleasure in looking at things.
His poems might all have been written by a blind man in a world of
blind men. In *The Fever* he gives you the thought thus:

> These burning fits but meteors be,
>   Whose matter in thee is soon spent.
> Thy beauty, and all parts, which are thee,
>   Are unchangeable firmament.

The mediation of the senses is spurned. Brain does all.

And as Donne saw everything through his intellect, it follows,
in some degree, that he could see everything humorously. He could
see it the other way, too. But humour was always at his command.
It was part of his realism; especially in the bulk of his work, his
poems dealing with love. There is no true lover but has sometimes
laughed at his mistress, and often at himself. But you would not
guess that from the love-songs of many poets. Their poems run the
risk of looking a little flat. They are unreal by the side of Donne.
For while his passion enabled him to see the face of love, his
humour allowed him to look at it from the other side. So we behold
his affairs in the round.

But it must not appear that his humour, or his wit, and his
passion, alternated. The other two are his passion's handmaids. It
should not be forgotten that Donne was one of the first great
English satirists, and the most typical and prominent figure of a
satirical age. Satire comes with the Bible of truth in one hand and
the sword of laughter in the other. Donne was true to the reality of

his own heart. Sometimes you hear the confident laughter of lovers who have found their love:

> I wonder, by my troth, what thou and I
> Did till we loved? were we not weaned till then?
> But sucked on country pleasures, childishly?
> Or snorted we in the Seven Sleepers' den?

and there is the bitterer mirth of the famous—

> For God's sake, hold your tongue, and let me love.

He could combine either the light or the grave aspects of love with this lack of solemnity that does but heighten the sharpness of the seriousness. His colloquialism helped him. It has been the repeated endeavour of half the great English poets to bring the language of poetry, and the accent and rhythm of poetry, nearer to those of the intensest moments of common speech. To attempt this was especially the mark of many of the greatest of the Elizabethans. Shakespeare's 'Prithee, undo this button!' finds its lyrical counterpart in several of Donne's poems. Yet he did not confine his effects to laughter and slang. He could curiously wed fantastic imagination with the most grave and lofty music of poetry; as in the great poem where he compares his wife to the stationary leg of a compass, himself to the voyaging one:

> And though it in the centre fit,
>   Yet when the other far doth roam,
> It leans and hearkens after it,
>   And grows erect as that comes home.
>
> Such wilt thou be to me, who must,
>   Like the other foot, obliquely run;
> Thy firmness makes my circle just,
>   And makes me end where I begun.

For indeed, while the quality of his imagination was unique and astonishing, he expressed it most normally as a great poet, with all the significance and beauty that English metre and poetry can give:

> O more than moon,
> Draw not up seas to drown me in thy sphere!

and –

> Thou art not soft, and clear, and straight, and fair,
> As down, as stars, and cedars, and lilies are;
> But thy right hand, and cheek, and eyes, only
> Are like thy other hand, and cheek, and eye –

contain as much inexplicable loveliness and strangeness as any of
the writings of the Romantics. The mere technique of his poetry
has been imitated and followed by many of all the poets who followed
him and loved him, from Dryden to Swinburne. It is a good thing
that he is slowly spreading from that select band of readers to a
wider public. This edition has opportunely appeared at the time
of the spreading of his fame. It is fitting he should be read in an age
when poetry is beginning to go back from nature, romance, the
great world, and the other fine hunting-places of the Romantics,
by devious ways and long *ambages*, to that wider home which Donne
knew better than any of the great English poets, the human heart.
'The heart's a wonder.'

(*Poetry and Drama*, June 1913)

From *John Webster and the Elizabethan Drama*

I

'What is Art?' is a question which most writers on subjects connected
with literature, painting, plays, music, society, or life, are ready
with an equal cheerfulness to ask or to answer. They may be right;
but to me they seem to make a gigantic, unconscious, and probably
unjustifiable assumption. It is quite doubtful, and it is nowadays
continually more doubted, whether the word 'Art' has properly
any meaning at all. But it has so obsessed men's minds, that they
start with an inevitable tendency to believe that it has a meaning. In
the same way, those who believe in Art are generally inclined to
believe in a single object at which all Art, that is to say all the arts,
aim: Beauty. It may turn out to be true that both Art and Beauty
are real and useful names; but the attitude of mind that assumes
that they are is deplorable. The most honest and most hopeful
course to pursue, is to say that there are certain kinds of human
activity which seem to hang together in classes, such as reading
books, hearing music, seeing pictures; and to examine our states of

mind while we follow these pursuits, to see how far they are of one kind in each 'art', and in all, and whether *all* successful works of art do seem to us to have some quality in common which can be called Beauty.

The situation seems to me as if men had agreed to say 'The emotions caused in human beings by pins, walking-sticks, feathers, and crowbars, acting through the tactile sense, are all of one unique kind. It is called Grumph. Pins, etc., are called the grumphs. Grumph is one of the holiest things in this melancholy world,' and so forth. And soon they'd say, 'But, philosophically, what *is* Grumph?' Then they'd argue. They would come to some conclusion which, as you cannot tickle with a crowbar, would preclude tickling with feathers; and they would excommunicate all those who used feathers for tickling with the formula, 'That is not Grumph!' They would write Treatises on any one grumph, on the 'Pin-grumph', say, carefully keeping in mind all the time that what they said would have to be more or less true of the other grumphs too. Some would lay great importance on the fact that, as you were tickled with feathers, you were, in a way, also tickled by being beaten with a walking-stick. Others would discover the ferule of the pin, and the quill, shaft, and two vanes of barbs of the crowbar. An Oxford don would arise to declare that all grumph continually approximated to the condition of pins. . . .

I have put the affair, as I see it, in a figure, and with other names, in order to show its unreason more clearly, and far more shortly, than is possible if the prejudice-clad and elusive word 'Art' is used. In either case, the sensible reply to it all is, 'We have sticks and pins, plays and poems. These we know. These are, as certainly as anything is, real classes of things. Begin from them, and from the emotions they move. And see if thence you climb upwards to Grumph, to Art.'

* * *

II

By the middle of the sixteenth century, the drama was in an inchoate condition. Interludes of all kinds, moral, religious, controversial, and farcical, were being played by all sorts of audiences, besides the rough beginnings of popular tragedy and comedy, and

many survivals of the old religious plays. In the sixties the real
Elizabethan drama began; and one of the chief influences in working
the change was the classical one. It came from above, and from
amateurs. It was started, it is noteworthy, by people with a fixed,
conscious, solemn, artistic aim. They wanted to have tragedies in
the real classical way; so they imitated, queerly enough, Seneca!
English literature has always been built on a reverent misunder-
standing of the classics. Anyhow, anyone is good enough to be a god.
The worst art has always been great enough to inspire the best. The
iron laws of heredity do not affect literature; and Seneca may father
Shakespeare as Macpherson fathered the Romantic Movement.

. . . The influence of Seneca, and, vaguely, what was thought to
be the classical tradition, in accordance with the misunderstood laws
of Aristotle, came primarily by two streams, through Italy and
France. *Tancred and Gismunda* was influenced by the Italian Sene-
cans; Kyd translated Garnier. Italy, of course, the romantic home
of all beauty and art, had the most influence. But culture came from
France. The English began translating Seneca for themselves in the
sixties and seventies. As far as can be seen, the position in the
eighties, when Marlowe and Kyd were about to fling English
tragedy as we know it shouting into the world, was that the popular
stage was scarcely touched at all by this classical, Senecan movement; the children's companies and ordinary court plays were only
partly and patchily affected; but private performances in the Inner
Temple and Gray's Inn had proudly and completely adopted the
Senecan (or, generally, classical) style. As these were often given
before the Queen, they had great influence in spreading the impression that this type of tragedy was the highest, the only type
intellectual and cultivated people could aspire to. The Senecan
boom did not leave much directly to Elizabethan drama; far less
than is generally made out. It left perhaps a ghost tradition, the
much-advertised and over-valued 'revenge motive', and the tendency
to division into five acts. But indirectly it had value in tightening
up the drama, pulling the scattered scenes which appeal to the
English, a little, but not too much, into one play. And it was of vast
use as an ideal. It enabled the dramatists to write for their audiences
but above them. It set the audiences an æsthetic standard, shook
them into artistic morality. Left to itself, this movement would
have, and did, become academic, cold, dead. But Fulke Greville,
Alexander, even Ben Jonson, did not get the full benefit of it. The

best of it, and the best of the popular stage, were torn out, combined, and revitalised by Kyd and Marlowe. Towards that the times were ripening. The drama was getting a standing, the first important step. It was at once popular and fashionable. And, though a few Puritan fanatics had started a protest, the main mass of the people were against them. That gradual depletion of the theatre-audiences which took place during the next century, when *bourgeois* democracy slowly became one with Puritanism, had not commenced. The establishment of fixed theatres in London must have raised the level of the performances; and, the second important step, it was educating and preparing an audience. For an audience must be trained and trained together, as much as a troupe of actors. It is equally one of the conditions of great drama.

III

Soon after Lyly began to breathe into comedy (with which I am not concerned) a movement that was near to being life, and a prettiness that was still nearer beauty, Kyd and Marlowe blew life, strength, and everything else into tragedy. To say that they grafted the energy of popular tragedy on the form of classical, would be to wrong by a soft metaphor their bloody and vital violence. It was rather as if a man should dash two dead babies together into one strident and living being. Kyd, of course, does not really stand by Marlowe. But he seems further below him than is fair, because Marlowe's genius was more literary, and so lives longer. Both brought light and life to tragedy. Kyd filled Seneca's veins with English blood. He gave his audience living people, strong emotions, vendetta, murder, pain, real lines of verse, and stiffly enough, the stateliness of art. He thrilled a torch in the gloom of the English theatre. Marlowe threw open a thousand doors, and let in the sun. He did it, in the prologue to *Tamburlaine*, with the superb insolence and lovely brutality of youth. His love of the body, his passion for the world of colour and stuff, his glorious atheism, 'giantism 'gainst Heaven', were trumpets in that morning. The blood still sings to them. Marlowe is less representative, stands clearer of his period, than almost any Elizabethan. He was of no school, had no followers. Others, Shakespeare for instance, caught something of his trick of blank verse, or tried a play or two in his manner. But there was no body of drama that partook of the atmosphere of ferocious, youthful, passionate tragedy that distinguishes Marlowe's work. He stands rather, in his joy of the world, and irreligion, as the herald of the whole age, and of that short song of passion it could utter before the beginning of the night. His loneliness is explicable. It was not only that no contemporary was old and great enough to take all he had to give. But his dramatic method was unique. He was not a dramatist in the way the others were. He was – in this something like the young Shakespeare, but far more so – a lyric writer using drama. 'Plot' does not matter to him. Each scene he works up into an intense splendid lyric. They are of different kinds, but put together they have unity. The whole is a lyric drama. No one else, except, conceivably, Webster, in a slight degree, used this artistic method. Marlowe was an extreme *pointilliste*. He produced his whole effect by very large blobs of pure colour, laid on side by side. The rest were ordinary semi-impressionists, with a tale to tell. Only Webster more than rarely achieved expressionism.

One other gift Kyd and Marlowe, especially Marlowe, gave their contemporaries; blank verse. Before them was the Stone Age; they gave the poet a new weapon of steel. Marlowe was drunk on decasyllables, the lilt and clang and rhetoric of them. How he must have shouted, writing each line of *Tamburlaine*! . . .

IV

There was a period – 1600–1610 are the rough inside limits – that stood out an infinity above the rest. Nearly all the good stuff of Elizabethan drama was in it or of it. Except in comedy, there are only the lonely spring of Marlowe and the Indian summer of Ford outside it. And it is not only that it was Shakespeare's great time. That is partly both cause and effect, and our great good fortune.

The whole age, in drama and beyond, was alive with passion and the serious stuff of art. Nor was it only that so much of great merit was produced in this short time. Nearly all the work of the period shared, apart from its goodness, in a special atmosphere. It is extremely important to recognise the absolute distinctness and supreme greatness of this period, its sudden appearance and its swift and complete end. There is only space here to hint at its characteristic features. It was heralded (poetry is generally a few years ahead of drama) by Shakespeare's sonnets, and the poems of Donne – who, in spite of Ben Jonson, did not write all his best things before 1598.

Poets, and men in general, had reached a surfeit of beauty. The Renaissance joy in loveliness, the romantic youthfulness of the age, the wave of cheerful patriotism, all passed at the same time. Boyhood passed. Imagination at this time suddenly woke to life. Its flights were to the strangest corners and the pitchiest barathrum of the deep. Intellect was pressed into the service of the emotions, and the emotions were beaten into fantastic figures by the intellect. The nature of man became suddenly complex, and grew bitter at its own complexity. The lust of fame and the desire for immortality were racked by a perverse hunger for only oblivion; and the consummation of human love was observed to take place within the bright, black walls of a flea. It seemed as though all thought and all the arts at this time became almost incoherent with the strain of an inhuman energy within them, and a Titanic reaching for impossible ends. Poetry strove to adumbrate infinity, or, finding mysticism too mild, to take the most secret Kingdom of Heaven by storm. Imagination, seeking arcane mysteries, would startle the soul from its lair by unthinkable paradoxes. Madness was curiously explored, and all the doubtful coasts between delirium and sanity. The exultations of living were re-invigorated by the strength of a passionate pessimism; for even scepticism in that age was fecund and vigorous, and rejoiced in the whirling gloom it threw over life. The mind, intricately considering its extraordinary prison of flesh, pondered long on the exquisite transiency of the height of love and the long decomposition that death brings. The most gigantic crimes and vices were noised, and lashed immediately by satire, with the too-furious passion of the flagellant. For Satire flourishes, with Tragedy, at such times. The draperies of refinement and her smug hierarchy were torn away from the world, and Truth held sway there with his terrific court of morbidity, scepticism, despair, and life. The veils of romanticism were stripped away; Tragedy and Farce stood out, for men to shudder or to roar.

*   *   *

V

Light has interestingly been thrown of late on Webster's method of composition. It had long been known that he repeats a good many lines and phrases from himself and from other people: and that a great deal of his writing, especially in his best and most careful work, has the air of being proverbial, or excerpt. John Addington Symonds remarked with insight a good many years ago that Webster must have used a note-book. His plays read like it. And now Mr Crawford has discovered some of the sources he compiled his note-book from. It would be useless to repeat Mr Crawford's list with a few additions, or to examine the instances one by one. Nearly, not quite, all his cases seem to me to be real ones. There are certainly quite enough to enable one to draw important inferences about Webster's way of working. These instances of borrowing are very numerous, and chiefly from two books, Sidney's *Arcadia*, and Montaigne – favourite sources of Elizabethan wisdom. They are very clearly marked, and consist in taking striking thoughts and phrases in the original, occasionally quite long ones, and rewriting them almost verbally, sometimes with slight changes to make them roughly metrical. . . .

There are three explanations of all this. Either Webster knew the *Arcadia* so well that he had a lot of it by heart. Or he had the book and worked from it. Or he kept a note-book, into which he had entered passages that struck him, and which he used to write the play from. It seems to me certain that the third is the true explanation. We know that Elizabethan authors did sometimes keep note-books in this way. Bacon did so, and Ben Jonson, whom Webster admired and rather resembled, worked most methodically this way. The memory theory could scarcely explain the verbal accuracy of so many passages. But there are other considerations, which make the note-book probable. The passages from the *Arcadia* or from Montaigne came very often in lumps. You will get none, or only one or two, for some scenes, and then twenty lines or so that are a *cento* of them, carefully dovetailed and worked together. It is very difficult to imagine a man doing this from memory or from a book. But it is exactly what would happen if he were using a note-book which had several consecutive pages with *Arcadia* extracts, several more with Montaigne, and so on. . . .

A good many of these passages Webster copied out identically, except sometimes for a few changes to make them go into rough verse. Others he altered in very interesting ways. It was not necessarily part of his goodness as an author to alter them. His genius comes out equally in the phrases he used to produce far greater effect than they do in the original, by putting them at some exactly suitable climax. We are getting beyond the attitude, born of the industrial age and the childish enthusiasm for property as such, which condemns such plagiarism, imitation, and borrowing. The Elizabethans had for the most part healthy and sensible views on the subject. They practised and encouraged the habit. When Langbaine, in his preface to *Momus Triumphans*, 'condemns Plagiaries' (though he is only thinking of plots, even then), it is a sign of the decadence towards stupidity. The poet and the dramatist work with words, ideas, and phrases. It is ridiculous, and shows a wild incomprehension of the principles of literature, to demand that each should only use his own; every man's brain is filled by thoughts and words of other people's. Webster wanted to make Bosola say fine things. He had many in his mind or his note-book: some were borrowed, some his own. He put them down, and they answer their purpose splendidly.

> I stand like one
> That long hath ta'en a sweet and golden dream;
> I am angry with myself, now that I wake.

That was, or may have been, of his own invention.

> The weakest arm is strong enough that strikes
> With the sword of justice.

That he had found in Sidney. There is no difference. In any case the first, original, passage was probably in part due to his friends' influence; and the words he used were originally wholly 'plagiarised' from his mother or his nursemaid. 'Originality' is only plagiarising from a great many.

So Webster reset other people's jewels and redoubled their lustre. 'The soul must be held fast with one's teeth . . .' he found Montaigne remarkably saying in a stoical passage. The phrase stuck. Bosola, on the point of death, cries:

> Yes I hold my weary soul in my teeth;
> 'Tis ready to part from me.

It is unforgettable.

Webster improved even Donne, in this way; in a passage of amazing, quiet, hopeless pathos, the parting of Antonio and the

Duchess (*Duchess of Malfi*, III. 5), which is one long series of triumphant borrowings:

> We seem ambitious God's whole work to undo;
> Of nothing He made us, and we strive too
> To bring ourselves to nothing back,

Donne writes in *An Anatomy of the World*.

> Heaven fashion'd us of nothing; and we strive
> To bring ourselves to nothing,

are Antonio's moving words.

This last example illustrates one kind of the changes other than metrical Webster used to make. He generally altered a word or two, with an extraordinarily sure touch, which proves his genius for literature. He gave the passages life and vigour, always harmonious with his own style. You see, by this chance side-light, the poet at work, with great vividness. 'Fashion'd' for 'made' here, is not a great improvement; but it brings the sentence curiously into the key of the rest of the scene. The metrical skill is astounding – the calm weight of 'fashion'd'; the slight tremble of 'Heaven' at the beginning of the line; the adaptation from Donne's stiff heavy combative accent, the line ending with 'and we strive too', to the simpler easier cadence more suited to speech and to pathos, '. . .; and we strive'; and the repetition of 'nothing' in the same place in the two lines.

. . . The description of Queen Erona is transferred to the Duchess again. Sidney says that in her sorrow, one could 'perceive the shape of loveliness more perfectly in woe than in joyfulness.' Webster turned this, with a touch, to poetry in its sheerest beauty.

> BOSOLA You may discern the shape of loveliness
> More perfect in her tears than in her smiles.

It is just this substitution of the concrete for the abstract – which is the nearest one could get to a definition of the difference between a thought in good prose and the same thought in good poetry – that Webster excels in. Even where his adjectives gain, it is in this direction.

> Or is it true that thou wert never but a vain name, and no essential thing?

says Sidney in a long passage on Virtue. Webster makes it a shade more visual, and twenty times as impressive:

> Or is it true thou art but a bare name,
> And no essential thing?

So Bosola gives life to a meditation of Montaigne. Montaigne's democratic mind pondered in his study on the essential equality of men. 'We are deceived,' he says of princes; 'they are moved, stirred, and removed in their motions by the same springs and wards that we are in ours. The same reason that makes us chide and brawl and fall out with any of our neighbours, causeth a war to follow between princes; the same reason that makes us whip or beat a lackey maketh a prince (if he apprehend it) to spoil and waste a whole province. . . .' Bosola is the heart of democracy. 'They are deceived, there's the same hand to them; the like passions sway them; the same reason that makes a vicar to go to law for a tithepig, and undo his neighbours, makes them spoil a whole province, and batter down goodly cities with the cannon.' The tithepig carries you on to Parnassus; Bosola has the vision of an artist.

The liveliness of the 'there's' for 'there is' in the last quotation is typical. Webster, like all the great Elizabethans, knew he was writing for the ear and not the eye. They kept in close touch, in their phrases, rhythms, and turns, with speech. Their language was greater than speech, but it was in that kind; it was not literature.

But there is one example of adoption and adaptation where Webster stands out quite clear as the poet, with the queer and little-known mental processes of that kind of man suddenly brought to the light. Montaigne has a passage:

> Forasmuch as our sight, being altered, represents unto itself things alike; and we imagine that things fail it as it doth to them: As they who travel by sea, to whom mountains, fields, towns, heaven, and earth, seem to go the same motion, and keep the same course they do.

The sense is clear and on the surface. He is illustrating the general rule by an interesting instance from ordinary experience. When you go in a train, or a boat, the sky, the earth, and its various features, all seem to be moving in one direction.[1] In *The White Devil*

---

[1] Note, though, that Montaigne has made a slip. They really appear to be moving in the *opposite* direction to yourself. Webster takes the idea over, mistake and all.

Flamineo is tempting Vittoria with the happiness Brachiano can give her.

> So perfect shall be thy happiness, that, as men at sea think
> land and trees and ships go that way they go, so both
> heaven and earth shall seem to go your voyage.

Webster took this instance of Montaigne's and used it to help out quite a different sense. He used it as a simile of that elusive, unobvious, imaginative kind that illuminates the more that you can scarcely grasp the point of comparison. But he did more. He was led to it by thinking, as a poet thinks, only half in ideas and half in words. Or rather, with ordinary people, ideas lead to one another, suggest one another, through ideas. With poets they do it through words, quite illogically. The paths of association in the brain are different in the two cases. A word is an idea with an atmosphere, a hard core with a fringe round it, like an oyster with a beard, or Professor William James's conception of a state of mind. Poets think of the fringes, other people of the core only. More definitely, if the dictionary meaning of a word is a and the atmosphere x, the poet thinks of it as $(x + a)$, and his trains of thought are apt to go on accordingly. So here, Webster found, vaguely, 'heaven and earth' ... 'going the same motion' ... and he leapt to the mystical conception of supreme happiness. He took 'heaven and earth' from their original, half material, significance, and transfigured them. He took them from the illustration and put them into the thing illustrated. The meaning of the original suggested one thing to his mind, the words another; he combined them, in another world. And the result is a simile of incomprehensible appropriateness and exquisite beauty, an idea in a Shelleyan altitude where words have various radiance rather than meaning, an amazing description of the sheer summit of the ecstasy of joy.

The note-book habit suited those idiosyncrasies of Webster's slow-moving mind which distinguished him from the ready rhetoric of Fletcher and the perpetual inspiration of Shakespeare. The use of such a thing by a poet implies a difference from other poets in psychology, not, as is often ignorantly supposed, in degree of merit. It merely means he has a worse memory. All writers are continually noting or inventing phrases and ideas, which form the stuff from which their later inspiration chooses. Some have to note them down, else they slip away for ever. Others can note them in their mind and yet feel secure of retaining them. The advantage of this method is that you unconsciously transmute all 'borrowed' ideas to harmony with your own personality – that when you hunt them out to reclaim them you find them slightly changed. The disadvantage, under modern conditions, is that you may commit the most terrible sin of plagiarism, and lift another man's work, and display it in a recognisable form, without knowing it. So Meredith in one of his last and best lyrics, an eight-lined poem called 'Youth and Age', repeats a line identically from Swinburne's best poem, *The Triumph of Time*; and all unconsciously. The disadvantage of the note-book method is that you have to perform the operation of digesting your trophy, harmonising it with the rest of the work, on the spot. Webster does not always do this successfully. There are passages, as we have seen, where he too flagrantly helps himself along with his note-book. But as a rule he weaves in his quotations extraordinarily well; they become part of the texture of the play, adding richness of hue and strength of fabric. In *The White Devil*, in the scene of astounding tragical farce where Flamineo persuades Vittoria and Zanche to try to murder him with bulletless pistols, the quotations from Montaigne come in entirely pat. For it is not, generally, when the play goes slowest that Webster has most recourse to his note-book. The swift passion of Ferdinand's interview with the guilty Duchess (*Duchess of Malfi*, III. 2) is, if you enquire closely, entirely composed of slightly altered passages from the *Arcadia*. This detracts no whit from its tumultuous force.

The chief value of working through a note-book, from a literary point of view, is this. A man tends to collect quotations, phrases, and ideas, that particularly appeal to and fit in with his own personality. If that personality is a strong one, and the point of his work is the pungency with which it is imbued with this strong taste, the not too injudicious agglutination of these external fragments will vastly enrich and heighten the total effect. And this is, on the whole, what happens with Webster. The heaping-up of images and phrases helps to confuse and impress the hearer, and gives body to a taste that might otherwise have been too thin to carry. Webster, in fine, belongs to the caddis-worm school of writers, who do not become their complete selves until they are incrusted with a thousand orts and chips and fragments from the world around.

*　　*　　*

8
Drama

Brooke wrote from the South Seas: 'All I want in life is a cottage, and leisure to write supreme poems and plays.' And in a lengthy letter of advice to Reginald Berkeley, he recommends the writing of one-act plays: 'They're quicker, harder technically, and far better practice.' There is no doubt that he took a keen practical interest in the theatre, and that he looked upon *Lithuania* as, for him, a significant experiment. It was so, says Maurice Browne, 'partly because his medium compelled him to work within limitations which admitted of no redundancy or elaboration, partly because in it he was concerned with the expression of character, not of personal feeling, and partly because he felt that it was his first, important stepping-stone toward tragedy'.

Clearly influenced by the starker horrors of Elizabethan tragedy, he followed the example of the Elizabethans in not thinking it necessary to invent his own plot. Indeed, he could hardly have taken a more worn one. It goes back at least as far as Lillo's *Fatal Curiosity* of 1736, which in turn was based on supposedly true events at Penryn a century earlier. In the nineteenth century, travelling harpists and fiddlers in Wales were singing a song with the same theme, called 'Y Nodyn Du' ('The Black Mark', by which the mother recognized her son). And there was a Victorian play (*Vae Victis* by Mrs Oscar Beringer) which used the same plot. According to Robert Ross, however, Brooke found his story in a newspaper. And there is another report, claiming like Ross's to be at first hand, that he picked it up while travelling in Europe. Whatever its origin, Brooke added one refinement to the usual version: he introduced a bestial daughter to perform the deed!

His friend, John Drinkwater, found the play 'home-spun, almost threadbare in texture', but 'not without the beauty that none but a poet could have achieved'. He suggests that its 'spare prose idiom' may have been influenced by Masefield's early plays; and Masefield, it appears from the letter to Berkeley, had gone carefully through the script with him. Most characteristic of its author are the man's physical disgust at the sensation and taste of sickness, and the sense of the callousness of people:

'I've got to go quietly', he said. Laugh! we were nearly sick.

But the play is slight (Brooke thought so too). And my excuses for including it are that it shows promise, that it suggests the further range of his gifts, and that – among his dramatic pieces – there is nothing better.

Indeed, there is little else. I have read through the scripts of plays performed during the Swiss holidays (though they were group productions, the 'Brooke' is usually self-apparent, and pervasive); but they were party pieces merely, and quite unpublishable. There is, too, the sketch of a translation of Wedekind's *Frühlings Erwachen*. But the only other dramatic work which deserves attention is the verse epilogue to a novel, *The Death of John Rump*, read first for the Carbonari (see chapter 2). It was the item about which, in selecting the poems for the posthumous volume of 1915, Marsh confessed to most hesitation. Though he finally rejected it (as, more recently, did Geoffrey Keynes, after considering it for a new edition of *The Poetical Works*), he included it in his autobiography, *A Number of People*, acclaiming it (with justice) 'a delightful thing'. In placing it after *Lithuania*, I have broken with chronology to allow it its rightful place as a link between the drama and the poems.

Lithuania

The inside of a hut in Lithuania. Table in centre. To the left of the table a ladder up to the upper storey. Behind, in the back wall, a long low window, doors in the right end of the back wall and the near end of the left wall. Projecting from the right wall, a large stone stove. Beyond it, a dresser with a basin, etc. It is early night in autumn. Outside the window is a space of moonlight; pine trees are vaguely visible beyond.

At the left end of the table, facing sideways, is sitting the STRANGER, *finishing a meal. The* DAUGHTER *is sitting on a stool before the stove,*

back to the audience, occasionally glancing at the STRANGER. *The*
MOTHER *is moving to and fro with plates, food, etc., between the table,*
the stove, and the dresser. There is a lamp on the table.
The STRANGER *is in young middle-age, expensively, rather flashily*
dressed, medium height, rather weakly built, with black, greased hair,
moustache, and a small pointed beard. Excitable manner. The MOTHER
is fifty or more, medium height, strongly built, but worn and rather bent;
thin face; quiet and occasionally voluble.
The DAUGHTER *is just past her youth, a little shorter than the* MOTHER,
but squarer, heavy-faced, and immobile.

STRANGER (*pushing chair back, and drinking vodka*) That's good.
That's good. I think I'll be turning in now. I'm dog-tired after that
tramp through the woods. By Jove, I was lucky to find this house!

MOTHER   If you'd bide a small bit – my man'll be in from the fields
any minute now.

STRANGER (*getting up*)   And aren't you two women afraid, being
alone in a lonely house like this, these evenings? . . .

MOTHER   What's there for fear? Who'd want anything here, to
rob us? And is it likely anyone'd want me? And Anna – Anna'd
give them more than they came for. She's stronger than most men.

STRANGER (*rather uneasily, bowing slightly*)   Your daughter's a very
well-built girl.

MOTHER   She's strong. She has to work in the fields with her Dad.

STRANGER   Ah, I suppose it's hard enough to keep things going,
with only one man in the family – or (*quickly*) you have some sons,
no doubt?

MOTHER   No. There was one. He ran off when he was thirteen.

STRANGER (*with a nervous, polite little laugh*)   It's a pity. Women
want someone to protect them, I always think. Now wouldn't you,
as a mother, welcome him if ever he came back again to help you
in your old age?

MOTHER (*undecidedly*)   Well, I don't know—

DAUGHTER   He was drowned.
(*Short pause*)

STRANGER   Oh! I beg your pardon – but your husband, does he leave you alone—
(*A man's shout, from some distance*)

MOTHER   That's him. I'll go and meet him. If you'd bide a minute – I'd rather you saw him before you go to bed.

(*Exit*)

(STRANGER *strolls, rather swaggeringly, to the stove*)

STRANGER (*apparently with slight suppressed excitement*)   I suppose a fine young girl like you must sometimes be sick of a life of working, working, in this gloomy place – beautiful as it is.

DAUGHTER (*looks at him steadily*)   Um—

STRANGER   I'll warrant there's not much fun round here; not many young men, no dancing and so on: ah, you ought to be in a big town!

DAUGHTER (*half to herself*)   I have my fun—

STRANGER   It's wonderful in a big city! The glare and the roar of the streets. Your blood swims with it. It's a shame you should never know it. Don't you see that you'll only grow hard and worn here; stiffer and duller every day; working, working, working; then you'll be like your Mother, and at last you'll shrivel and be ugly; and then you'll die. Now; what'd you say (*laughing a little rather hysterically*) if some good fairy suddenly came (*looking at her*) and promised to take you to a big city and show you everything, and buy you dresses and jewels, and give you the best of everything, like a lady?
(*Pause*)

DAUGHTER (*gets up suddenly and crosses to him, limping slightly*)   I'm lame. A dog bit me. Would you like to see? (*Pulls up her skirt and down her stocking and shows place under knee.*) Are ladies' legs like that? See that cut? (*holding out her hand*). That's a big nail did that. What'd they say in cities to that hand? Feel! (*She grips him with her right hand, just above the knee, and looks up smiling slightly. He gives a little exclamation and draws back, rather embarrassed.*) Have you ever felt a lady's hand like that? (*A small pause. She lets go, and goes, swinging, across to the ladder and slowly up it, and, turning to the right, exit.*)

(*He sits down, his hand on his leg.*)
(*Enter* FATHER *and* MOTHER. *The* FATHER *is of middle height, not very broad, aged about fifty, clean-shaven, of a rather excitable manner, dark-brown hair beginning to go grey.*)

MOTHER   This is my husband.

STRANGER (*going towards him, looking hard at him; a little nervously*) Are you the master of the house? How do you do? Your wife was kind enough to promise me a bed here. I got lost in the forest, and benighted. I was very lucky to find a house.

FATHER   How were you in the wood, dressed like that, sir?

STRANGER (*slight agitation*)   I'd lost my way. I was trying to walk to Mohilev. It was so fine – I'm very fond of walking – I thought I'd like to walk. I'm going round the small towns of this part on – business. Government business.

FATHER   Mohilev? You're a lot out of your way. You must be tired as a horse. And with that bag. You might have been robbed.

STRANGER (*opening the bag*)   Oh, there's nothing much but papers in the bag. But (*excitedly*) I've a lot of money about me (*fumbling, and pulling some notes from under his waistcoat*). See. There's a lot of money! It'd buy this house twice over, and all in it. I dare bet you've never seen as much money as that on this table in your life before. (*Pulls out some more, laughing hysterically. Finishes the glass of vodka.*)

FATHER (*looking up at him*)   No, Baron.
(*A pause.* MOTHER *goes to the stove*)

MOTHER   It's not safe, walking in these woods with all that upon you.

STRANGER   I didn't meet a soul the whole day, or see a house. This was the first I came to. I came on it straight out of the forest – from the west there. I *was* glad to see the light!
(*Short pause.* DAUGHTER *comes back quietly across back of room and sits down; meanwhile* STRANGER *continues*)
It must be frightfully lonely here. I should think it would get on one's nerves. To hear the wind in the branches, and watch the night coming on, month after month. I declare I began to feel quite

queer to-day walking all day alone among the trees. A merry company for me!
(*Short pause*)

FATHER   There's a fistful of houses down below in the valley; three minutes down. You didn't go to them, Baron; they lie east. There's people there.

MOTHER (*setting table again*)   *He* goes down to them.

FATHER   And there's work enough to be done about the fields.

STRANGER   But in winter you must find time hang heavy on your hands?

FATHER   Ah – winter's coming.

STRANGER   I expect you'll all be glad when you've saved up a bit and go away and live by some town.

FATHER   That – that'll be when the rams milk – when God wakes from his snoring and remembers his poor.

MOTHER (*reproving mechanically*)   Oh, Ivan!

FATHER   There's no living off this land.
(*Pause*)

STRANGER   Well, I'm dog-tired after that tramp through the woods. I think I'll be turning in. It must be late?

FATHER   It should be after eight.

STRANGER (*laughing*)   Why, I declare, you've no clock! (*Pause. Laughing aloud.*) Why, you'll not know what time to go to bed! I must leave you my watch for the night. I really must. (*Taking his watch out of his waistcoat.*) Look! It's good gold, all of it! I'll hang it up there. I'll bet you've never seen a gold watch hanging up on your wall, eh?

(DAUGHTER *looks at* MOTHER *behind his back*, MOTHER *at* DAUGHTER. FATHER *looks at each of the three, drumming on the table. Pause.*)

MOTHER (*taking up the lamp*)   Shall I show you to bed, Baron?

STRANGER   Yes. I really must turn in. (*Turns to the watch.*) There, what do you say to that! (*Goes up to* DAUGHTER.) Good-night, my little Anna. (*Puts hand on her shoulder and presses it.*) Good-night!

(*She stands stiffly up, dropping a slight curtsey.* STRANGER *turns to* FATHER.) Good-night! Good-night! I'm afraid I've robbed you of the best part of your meal. I must apologise! But I'll pay for it. You shan't regret your hospitality. (*Goes up towards him as if to shake his hand or embrace him, hesitates, and passes on after* MOTHER, *up the ladder.*)

FATHER (*after him*) It's poor food; but you're welcome to it.

MOTHER (*up the ladder*) It's a poor room for *you* – we sleep to the right here. You'll not be troubled if you hear us moving— (*Exeunt, talking.*)
(*Light from stove,* R. DAUGHTER *standing at stove.*)
(FATHER *sits down to eat at* R. *end of table, facing audience.*)

FATHER (*eating*) You're always talking about men; there's one for you. Why don't you go to him? He was looking at you. And he's drunk a lot.

DAUGHTER (*bringing soup and pouring it out*) He's an undersized, white-handed, dirty little man.

FATHER You're afraid. You're always afraid.

DAUGHTER He's not a man. He's a little, weak, chattering half a man; like you.

(FATHER *turns round savagely and catches her with a wrench by the upper arm. A spoon is knocked from her hand*)

DAUGHTER (*twisting her arm free and hitting his hand down; without raising her voice*) If you hit me, I'll kill you. (*Goes to seat* R. *front, and sits down with her back to the audience.*)

MOTHER (*enters with lamp, places it on table, and puts it out*) Have you brought anything?

FATHER No. There's a curse on these woods. There's not a hare nor a bird in them. They're as quiet as the dead.

MOTHER (*sits down on the further side of the stove, three-quarters face to the audience*) We can't get through the winter. We've nothing.

FATHER I'm hungry. There's never food enough in this bloody house. There's no living off this land.

MOTHER I gave him all there was. I knew he was a rich man. We'll get enough from him for eight days, maybe.

FATHER   And then?

MOTHER   We've always got through—

FATHER (*getting up excitedly*)   I'm sick of it, I say. I'll go off to the towns. There's money there. Why should I stay here and work for you two as well as myself? I'll go off alone. (*Catches sight of watch.*) Look at that! Why should he have that and we be starving? It would keep us a year. How did he get it? Who is he? Why did he talk like that?

MOTHER   He had drunk. He is a rich man.

FATHER   He's mad, I say. Who ever heard tell of a man walking through these woods because he liked it, if he wasn't mad? And in that coat, and with a bag?

DAUGHTER   No one saw him come.

MOTHER   If he's mad, we might get a reward for keeping him. His parents would be very rich.

FATHER   He's not mad. But he's queer. Something was driving him mad. Why should he have come here? All that money – the way he talked – do you think it's his?
(MOTHER *and* DAUGHTER *look at each other, scarcely moving their heads, at intervals through the conversation.*)

MOTHER   If it's not his—

FATHER   He looked like a thief. He's a thief's manner. He stole it, I say. He's escaping, hiding. That's why he came here.

DAUGHTER   No one knows he's here.

MOTHER   If he's a thief, we might get a reward for giving him up, or something.

FATHER (*snatching down watch*)   This gold thing, and all that money, what right has he to it? There may be people starving because he stole it. He looked like a thief.

DAUGHTER   He was a little, weak, under-sized man—
(*Pause*)

FATHER (*leaning against the end of the table*)   I'm working, and keeping you two, and doing my best, and I'm starving. And he's a thief and alone, and he has all that money. If there were a God, would He let that be?

MOTHER Ivan!
(*Pause*)

FATHER (*as if unwillingly, and still louder*) We've as good right to it as him. What's money to a hunted man, alone?

MOTHER Hush! You'll wake him!

FATHER (*much lower*) What do I care if he hears?
(*Pause*)

DAUGHTER He'll sleep deep, being tired.
(*Pause. The light from the stove is lower*)

FATHER Why do you look at me?
(*Pause*)

MOTHER (*her hands fumbling; drawing silently closer to the stove*) We'll never get through the winter.
(*Pause*)

FATHER (*shrilly*) Why do you look at me? What are you both thinking? I don't know what you're thinking.
(*Pause*)

MOTHER You're shaking, Ivan. You're making the table rattle—
(*Pause*)

FATHER Why are you looking at me? I can't see your eyes.
(*Longer pause*)

FATHER (*nearly crying*) I killed a man in fight, once – in fight. My God, I – not—
(*Small pause. They all rise silently*)
I must think. Say something. To-morrow—

DAUGHTER Now.

FATHER To-morrow.

MOTHER Now.

FATHER He's our guest—

MOTHER He's a thief.
(*Small pause.* DAUGHTER *begins to light lamp*)

MOTHER (*very low and quick*) He's asleep – only once! He can't struggle. We'll hold him. No one'll ever know. We *must* have the money. You're a coward!

(FATHER *mechanically pulls knife out of sheath, takes lamp mechanically from* DAUGHTER, *and makes a few steps towards the ladder. The women follow.*)

FATHER I can do it. (*Takes a few steps; looks back.*) You're filthy. Stay here. You're not to touch him. I'll do it. (*Goes up ladder quickly and quietly. The* DAUGHTER *stands by the bottom of ladder, leaning against it.* MOTHER *goes back towards stove.*)

(*Long pause. Slight sounds.*)

(DAUGHTER *puts one foot slowly on bottom rung of ladder. Suddenly* FATHER *appears and comes down. Puts lamp on table. Leans against table, shivering.*)

(MOTHER *comes forward. Pause*)

(FATHER *nods*)

DAUGHTER The knife's clean.

MOTHER Did you?

FATHER I – (*crumblingly*) no! I feel dead-sick. I couldn't. I didn't go in. I've been working all day. I'm sick. (*Coughs and retches slightly.*)

MOTHER You *must*—

FATHER I can't – like this. Vodka. I want drink in me.

MOTHER He drank it. You *must*.

(FATHER *goes unsteadily to back of stage. Puts on his coat.*)

FATHER (*fumbling in his pocket*) I'm going down to the shop to get drink. I've got a few *kopeks*. I'll get so I can do it. I'll drink till I'd stick Almighty God. (*Straightens himself, speaks more controlledly.*) When I come back you'll see: I'll be ready to knife anybody. I tell you I'm tired now, and sick. You can't kill a man when your throat's full of stink, and you're going to be sick. I've been working all day. (*Fumbling at the door.*) I'll be back in no time. I swear I'll kill him. I'll drink murder into me. My God! (*Exit by the door,* R.B.)

(*His figure is seen passing the window, going across to the left, running, rather slowly.*)

(MOTHER *and* DAUGHTER *watch him cross; then listen a moment. No sound from above.* MOTHER *puts out the lamp. They sit down by the stove in their usual places,* DAUGHTER *with her back to the audience. The* DAUGHTER *opens the mouth of the stove, puts log of wood in, and leaves the mouth open. A certain amount of light comes out.*)

DAUGHTER He's a coward.

MOTHER He's all right.

DAUGHTER He's a coward.

MOTHER He's not that. He thinks so much. *You* can't understand. He'll be all right when he's got drink in him. It'll stop him thinking.

DAUGHTER If I'd started off to kill a man, I wouldn't need to stop to drink.

MOTHER You'd – I was afraid we wouldn't get him to do it.

DAUGHTER He'll get drunk.

MOTHER He's not got enough money to get drunk on. – Besides, he knows what he's gone for.

DAUGHTER He's gone to get away.
(*Short pause*)
It's hard, waiting.

MOTHER He'll do it when he comes back. (*Gets up and goes to foot of ladder, and wanders back again. Standing.*) I know him. (*Takes down watch and examines it.*) Do you think he's a thief?

DAUGHTER I don't know. We'll be rich. We'll get away from here.

MOTHER (*hangs up watch*) It's the same anywhere. But we won't starve then.

DAUGHTER It's Hell, waiting.
(*Pause*)
One must do things straight, and not think. It'll be harder.

MOTHER (*going irresolutely towards the window*) It's bright outside. (*Suddenly*) No one can have seen in, can they? When *he* was at supper? (*Turns.*)

DAUGHTER No. They couldn't see from the road.

MOTHER (*comes back and sits down*) Anyhow, who could come by here at night?

DAUGHTER   They come here, sometimes.

MOTHER   'Sometimes!' They come a lot to see you, don't they? –
Young men. Twice a year! When I was a girl—

DAUGHTER   You're always jealous of me—
(*The voices get a little shrill, naggingly, not angrily.*)

MOTHER   Jealous! When I was a girl, I'd a dozen after me.
(STRANGER *appears silently, at top of ladder, in shirt and trousers,
bare-foot and comes quietly down, holding a burning match in his left
hand, looking rather dazedly excited.*)

DAUGHTER   It's a dirty thing to be old and jealous.

MOTHER   You've always hated me. I'm your mother; it's wrong
to hate your mother – you're not natural.

DAUGHTER   It's you hate me. You're my mother, right enough.
I've seen love turn—

MOTHER   You don't know what it is to be a mother. You never will,
very like.
(*The* STRANGER *reaches the bottom of the ladder. It creaks. The*
DAUGHTER, *at the second creak, looks round and stares agape; startled.
The* MOTHER *sees her face, breaks off, looks round, and jumps up
exclaiming.*)
(*Short pause*)

MOTHER   What do you want?

STRANGER   Oh! Isn't your husband here?

MOTHER   He's gone out. – Has anything disturbed you, Baron?

STRANGER   No – you see – no: I wanted to speak to him. I thought
– I wanted to do it to-night. It doesn't matter. When will he be
back?

MOTHER   I – I don't know—

DAUGHTER   Not for hours, maybe. He comes back very late.

STRANGER (*advancing a step or two*)   Oh, to-morrow'll do.

MOTHER (*going quickly to the window*)   It's very cold. (*Folds rather
old wooden shutters across and bars them with a great rusty iron bar.*

The STRANGER *is staring with a vague uneasiness about*.) We'll lock up and go to bed. My man comes in later. Did you want anything, Baron?

STRANGER   No, I only thought, if he was here; – I'd something I wanted to get clear before I could sleep. It's nothing. (*Drifts back to the ladder.*)

MOTHER   We didn't disturb you, Baron – our talking?

STRANGER   Oh no, I assure you: I – I went to sleep for a bit and woke up suddenly. I felt, somehow, I shouldn't go to sleep again until I'd got clear—

MOTHER   You'll sleep sound enough, Baron. You'll not hear anything.

STRANGER (*more abruptly*)   Yes. I'm sorry to have startled you – A fancy. . . . To-morrow'll do – I'll sleep like a log. (*Starts climbing up ladder.*)

MOTHER (*still in front of window*)   Yes. You must be tired. (DAUGHTER *stands up. Exit* STRANGER. MOTHER *comes forward.* MOTHER *and* DAUGHTER *converse in whispers.*)

MOTHER   What did he mean? Why did he come down?

DAUGHTER   I don't know.

MOTHER   Had he heard?

DAUGHTER   I don't think so. Perhaps he woke up frightened.

MOTHER   Or he's mad.

DAUGHTER   He was queer all the time.

MOTHER   Could he have been drunk – on that little? Men do queer, restless things when they're drunk—

DAUGHTER   Will he come again?

MOTHER   It makes it worse – that he's like that, – that—
(*Knock at door,* R.B. *The women clutch at each other, and stand looking round. Knock again.* MOTHER *whispers,* 'We must open'. DAUGHTER *nods.* MOTHER *goes over to door.* DAUGHTER *moves quickly to fireplace and takes watch down and thrusts it in her bosom.* MOTHER

opens door slightly: looks out: opens it wider, saying, 'Ah, step in, Paul', and admits a young man, carrying a hare. The young man stamps his feet, and takes off his coat. He is rather tall, neutral coloured, solid-faced, aged twenty-five, clean shaven.)

MOTHER   You're calling very late—

YOUNG MAN   It's not half-past eight. I only stepped in for a minute.

MOTHER   I was just tidying up. We go to bed early. (*Keeps looking round towards the ladder.*)

YOUNG MAN   I just stepped in to bring you this (*throwing hare on table*).

MOTHER   It's very good of you (*taking it up and looking at it*).

YOUNG MAN   I'd like to get warm a minute.

(DAUGHTER *and* YOUNG MAN *come towards stove.*)

MOTHER (*takes lantern and goes towards ladder*)   I'll be putting straight, upstairs. (*Goes up ladder. To* DAUGHTER) You'll be coming soon.

(*Exit, right*)

(DAUGHTER *takes up hare, and handles it.*)

YOUNG MAN   It's close in here.
(*Pause*)
It's dirty and cold outside. Is your father here?

DAUGHTER   He's gone down, to drink.

YOUNG MAN   It's good of your mother to leave us.

DAUGHTER   She's putting straight, upstairs.

YOUNG MAN (*grinning*)   She's not moving about. There's no noise.

DAUGHTER   Never mind her!
(*Pause*)

YOUNG MAN   I didn't know you went to bed so early.

DAUGHTER   You've not often been.

YOUNG MAN   Maybe I'd not have come, if I'd known. – You're not very hospitable in this house.

DAUGHTER   It was good of you to bring this.

YOUNG MAN   I snared her to-day.

DAUGHTER   I wish – I think mother wants to shut the house up.

YOUNG MAN   Don't you want to see me?

DAUGHTER   It's not that. I'm very tired. You'd better go, Paul.

YOUNG MAN   You weren't in your fields to-day. I went to look.

DAUGHTER   I've done a lot. (*Comes up nearer to him.*) Go! Paul, I want to see you. Come; – any day. (*In sudden anger*) Go, will you?

YOUNG MAN (*putting a hand on each of her shoulders*)   Why do you never say things? I've never understood you.

DAUGHTER (*hitting his arm down and shaking herself free*)   Go! I'll see you again.

YOUNG MAN (*catching her quietly by the wrist as she hits his arm down*)   I'll stay a bit, maybe.

DAUGHTER (*pulls herself free*)   Go!

YOUNG MAN   What if I don't?

DAUGHTER (*seizing him by the upper arm in a passion and making him reel*)   Go, will you?

YOUNG MAN (*pulls her to him; they struggle*)   You're not so strong! (*After a second's struggle he kisses her on the mouth. Their mouths part, and she kisses him again. She is pressed back and strikes the edge of the table, which rattles. Released, she leans back against it. He grins.*)

DAUGHTER (*half whispering*)   You'll have something over!

YOUNG MAN   You're not so strong!

DAUGHTER   Go, for God's sake.

YOUNG MAN   I'll come again.

DAUGHTER   Yes; to-morrow.

YOUNG MAN (*picking up his coat*)   I'll come earlier, one day. Come out into the lane and meet me.

DAUGHTER   Yes.

YOUNG MAN (*putting on his coat*)   We'll have things to say.

DAUGHTER   I've got to go to bed now.

YOUNG MAN   Give me a kiss! (*She stands impassive. He kisses her.*)
Good-night.
(*Exit* YOUNG MAN, R.B. *She shuts the door after him, quietly*)

MOTHER (*comes quickly down*)   He's gone?
(DAUGHTER *nods.*)

MOTHER (*jerking her head towards the ladder*)   If *he* had come down
when Paul was here! . . .

DAUGHTER   Someone else may come in.

MOTHER   A lot of young men smell you out, don't they?

DAUGHTER   You fool! . . . We *must* have the money. I want to get
away from here.

MOTHER   Do you think anyone'd look at you in a town? They like
them fine made there.

DAUGHTER   He *must* come soon. He must do it. (*Sits down.*)
(*Pause*)

DAUGHTER   He's been away an hour.

MOTHER   Five minutes, more like.
(*Pause*)

MOTHER (*starting suddenly up*)   What was that?

DAUGHTER   What?

MOTHER   A step.

DAUGHTER   Where?

MOTHER   Outside. It's Ivan.

DAUGHTER   I heard nothing.

MOTHER   Perhaps it's somebody else.
(*Pause. Silence*)

DAUGHTER   It wasn't anything.

MOTHER   If he daren't, again, this time—

DAUGHTER   He's a coward.

MOTHER   He's tired. Perhaps he'll be drunk.
(*Pause*)

MOTHER (*shifting*)   I can't bear waiting. It's as if somebody's watching us.
(*Pause*)
(DAUGHTER *rises and limps over to a box on ledge beyond the stove; rummages there.*)

MOTHER (*huskily*)   What are you doing?

DAUGHTER   These knives are old and weak.

MOTHER   You— Sit down. He'll come.

DAUGHTER (*stooping over box of firewood*)   I'll go mad, waiting. (*Rises with an axe in her hand.*) This isn't very sharp, but it's heavy.

MOTHER   What do you mean?

DAUGHTER (*lighting the lamp on the table*)   Hush. We can do it.

MOTHER (*getting up*)   You mustn't. Do you think—?

DAUGHTER   He's a weak little man. Take off your skirt and throw it over him up to the neck and hold it down so as he can't get his hands out. Hold fast.
(MOTHER *slips off her outer skirt.* DAUGHTER *takes up the lantern.*)

MOTHER (*going to the ladder*)   Come on quickly, for Christ's sake. Oh, thank God!

DAUGHTER   We'll put the lantern on the shelf.
(*They go quietly up the ladder –* DAUGHTER *first – and disappear left.*)
(*Pause*)
(*Slight muffled noises. A shout. A crashing thud. A groan broken by a thud. A succession of rather regular heavy thuds. While these are still going on there is the sound of quick steps above, and the* MOTHER *comes, half falling down the ladder, sobbing quietly. The thuds cease.*)

MOTHER (*collapsing on to a stool at the table*)   O Christ! Stop! Stop! O Christ!

(DAUGHTER *comes slowly downstairs, the light in one hand, holding the axe stiffly down with the other; drawing long, difficult, audible breaths.*)
(*The* MOTHER *ceases sobbing.*)

MOTHER Why did you go on hitting?

DAUGHTER (*putting lamp on table*) I couldn't help it.

MOTHER You went on and on. I thought you were mad. He cried out on his mother, at first.

DAUGHTER (*standing*) He didn't.

MOTHER He cried on his mother. She'll never know. You went on and on hitting. You were horrible. Why did you?

DAUGHTER I couldn't stop.
(*Goes round and stands by the stove.*)

MOTHER Why did you go on and on hitting? I thought you were mad. I hated you.

DAUGHTER I couldn't help it.
(*Pause*)

MOTHER Why are you still holding that thing?
(DAUGHTER *goes up beyond the stove and throws axe into wood-basket. Returns and sits in her seat, back to audience.*)

MOTHER I'll never use that skirt again.

DAUGHTER You'll never need to.
(*Pause*)
(MOTHER *begins slowly clearing remains of supper away.* DAUGHTER *puts her head in her hands and begins sobbing.*)

MOTHER Well, he won't move now. We'll make Ivan bury him out in the woods, to-night, or to-morrow. We'll get away from here before the thick of winter.
(*Faint noise from outside, some distance away.*)
We'll have plenty— What's that? It's Ivan coming back.
(*Noise louder and increasing.*)
Get ready, lass. It's done. There's someone with him. I hear talking. Perhaps it's somebody else. Get up – look yourself. We must be ready.

DAUGHTER (*jumping up*) It's done. We can tell him it's done. I'm glad. We can get away. We'll be rich. I'll wear silk.

MOTHER (*breaking in*) It's Ivan. I hear his name. Who's he bringing with him? Is he mad?

DAUGHTER He's drunk.
(*Rattling at door* L. *front.*)

MOTHER He's arrested. (*Goes to door and opens it.*)
(VODKA-SHOP-KEEPER *and* HIS SON *enter, the* FATHER *between them.* VODKA-SHOP-KEEPER *a tall, blond, jolly man of about forty, hairy face, and inclined to be stout. His* SON, *eighteen, slight, rather darker, and self-conscious.*)
(VODKA-SHOP-KEEPER *holds a boot in his right hand. His* SON *holds a vodka bottle. They are supporting the* FATHER, *who is drunk, dazed-looking and dragging. He has only one boot on. The* VODKA-SHOP-KEEPER *and his* SON *are also slightly drunk;* VODKA-SHOP-KEEPER *excited,* SON *sly and flushed.* MOTHER *and* DAUGHTER *both standing.*)

V.-S. Evening, missus! We've brought your man home. (*Laughing.*)

MOTHER Ivan—?

V.-S. He wanted to come alone. He said he had something to do. (*Laughs.*) He said he had to go quietly. He *would* take his boot off. (*Holds boot up.*) We couldn't stop him. He couldn't get the other off. Said he had to go '*quietly*'. You should have seen him going quietly – (*laughs*) – my God!
(FATHER, *asleep, collapses at the foot of the ladder*)

V.-S. Here – hold up. He's gone dazed from the open air. Give him a drop to wake him up. (SON *pours from bottle into glass left on table, shakes* FATHER *and makes him drink it.*)

V.-S.'s SON He came into the shop shivering and white. My God! 'Drink', he says. I gave him a glass. He drank two before he spoke. 'I've got something to do', he said. (*Giggling.*)

V.-S. When I came in he was drunk – blind. He can't have eaten all day, getting like that on three glasses. He was talking big about his Luck. We all had a glass to his Luck. 'As much as you like, now,' I said.

FATHER (*suddenly*) Hush! (*Tries to begin to climb ladder – falls against it.*)

MOTHER (*screaming*) Ivan!

v.-s. (*delightedly*)   That's it. Oh, he's all right. He won't hurt himself. You should 'a' seen him hopping along in the mud like a lame hare. 'I've got to go quietly', he said. Laugh! we were nearly sick. 'I've Luck', he said. 'God's good to me.' 'Here's to God', I said. '*I* know your luck. No more starving now!' We all drank. (*Pours out, and drinks from glass.*)

(MOTHER *and* DAUGHTER *stare suddenly at him.*)

(FATHER *rises to his feet and stands wavering – holds up one hand.*)

FATHER   Quietly! Quietly! (*Nods his head.*)

(MOTHER *runs to him and holds him by the arm, still staring at* VODKA-SHOP-KEEPER.)

v.-s.'s SON (*giggling*)   He kept saying it. 'Quietly,' he said. Didn't he, Dad? 'I've something to do – *quietly*', he said. 'Not a sound', he said. He took his boot off and hopped through the mud like – like – a lame hare!

MOTHER (*to* VODKA-SHOP-KEEPER)   You know—

v.-s. (*grinning*)   Rather.

MOTHER (*calmly*)   Of course, you share – the Luck.

v.-s. (*cheerfully*)   I get what comes to me. I told him so. We all get a little. It's a great day. He's up there, I suppose (*nodding to the upper storey*).

(MOTHER *nods.*)

v.-s.   Tired, eh? (*Laughs.*)

MOTHER (*after a short pause, leaving go of Ivan*)   You see— (*Begins again.*) He told you?

v.-s. (*expanding*)   Rather! First in the village he came to.

(FATHER *drinks again.*)

I'd never have known him. He knew me – after twenty years! We had a glass. He told me of his joke. 'I'll be the first to congratulate them in the morning', I said. ''Tisn't often one gets a son back! Ivan'll be glad of a son!

(*Pause. Ivan waves his glass, puts on an air of mystery, says 'Somethin' to be done', sits down on the ladder and goes into a doze. His glass crashes to the ground.*)

MOTHER (*vacantly*)   Son. . . . Son . . . (*leaning on table*).

(DAUGHTER *stands stiff.*)

V.-S. (*roaring with laughter*) It's turned all their heads! He said to me, 'I've such a game on. I'll knock and say I'm a rich man who's lost his way in the woods, and I want a night's lodging, and I'll show 'em my money, and I'll watch 'em and see 'em all again, and then in the morning I'll say: "Behold your son which was lost and is found!"'' Excited – wasn't he just. 'You'll never keep the secret all night', I said. And he hasn't. I knew he wouldn't. 'I'll be the first to congratulate them in the morning', I said. And I'm doing it to-night! (*Drinks from bottle.*)
(*Pause*)

MOTHER (*looking down at the table*) You knew him?

V.-S. (*blearily*) Bless you, yes! – when he talked of old times. What are you all looking like that for? Didn't he come on here?

DAUGHTER He did.
(*Pause.* VODKA-SHOP-KEEPER *stares resentfully*)

V.-S. You're not very cheerful.

MOTHER (*goes suddenly to her chair, saying*) He cried out 'Mother!'
(*Sits down.*)

V.-S. (*genially*) I'll be bound he did!

FATHER (*waking up suddenly*) Something to be done.
(MOTHER *suddenly screams.*)

DAUGHTER Stop it, Mother!

V.-S. What is it? What have you done?
(VODKA-SHOP-KEEPER *and his* SON *step a little backward towards door,* L.F. MOTHER *continues crying and sobbing loudly.*)

V.-S. (*to* DAUGHTER) Why are you looking like that? Didn't he tell you who he was?

DAUGHTER No.

V.-S. What have you done? Where is he? (*Raises his head suddenly and shouts*) Ivan! Young Ivan! Ivan!

FATHER (*fumbling with his other boot*) Not a sound.
(*Pause*)

MOTHER He cried out 'Mother!' You went on and on hitting.
(*Screams.*)

v.-s. What have you done? You've— (*Backs towards the door, staring – the* SON *behind him*).

v.-s.'s SON She's got something on her hands, Father!
(MOTHER *still screaming.*)

DAUGHTER Stop it, Mother!
(FATHER *starts clambering up ladder, stumbling.*)
(SON *slips out of door.*)

v.-s. You've— (*Hurries out, slamming door*).
(MOTHER *screaming.*)

DAUGHTER Stop it, Mother!

FATHER (*vaguely, with immense air of mystery and determination*)
Very softly now. Quietly, quietly! Quietly— (*Falls on to the ladder.*)

DAUGHTER They'll put me in prison!

CURTAIN

Death of John Rump

... It may have become apparent that personally I do not approve of John Rump. He was a failure. He might have been a thousand splendid things. He was – an English Gentleman. He might have seen – he was blind; have heard – he was deaf. Infinite chances lay about him – he was an English Gentleman.

Yet we may pity him now, lying there through that long March night, helpless in the hands of his like. In that stuffy room were no watching angels, no 'Justice and Mercy of God', no 'Death as an Emperor with all his Court'. No sublimity or solemnity of leaving this world was there; no awe and pomp of dying; but worry, heat and tangled bed-clothes; an incompetent doctor, and tired-eyed, gulping relations; injections of oxygen and God knows what; and, bared of gentility, John Rump, blue-lipped, fighting for breath, helpless and pitiable as a blind kitten in a water-butt, or an insect crushed underfoot; drugs and fuss, gasping and snivelling.

Outside, in the snow-covered town, perfectly silent under the faint approach of morning, were peace and mystery, colour and beauty and joy; things that John had never known.

Epilogue in Heaven

(Everywhere there is a subdued air of expectancy. The archangels, massed effectively at the back, are wearing scarlet for the occasion. The harps and trumpets tune up. St. Cecilia waves the bâton. The first semi-chorus of angels on the left sings:)

Home out of time and space,
    The wanderer is turning
        Immortal feet;
The white and eager face,
    The thirsting mouth and burning
        Eyes we'll regreet, –
One that has found his grace,
    One that has staked his yearning,
        One out of imperfection grown complete.

(Second semi-chorus on the right)

What will he bear with him, what will he bring to us
    From the world where laughter and love are rife,
Great dreams to report to us, songs to sing to us,
    Spoils well won from the heart of the strife?
Will he come like a glad-eyed silent lover,
    Or slow and sorry that all is over,
Or sudden and splendid and swift as the spring to us,
    Fresh and laughing from lovely life?

(Full chorus)

As the ending to a story,
    As the light dies in the West
        When the birds turn home at even,
            Glad and splendid will he come,
He the victor into glory,
    He the weary to his rest,
        The immortal to his heaven,
            The wanderer home.

FIRST SERAPH (*pointing downwards*) I see a speck immediately below.

MANY LITTLE CHERUBS Bravo! Bravo! Bravo!

SECOND SERAPH I see it too. A black speck. Very far!

CHERUBS   Huzza! Huzza! Huzza!

THIRD SERAPH (*excitedly*)   'Tis him! 'Tis him! upon his upward way!

CHERUBS   Hurray! Hurray! Hurray!

GOD (*rising*)
    I do espy him like a *fretful midge*,
    The while his wide and alternating vans
    Winnow the buxom air. With flight serene
    He wings amidst the watery Pleiades;
    Now Leo feels his passage, and the Twins;
    Orion now, and that unwieldy girth
    Hight Scorpio; as when a trader bound
    For Lamda or the isle of Mogador,
    Freighted with ambergris and stilbrium,
    And what rich odours . . .

(The remaining 127 lines are lost in the increasing hubbub. Enter, from below on the left, JOHN RUMP in top-hat, frockcoat etc., bearing an umbrella. He stands impassive in the middle.)

GOD

    John Rump, of Balham, Leeds, and Canterbury,
    Why are you wearing hideous black clothes?

RUMP

    Because I am an English Gentleman.

GOD

    John Rump, we gave you life and all its wonder.
    What splendid tidings have you got to tell?

RUMP

    God, I have been an English Gentleman.

GOD

    Infinite splendour has been in your power;
    John Rump, what have you got to show for life?

RUMP

    God, I have been an English Gentleman.

GOD (*rising angrily*)
    Was it for this we sent you to the world,
    And gave you life and knowledge, made you man,

Crowned you with glory? You could have worked and laughed,
Sung, loved, and kissed, made all the world a dream,
Found infinite beauty in a leaf or word ...
... Perish eternally, you and your hat!

RUMP (*not wincing*)
    You long-haired aesthetes, get you out of heaven!
I, John Rump, I, an English Gentleman,
Do not believe in you and all your gushing.
I am John Rump, this is my hat, and this
My umberella. I stand here for sense,
Invincible, inviolable, eternal,
For safety, regulations, paving-stones,
Street lamps, police, and bijou-residences
Semi-detached. I stand for sanity,
Comfort, content, prosperity, top-hats,
Alcohol, collars, meat. Tariff Reform
Means higher wages and more work for all.
(As he speaks, GOD and the seraphic multitude grow faint, mistier
and mistier, become ineffectually waving shadows, and vanish. The
floor of Heaven rocks ... the thrones and the glassy sea ... all
has vanished. JOHN RUMP remains, still and expressionless, leaning
on his umbrella, growing larger and larger, infinitely menacing,
filling the universe, blotting out the stars ...)

9
Poetry

I

Brooke was from the first a deliberate poet. His earliest verses, written at the age of ten after seeing a great wave break over the sea-front, show concern for his newly acquired knowledge that blank verse should have five feet with two beats in each foot. Here is the remarkable last line:

One day Poseidon grown strong will conquer.

His lack of sympathy with *vers libre* has been noted. In the review of Pound's *Personae* he wrote:

It is certain (thanks in part to Mr. Saintsbury), that the foot is immensely important in English prosody. It is still more certain that the line is. Otherwise *Lorna Doone* and much of Dickens would be pure verse.

And in one of his earliest notices for *The Cambridge Review* he chided the President of Magdalen College, Oxford, T. H. Warren, for the metrics of *The Death of Virgil*:

The blank verse is pedantic, but not from lack of licence. Several lines have a foot too many.

Marsh, one may think, in that famous phrase of D. H. Lawrence's, was not the only 'policeman of poetry'.

He would often speak of the difficulties confronting a poet who was anxious to study the technique of his craft. For any other art one could have found a school where certain rules were taught and methodical criticism offered. As the only substitute for this, he constantly sought good models. Reviewing *The Memoir* in *The Times Literary Supplement*, Virginia Woolf wrote:

> He had read everything, and he had read it from the point of view of a working writer. In discussing the work of living writers he gave you the impression that he had the poem or story before his eyes in a concrete shape, and his judgments were not only very definite but had a freedom and a reality which mark the criticism of those who are themselves working in the same art. . . . To work hard, much harder than most writers think it necessary, was an injunction that remains in memory.

Evidence of the hard work and an indication of his methods of composition may be found in a few surviving notebooks. One of these, dating from Grantchester days, contains material of three sorts. There are, first, a number of notes on the technical structure of poems he has been reading. These serve only to illustrate his interest in prosody. Secondly, there are lists of words such as 'syllabub', 'paravent' and 'postule' which he has culled, chiefly, from the poems of Browning, and also from Keats and Milton. These lists of words throw little light on the origins of individual poems – though there is mention that 'arval-bread' = baked-meats (see 'Ambarvalia' *P.W.* 91); and use was to be found later for 'queasy' ('Jealousy' *P.W.* 128). But they do show – and this is more important – his passionate interest in words, words which are at least of the same kind as in the poems; and they point, too, to something that was fundamental to his writing. Walter de la Mare has said that, for Brooke, 'words . . . are absolute symbols; they mean precisely what they say and only what they say'. And, whereas de la Mare found words to be 'obstinate and artificial symbols' – found them, he once said, a restriction upon expression rather than a means of it – words were, for Brooke, not only a means of expression, but often the motive for it. 'Oh, it sets me singing', is the unkind response to news that Marsh has torn a ligament.

Isn't ligature – or is it ligament? – a lovely word?

> 'Is it prudent? is it Pure?
> To go and break a ligature?'

'With lissom ligament
My lovely one she went
And trod the street
On quiet feet.'

'A word,' said Brooke in a passage I have quoted from *John Webster*, 'is an idea with an atmosphere, a hard core with a fringe round it, like an oyster with a beard. . . . Poets think of the fringes.'

The third sort of material contained in the Grantchester note-book is a garnering of quotations, chiefly from the letters of Shelley, and also from Keats, Shakespeare, Yeats and Dryden. This in itself would not be remarkable; many people, and writers especially, keep commonplace books. But the interest of Brooke's quotations is that so many of them express ideas which are embodied, in some form or other, in the poems. Here are three instances:

And that deep torture may be called a Hell
When more is felt than one hath power to tell.

(Shakespeare)

This is the antithesis of the idea expressed in 'Dead Men's Love' (*P.W.* 83), where two lovers only discover they are in Hell by their total absence of feeling. Again:

Some of us have in a prior existence been in
love with an Antigone, and that makes us find no full
content in any mortal tie.

(Shelley, letter to John Osborne, 1821)

Compare Brooke's 'The Young Man in April' (*P.W.* 57). Finally:

Leave Mammon and Jehovah to those who delight in
wickedness and slavery – their altars are stained with blood
and polluted with gold, the price of blood. But the shrines
of the Penates are good wood-fires or window-frames inter-
twined with creeping plants; their hymns are the purring of
kittens, the hissing of kettles; the long talks over the past
and dead, the laugh of children, the warm wind of summer
filling the quiet house, and the pelting storm of winter
struggling in vain for entrance.

(Shelley, letter to Peacock, 1816)

There is no need to list the occasions when Brooke worshipped at the shrines of the Penates; in this he was consistent and devout.

Again from *John Webster*: 'A man tends to collect quotations, phrases, and ideas, that particularly appeal to and fit in with his own personality.' He belonged to 'the caddis-worm school of writers'; and though not, in truth, a plagiarist, he practised what Ben Jonson held to be 'the third requisite in our poet, or maker', the art of 'Imitation'.

It should not be adduced that Brooke depended always on literary stimuli for his poems: far from it. More often, as other notebooks show, they begin by his 'collecting a few words, detaching lines from the ambient air', or – I quote from one of his last letters – 'collaring one or two of the golden phrases that a certain wind blows from (will the Censor let me say?) Olympus, across these purple seas'. The notebooks show how these phrases would then be pieced together, amplified, modified, with blanks left for the unforthcoming word, so that the manuscript at this stage would resemble a jigsaw puzzle with pieces missing from it. 'Have you seen Rupert's notebooks,' Jacques Raverat once asked, 'and all the drafts of sonnets with the blanks left in for the "O God"s?' The manner in which one of these last pieces was supplied has been recorded by Leonard Woolf. 'At one moment he said: "Virginia, what is the brightest thing you can think of?" "A leaf with the light on it", was Virginia's instant reply.' And a blank space towards the end of 'Town and Country' (*P.W.* 123) was filled in immediately:

Child-like we lean and stare as bright leaves stare.

An interesting example of the later stages of Brooke's 'carpentry' is given in the *Memoir*, where Marsh prints the first and final drafts of the 'Psychical Research' sonnet. Hassall is more ambitious in printing drafts of 'Seaside' with a conjectural commentary.

II

It must be remembered, then, in reading the early poems that many of them were little more than a young man's exercises in mastering his tools. With the appearance of the Keynes edition, the number of these published exercises was greatly increased: thirty-eight poems were added to the eighty-two previously collected. Sir Geoffrey sought to justify this increase in the *corpus* by saying that 'when a poet has passed his third decade of posthumous fame and has come to be accepted as a national possession, his early efforts acquire an interest for the evidence they afford of the influences at work during formative years'. But such evidence was before this only too readily available. Brooke had himself deemed all the new poems unworthy of inclusion in the only volume to appear in his lifetime. They add little more than what he himself called 'unimportant prettiness', and could be a further barrier to a fair appraisal.

It follows that I have excluded them, and likewise most of the early poems, though reference to a few of them is made here. Lest it should then seem inconsistent or perverse to have included three poems not in Keynes, I must offer my own justification. I do not pretend that any of them is representative of Brooke at his best, or second best, though none could discredit him as so many of the early poems may. The Sicilian Octave ('An Evil Time') was the first of his poems to be printed in the *Westminster Gazette*, in which the weekly competitions, later continued in the *Saturday Westminster*, provided him not only with financial gain but practice in his craft. The poem – or octave – has not only an historical interest; it shows more clearly than most of his work at this time the deliberateness I have referred to. The other two poems are translations, of which there are no examples in the *Poetical Works*. The (characteristically) free translation of Horace (Liber 1, Carmen 38) was written in the copy of Horace he used when at Rugby. The translation of Christian Wagner was written, before he knew German, from a literal version by Geoffrey Keynes. It was to win his second prize in the *Westminster*, and was the subject of the entertaining 'Comment' I have printed as an appendix to it.

III

There was one serious weakness in the course of apprenticeship Brooke prescribed for himself, and for this he could hardly be blamed: it was the fault of the times. It is hard to think of more unfortunate models for a young poet than Swinburne and the poets of the decadent nineties – unless it be Brooke himself, as reflected in the juvenilia of some later poets. Like Swinburne, Brooke never quite succeeded in fusing body and soul, which is one reason why, as Patric Dickinson has said, he appeals to adolescence 'eternally caught in the same predicament'. And, just as the neo-Brookes seem to be most attracted by the 'red mournful roses', the 'little creeping shadows' and 'white lips of desire' of *their* master, so Brooke, too, fell victim to some of the worst faults of *his*.

The most common blemishes of the early poems are what he later referred to as 'romantic devices – devices, that is, which aim at the beauty or power of some single line or part of the work of art, rather than at the effect of the whole', and of which he gives as an example:

Fog's tenebrous opal dream swooned thwart the lamps.

He never entirely outgrew his inclination to 'load every rift with ore'; and even this self-parody – and an entry in the Grantchester notebook:

... twittered the epithalamion of day and darkness, and the occident was scarlet with hymeneal flames

– shows that such loadings of the rifts, though he rejected them critically, continued to hold a fascination for him.

Dowson, too, whom he commended to the Rugby sixth form in a paper on 'Modern Poetry', was not a helpful influence. Quoting the remark of Hugo to Baudelaire: 'You have created a new shudder', Brooke suggests that one might say of Dowson: 'He has created a new sigh.' Such sighs may be heard in 'The Path of Dreams' (*P.W.* 194), 'In January' (*P.W.* 187), 'Evening' (*P.W.* 184), 'Sorrow' (*P.W.* 182), 'The Lost Lilies' (*P.W.* 172), to take but a few examples from Sir Geoffrey's additions to the poems. Slightly more successful are the Dowsonian alexandrines of 'Day that I have loved' (*P.W.* 142). There is, furthermore, an obvious link with Dowson in 'Dead Men's Love' (*P.W.* 83): compare the lines of 'Amor Profanus':

In vain we stammered: from afar
Our old desire shone cold and dead:
That time was distant as a star,
When eyes were bright and lips were red,
And still we went with downcast eye
And no delight in being nigh,
Poor shadows most uncomforted.

'Dead Men's Love' was one of the poems ('Dawn', 'Lust' and 'A Channel Passage' were others) which amply fulfilled Brooke's aim of shocking his first readers. Today the shock seems as dead as the poetry: we wonder why they bothered. But we can respect him for writing what came quickly to be known as the 'unpleasant poems'

– they were a healthy youthful reaction against mere prettiness –
and we can admire the determination with which he battled with his
publisher, Frank Sidgwick, for their inclusion.

I have included one of the unpleasant poems, partly to represent
them, and partly because of an interesting link with Brooke's
abetter in 'Decadence', St John Lucas. Lucas had written a novel,
which Brooke much admired, and here is the passage in it which
caught his imagination:

> Death laughed and took another skull in his hand.
>
>   'Lo, the skull of Helen,' he said: 'for whose sake the tall
> towers of Ilium fell headlong, and the heroes died in the dusty
> plain, and the gods themselves suffered wounds. Her body
> was sweet with strange perfumes, and the breath of her hair
> made men mad. But she grew old, and her bright hair
> became grey and thin; yea, Helen, the desire of Heaven,
> became a bald and withered hag who was fain even in
> summer to crouch over the fire. And then she was content
> to die, for Menelaus was palsied and querulous, and was ever
> upbraiding her concerning Ilium and Alexander; and the
> words were empty noise to her, and signified nothing.'

The two sonnets, 'Menelaus and Helen', show a slight advance on
Lucas.

IV

The earliest of Brooke's poems to suggest his better later work is
the sonnet, 'Seaside'. In the lines of the sestet

> . . . In the deep heart of me
> The sullen waters swell towards the moon,
> And all my tides set seaward . . .

we may look forward to that remarkable line from one of the last
fragments

> In Avons of the heart her rivers run.

But in another way the poem looks backward to a more profitable
influence; and we hear the new note in two slightly later sonnets,
in the lines

> When the high session of the day is ended
>   ('Day and Night', *P.W.* 115)

and

    Such long swift tides stir not a land-locked sea.
                (Sonnet: 'I said I splendidly loved you', *P.W.* 105)

Brooke, it will be clear, was working now on the Elizabethans. In 'Dust' he builds on an idea from Cowley's 'All-over Love':

> Hereafter if one *Dust* of me
>   Mixt with anothers *Substance* be,
> 'Twill *Leaven* that whole *Lump* with Love of thee.
>
>   Let Nature if she please disperse
> My *Atoms* over all the Universe,
>   At the last they eas'ly shall
>   Themselves know, and together call;
> For thy *Love*, like a *Mark*, is stamp'd on all.

If it be true that Swinburne is still present (and Shelley, too, in the epithet 'swift' applied to a woman's hair), words such as 'dance', 'gleam', 'eager', 'sweet', 'radiant', 'flame', and 'ecstasy' serve now to enliven and give warmth to the calculated metaphysics of Cowley. In some of the verses – in the fourth, fifth, sixth and seventh – there is an anticipation of the unforced lyrical quality of the best of his later poems, 'Retrospect' and 'Tiare Tahiti'.

v

W. B. Yeats has been reported as saying that, if Brooke could rid his poems of a 'languid sensualness', he would probably become a very great poet. This was said early in 1913 before the best of the poems had appeared. It is interesting to link the remark with the better known judgment (are not all his judgments well known?) of that most demanding critic, F. R. Leavis. Dr Leavis wrote:

> Brooke had a considerable personal force and became himself
> an influence. He energized the Garden-Suburb ethos with a
> certain original talent and the vigour of a prolonged
> adolescence. His verse exhibits a genuine sensuousness
> rather like Keats's (though more energetic) and something
> that is rather like Keats's vulgarity with a Public School
> accent.

As a general comment on the whole range of Brooke's poems this is brilliant. One must allow the charge of vulgarity in such instances as I have quoted; further, the Rugbeian was to speak again in the '1914' sonnets. But what is acutely perceptive is the comment on Brooke's sensuousness, which is allowed (notwithstanding Yeats) to be at least more energetic than Keats's. Yeats's charge of languidness looks back to the early poems – to the pre-Raphaelite 'Ante Aram' (*P.W.* 161) for example. There was a remarkable development in Brooke's later work, and of all the Elizabethans no one was more instrumental in furthering it than John Donne.

J. E. Flecker called Brooke 'our Donne Redivivus'. In Donne he found a great poet with whom he could feel in closest sympathy. If his two essays on him (chapter 7) serve as quite good introductions to Donne, they are excellent introductions to Brooke. It would be foolish to attempt to show instances of particular indebtedness in the poems. One could point to obvious connections such as that between 'Heaven' and Donne's 'The Baite', or his borrowing in 'Beauty and Beauty' (*P.W.* 66) the epithet 'scattering-bright' from 'Aire and Angels'. But Donne's influence is more subtle, more pervasive. We see it in the wit, the humour, the irony, the love of paradox, the tougher intellectual qualities of the later poems. 'Brooke mocked at the things – people, places and ideas alike – that he loved most tenderly, and loved the things he laughed at,' said Frances Cornford. And with his poems, as with Donne's, 'at any given moment . . . it is often impossible to discern which he is doing most'.

Brooke did not, like Donne, relieve the stress of passion by twisting iron pokers; but he attempted to reconcile an unhappy love by letting his mind dwell on 'things'. Thus, in one of the most characteristic of his sonnets, 'The Busy Heart':

> I would think of a thousand things,
>   Lovely and durable, and taste them slowly,
> One after one, like tasting a sweet food.
> I have need to busy my heart with quietude.

Above all, he shared with Donne the gift of dramatic distancing: as with Donne's, we see his affairs 'in the round'. The poet who turns back from his own room, leaving 'himself' in possession (see the Tchekoff review in chapter 7) seems close to Brooke's own experience. It cannot be claimed as more than an interesting coincidence that Donne's first published poem was written while serving in the Royal Naval Division before Cadiz, and was dedicated to a Cambridge man whose name was Brooke. But it may have been no accident that the *Songs and Sonets* were written mostly on Donne's visits to the continent, and that nearly all the best of Brooke's poems were written in Germany and the South Seas.

VI

It is easy to point to other influences in the poems: to the Milton of 'L'Allegro' in 'Grantchester'; to Drayton's 'The Parting' in 'The Chilterns' (*P.W.* 53); to Marvell's 'A Dialogue between the Soul and Body' in the 'Psychical Research' sonnet; to Meredith's 'Modern Love' sonnet 16 in 'The Hill', and to the idea of Meredith's whole sequence in Brooke's love sonnets from the South Seas. Hunting the influence, like hunting the symbol, can become an entertaining literary parlour game. But enough has been said of other voices. Brooke's own voice rings clearly in the later poems; and these require little by way of commentary: only a freshness of response in reading them.

'There is no one the least like him,' wrote Harold Monro on Brooke's death, 'though he had several imitators. No one has his frankness, no one his ingenuity, his incisiveness, or his humour – no one will pretend to have.' There is something in the physical toughness of the poems, in their muscularity, which is such as to make one feel that the man is active within the verse. As Walter de la Mare has said, Brooke's writing, whether in verse or in prose, is 'a kind of action'.

Donne-like as his humour may be, it has a quality peculiar to Brooke. There was a strain of the sentimental in him. In the early poems he indulged it, finding ample precedents among the decadent writers – though even then he can stand back and mock himself in his borrowed robes. When first he reacted against the sentimental he did so with a studied fierceness, as in the second of the sonnets, 'Menelaus and Helen': 'So far the poet . . .'. But in the later poems he was checked from worst excesses by the half-conscious play of his humour. This humour is not of the sort to provoke a laugh, nor often a smile, though the recognition of it may shadow 'soft and passingly, About the corners of [the] lips.' Its effect is seen most clearly, perhaps, in 'Grantchester' and 'Tiare Tahiti'. It is subtly at play in 'Mutability'; in 'The Night Journey' it checks the gathering momentum of flood and wind with the mock heroic: 'There is an end appointed, O my soul!' A like tone of mock solemnity is in the opening and concluding lines of 'The Great Lover'. In the '1914' sonnets there is for once no trace of this humour. As Dent said, the romanticism Brooke so much dreaded then came uppermost: the critical censorship of his humour failed him.

But, above all, the poems are charged with and surrender – at times with a surprising fulness – that 'individual and bewildering ghost', his personality. 'They seem as we read them', said de la Mare, 'to bring us into a happy, instant relationship with him. They tell us more than even friendship could discover unaided.' And they are free from those defensive barriers which poets so often build.

When you were there, and you, and you . . .

I think if you had loved me when I wanted . . .

These I have loved . . .

He assumed, indeed, and with a disarming sincerity, that his own fortunes must be nearest to his readers' hearts; we cannot read him with detachment. 'A man's poetry,' wrote H. W. Garrod, 'is, after all, only one part of his greatness; and indeed, only one part of his poetry.'

It is the chief value of Brooke's writing as a whole that it forms a living record of the man. It does not often take the reader beyond the shrines of the Penates. It is not for flights of fancy or for the deeper philosophic insights that we may read him; rather, for his sensitive response to a short but vivid life. As he wrote in his review of the Post-Impressionist Exhibition:

There are moments in the life of most of us when some sight suddenly takes on an inexplicable and overwhelming importance – a group of objects, a figure or two, a gesture, seem in their light and position and colour to be seen in naked reality, through some rent in the grotesque veil of accidental form and hue – for a passing minute.

A Sicilian Octave

An Evil Time came down with fateful feet
  And trod across the garden of my soul –
Before him grass and tender herbs were sweet,
  But still behind him desolation stole.
Stark thorns and thistle hedge a waste complete,
  Wide-spread beneath the adverse stars' control;
How shall the frail hands of my spirit meet
  The change – or make the marrèd beauty whole?

1905

Translation of Horace Liber I Carmen XXXVIII

  Fellow, I hate your pomp of Paris,
Those neat green garlands you propose.
  No longer seek the spot where tarries
    The last red rose.

  We only want some simple shrub
That will disgrace nor you, the stripling
  Waiter, nor me in village pub
    Placidly tippling.

c. 1906

God's Song Book
(*Translation of 'Liederbuch der Gottheit' by Christian Wagner*)

Glory of earth and sky and sea,
God's book of song He gives to me!
A child, I turn each page thereof,
And read, remembering His love.

Spring sunlight, upon fen and fold,
And every page is edged with gold!
Gay flowers between the leaves are pressed
To mark the songs we love the best.

1907

A Comment

God gives us, in earth's loveliness,
   His own great song-book, it is stated.
We stumble through, (and have to guess
   To whom or what it's dedicated!)

On first perusing, how we yearn to
   Mark every song! but soon, my friend,
The only page we want to turn to
   Holds two best words of all, 'The End'.

But, since we've got to read it through,
   Let us, as true philosophers,
Sit down, and critically review
   God's *very* minor book of verse.

One poem I've underlined – the best –
   (There's all sorts in God's poetry-book!):
But of the lot I most detest
   God's vulgar lyric 'Rupert Brooke'.

.   .   .

And, if you're lenient, and declare
   The faults and merits pretty equal,
At least you'll join my hearty prayer
   'Dear Author, *please* don't write a sequel!'

1907

Seaside

Swiftly out from the friendly lilt of the band,
     The crowd's good laughter, the loved eyes of men,
     I am drawn nightward; I must turn again
Where, down beyond the low untrodden strand,
There curves and glimmers outward to the unknown
     The old unquiet ocean. All the shade
Is rife with magic and movement. I stray alone
     Here on the edge of silence, half afraid,

Waiting a sign. In the deep heart of me
The sullen waters swell towards the moon,
And all my tides set seaward.
                              From inland
Leaps a gay fragment of some mocking tune,
That tinkles and laughs and fades along the sand,
And dies between the seawall and the sea.

1908

Sonnet

Oh! Death will find me, long before I tire
   Of watching you; and swing me suddenly
Into the shade and loneliness and mire
   Of the last land! There, waiting patiently,

One day, I think, I'll feel a cool wind blowing,
   See a slow light across the Stygian tide,
And hear the Dead about me stir, unknowing,
   And tremble. And *I* shall know that you have died,

And watch you, a broad-browed and smiling dream,
   Pass, light as ever, through the lightless host,
Quietly ponder, start, and sway, and gleam –
   Most individual and bewildering ghost! –

And turn, and toss your brown delightful head
Amusedly, among the ancient Dead.

April 1909

Menelaus and Helen

I

Hot through Troy's ruin Menelaus broke
  To Priam's palace, sword in hand, to sate
  On that adulterous whore a ten years' hate
And a king's honour. Through red death, and smoke,
And cries, and then by quieter ways he strode,
  Till the still innermost chamber fronted him.
  He swung his sword, and crashed into the dim
Luxurious bower, flaming like a god.

High sat white Helen, lonely and serene.
  He had not remembered that she was so fair,
And that her neck curved down in such a way;
And he felt tired. He flung the sword away,
  And kissed her feet, and knelt before her there,
The perfect Knight before the perfect Queen.

II

So far the poet. How should he behold
  That journey home, the long connubial years?
  He does not tell you how white Helen bears
Child on legitimate child, becomes a scold,
Haggard with virtue. Menelaus bold
  Waxed garrulous, and sacked a hundred Troys
  'Twixt noon and supper. And her golden voice
Got shrill as he grew deafer. And both were old.

Often he wonders why on earth he went
  Troyward, or why poor Paris ever came.
Oft she weeps, gummy-eyed and impotent;
  Her dry shanks twitch at Paris' mumbled name.
So Menelaus nagged; and Helen cried;
And Paris slept on by Scamander side.

1909

Dust

When the white flame in us is gone,
   And we that lost the world's delight
Stiffen in darkness, left alone
   To crumble in our separate night;

When your swift hair is quiet in death,
   And through the lips corruption thrust
Has stilled the labour of my breath –
   When we are dust, when we are dust! –

Not dead, not undesirous yet,
   Still sentient, still unsatisfied,
We'll ride the air, and shine, and flit,
   Around the places where we died,

And dance as dust before the sun,
   And light of foot, and unconfined,
Hurry from road to road, and run
   About the errands of the wind.

And every mote, on earth or air,
   Will speed and gleam, down later days,
And like a secret pilgrim fare
   By eager and invisible ways,

Nor ever rest, nor ever lie,
   Till, beyond thinking, out of view,
One mote of all the dust that's I
   Shall meet one atom that was you.

Then in some garden hushed from wind,
   Warm in a sunset's afterglow,
The lovers in the flowers will find
   A sweet and strange unquiet grow

Upon the peace; and, past desiring,
   So high a beauty in the air,
And such a light, and such a quiring,
   And such a radiant ecstasy there,

They'll know not if it's fire, or dew,
   Or out of earth, or in the height,
Singing, or flame, or scent, or hue,
   Or two that pass, in light, to light,

Out of the garden higher, higher. . . .
   But in that instant they shall learn
The shattering ecstasy of our fire,
   And the weak passionless hearts will burn

And faint in that amazing glow,
   Until the darkness close above;
And they will know – poor fools, they'll know! –
   One moment, what it is to love.

December 1909–March 1910

The Hill

Breathless, we flung us on the windy hill,
  Laughed in the sun, and kissed the lovely grass.
  You said, 'Through glory and ecstasy we pass;
Wind, sun, and earth remain, the birds sing still,
When we are old, are old. . . .' 'And when we die
  All's over that is ours; and life burns on
Through other lovers, other lips,' said I,
  'Heart of my heart, our heaven is now, is won!'

'We are Earth's best, that learnt her lesson here.
  Life is our cry. We have kept the faith!' we said;
  'We shall go down with unreluctant tread
Rose-crowned into the darkness!' . . . Proud we were,
And laughed, that had such brave true things to say.
– And then you suddenly cried, and turned away.

December 1910

Sonnet Reversed

Hand trembling towards hand; the amazing lights
Of heart and eye. They stood on supreme heights.

Ah, the delirious weeks of honeymoon!
  Soon they returned, and, after strange adventures,
Settled at Balham by the end of June.
  Their money was in Can. Pacs. B. Debentures,
And in Antofagastas. Still he went
  Cityward daily; still she did abide
At home. And both were really quite content
  With work and social pleasures. Then they died.
They left three children (besides George, who drank):
  The eldest Jane, who married Mr. Bell,
William, the head-clerk in the County Bank,
  And Henry, a stock-broker, doing well.

Lulworth, 1st January 1911

A Letter to a Live Poet

Sir, since the last Elizabethan died,
Or, rather, that more Paradisal muse,
Blind with much light, passed to the light more glorious
Or deeper blindness, no man's hand, as thine,
Has, on the world's most noblest chord of song,
Struck certain magic strains. Ears satiate
With the clamorous, timorous whisperings of to-day,
Thrilled to perceive once more the spacious voice
And serene utterance of old. We heard
– With rapturous breath half-held, as a dreamer dreams
Who dares not know it dreaming, lest he wake –
The odorous, amorous style of poetry,
The melancholy knocking of those lines,
The long, low soughing of pentameters,
– Or the sharp of rhyme as a bird's cry –
And the innumerable truant polysyllables
Multitudinously twittering like a bee.
Fulfilled our hearts were with that music then,
And all the evenings sighed it to the dawn,
And all the lovers heard it from all the trees.
All of the accents upon all the norms!
– And ah! the stress on the penultimate!
We never knew blank verse could have such feet.

Where is it now? Oh, more than ever, now
I sometimes think no poetry is read
Save where some sepultured Cæsura bled,
Royally incarnadining all the line.
Is the imperial iamb laid to rest,
And the young trochee, having done enough?
Ah! turn again! Sing so to us, who are sick
Of seeming-simple rhymes, bizarre emotions,
Decked in the simple verses of the day,
Infinite meaning in a little gloom,
Irregular thoughts in stanzas regular,
Modern despair in antique metres, myths
Incomprehensible at evening,
And symbols that mean nothing in the dawn.

The slow lines swell. The new style sighs. The Celt
Moans round with many voices.
                                    God! to see
Gaunt anapæsts stand up out of the verse,
Combative accents, stress where no stress should be,
Spondee on spondee, iamb on choriamb,
The thrill of all the tribrachs in the world,
And all the vowels rising to the E!
To hear the blessed mutter of those verbs,
Conjunctions passionate toward each other's arms,
And epithets like amaranthine lovers
Stretching luxuriously to the stars,
All prouder pronouns than the dawn, and all
The thunder of the trumpets of the noun!

January 1911

Thoughts on the Shape of the Human Body

How can we find? how can we rest? how can
We, being gods, win joy, or peace, being man?
We, the gaunt zanies of a witless Fate,
Who love the unloving, and the lover hate,
Forget the moment ere the moment slips,
Kiss with blind lips that seek beyond the lips,
Who want, and know not what we want, and cry
With crooked mouths for Heaven, and throw it by.
Love's for completeness! No perfection grows
'Twixt leg, and arm, elbow, and ear, and nose,
And joint, and socket; but unsatisfied
Sprawling desires, shapeless, perverse, denied.
Finger with finger wreathes; we love, and gape,
Fantastic shape to mazed fantastic shape,
Straggling, irregular, perplexed, embossed,
Grotesquely twined, extravagantly lost
By crescive paths and strange protuberant ways
From sanity and from wholeness and from grace.
How can love triumph, how can solace be,
Where fever turns toward fever, knee toward knee?
Could we but fill to harmony, and dwell
Simple as our thought and as perfectible,
Rise disentangled from humanity
Strange whole and new into simplicity,
Grow to a radiant round love, and bear
Unfluctuant passion for some perfect sphere,
Love moon to moon unquestioning, and be
Like the star Lunisequa, steadfastly
Following the round clear orb of her delight,
Patiently ever, through the eternal night!

c. 1911

The Fish

In a cool curving world he lies
And ripples with dark ecstasies.
The kind luxurious lapse and steal
Shapes all his universe to feel
And know and be; the clinging stream
Closes his memory, glooms his dream,
Who lips the roots o' the shore, and glides
Superb on unreturning tides.
Those silent waters weave for him
A fluctuant mutable world and dim,
Where wavering masses bulge and gape
Mysterious, and shape to shape
Dies momently through whorl and hollow,
And form and line and solid follow
Solid and line and form to dream
Fantastic down the eternal stream;
An obscure world, a shifting world,
Bulbous, or pulled to thin, or curled,
Or serpentine, or driving arrows,
Or serene slidings, or March narrows.
There slipping wave and shore are one,
And weed and mud. No ray of sun,
But glow to glow fades down the deep
(As dream to unknown dream in sleep);
Shaken translucency illumes
The hyaline of drifting glooms;
The strange soft-handed depth subdues
Drowned colour there, but black to hues,
As death to living, decomposes –
Red darkness of the heart of roses,
Blue brilliant from dead starless skies,
And gold that lies behind the eyes,
The unknown unnameable sightless white
That is the essential flame of night,
Lustreless purple, hooded green,
The myriad hues that lie between
Darkness and darkness! . . .

                                   And all's one
Gentle, embracing, quiet, dun,
The world he rests in, world he knows,
Perpetual curving. Only – grows
An eddy in that ordered falling,
A knowledge from the gloom, a calling
Weed in the wave, gleam in the mud –
The dark fire leaps along his blood;
Dateless and deathless, blind and still,
The intricate impulse works its will;
His woven world drops back; and he,
Sans providence, sans memory,
Unconscious and directly driven,
Fades to some dank sufficient heaven.

O world of lips, O world of laughter,
Where hope is fleet and thought flies after,
Of lights in the clear night, of cries
That drift along the wave and rise
Thin to the glittering stars above,
You know the hands, the eyes of love!
The strife of limbs, the sightless clinging
The infinite distance, and the singing
Blown by the wind, a flame of sound,
The gleam, the flowers, and vast around
The horizon, and the heights above –
You know the sigh, the song of love!

But there the night is close, and there
Darkness is cold and strange and bare;
And the secret deeps are whisperless;
And rhythm is all deliciousness;
And joy is in the throbbing tide,
Whose intricate fingers beat and glide
In felt bewildering harmonies
Of trembling touch; and music is
The exquisite knocking of the blood.
Space is no more, under the mud;
His bliss is older than the sun.
Silent and straight the waters run.

The lights, the cries, the willows dim,
And the dark tide are one with him.

Munich, March 1911

The Old Vicarage, Grantchester
(*Café des Westens, Berlin, May 1912*)

Just now the lilac is in bloom,
All before my little room;
And in my flower-beds, I think,
Smile the carnation and the pink;
And down the borders, well I know,
The poppy and the pansy blow . . .
Oh! there the chestnuts, summer through,
Beside the river make for you
A tunnel of green gloom, and sleep
Deeply above; and green and deep
The stream mysterious glides beneath,
Green as a dream and deep as death.
– Oh, damn! I know it! and I know
How the May fields all golden show,
And when the day is young and sweet,
Gild gloriously the bare feet
That run to bathe . . .
                              Du lieber Gott!

Here am I, sweating, sick, and hot,
And there the shadowed waters fresh
Lean up to embrace the naked flesh.
Temperamentvoll German Jews
Drink beer around; – and *there* the dews
Are soft beneath a morn of gold.
Here tulips bloom as they are told;
Unkempt about those hedges blows
An English unofficial rose;
And there the unregulated sun
Slopes down to rest when day is done,
And wakes a vague unpunctual star,
A slippered Hesper; and there are
Meads towards Haslingfield and Coton
Where *das Betreten's* not *verboten*.

εἴθε γενοίμην . . . would I were
In Grantchester, in Grantchester! –

Some, it may be, can get in touch
With Nature there, or Earth, or such.
And clever modern men have seen
A Faun a-peeping through the green,
And felt the Classics were not dead,
To glimpse a Naiad's reedy head,
Or hear the Goat-foot piping low: . . .
But these are things I do not know.
I only know that you may lie
Day-long and watch the Cambridge sky,
And, flower-lulled in sleepy grass,
Hear the cool lapse of hours pass,
Until the centuries blend and blur
In Grantchester, in Grantchester. . . .
Still in the dawnlit waters cool
His ghostly Lordship swims his pool,
And tries the strokes, essays the tricks,
Long learnt on Hellespont, or Styx.
Dan Chaucer hears his river still
Chatter beneath a phantom mill.
Tennyson notes, with studious eye,
How Cambridge waters hurry by . . .
And in that garden, black and white,
Creep whispers through the grass all night;
And spectral dance, before the dawn,
A hundred Vicars down the lawn;
Curates, long dust, will come and go
On lissom, clerical, printless toe;
And oft between the boughs is seen
The sly shade of a Rural Dean . . .
Till, at a shiver in the skies,
Vanishing with Satanic cries,
The prim ecclesiastic rout
Leaves but a startled sleeper-out,
Grey heavens, the first bird's drowsy calls
The falling house that never falls.

God! I will pack, and take a train,
And get me to England once again!
For England's the one land, I know,

Where men with Splendid Hearts may go;
And Cambridgeshire, of all England,
The shire for Men who Understand;
And of *that* district I prefer
The lovely hamlet Grantchester.
For Cambridge people rarely smile,
Being urban, squat, and packed with guile;
And Royston men in the far South
Are black and fierce and strange of mouth;
At Over they fling oaths at one,
And worse than oaths at Trumpington,
And Ditton girls are mean and dirty,
And there's none in Harston under thirty,
And folks in Shelford and those parts
Have twisted lips and twisted hearts,
And Barton men make Cockney rhymes,
And Coton's full of nameless crimes,
And things are done you'd not believe
At Madingley, on Christmas Eve.
Strong men have run for miles and miles,
When one from Cherry Hinton smiles;
Strong men have blanched, and shot their wives,
Rather than send them to St. Ives;
Strong men have cried like babes, bydam,
To hear what happened at Babraham.
But Grantchester! ah, Grantchester!
There's peace and holy quiet there,
Great clouds along pacific skies,
And men and women with straight eyes,
Lithe children lovelier than a dream,
A bosky wood, a slumbrous stream,
And little kindly winds that creep
Round twilight corners, half asleep.
In Grantchester their skins are white;
They bathe by day, they bathe by night;
The women there do all they ought;
The men observe the Rules of Thought.
They love the Good; they worship Truth;
They laugh uproariously in youth;
(And when they get to feeling old,

They up and shoot themselves, I'm told) . . .

Ah God! to see the branches stir
Across the moon at Grantchester!
To smell the thrilling-sweet and rotten
Unforgettable, unforgotten
River-smell, and hear the breeze
Sobbing in the little trees.
Say, do the elm-clumps greatly stand
Still guardians of that holy land?
The chestnuts shade, in reverend dream,
The yet unacademic stream?
Is dawn a secret shy and cold
Anadyomene, silver-gold?
And sunset still a golden sea
From Haslingfield to Madingley?
And after, ere the night is born,
Do hares come out about the corn?
Oh, is the water sweet and cool,
Gentle and brown, above the pool?
And laughs the immortal river still
Under the mill, under the mill?
Say, is there Beauty yet to find?
And Certainty? and Quiet kind?
Deep meadows yet, for to forget
The lies, and truths, and pain? . . . Oh! yet
Stands the Church clock at ten to three?
And is there honey still for tea?

The True Beatitude
(BOUTS-RIMÉS)

They say, when the Great Prompter's hand shall ring
 Down the last curtain upon earth and sea,
 All the Good Mimes will have eternity
To praise their Author, worship love and sing;

Or to the walls of Heaven wandering
 Look down on those damned for a fretful d——,
 Mock them (all theologians agree
On this reward for virtue), laugh, and fling

New sulphur on the sin-incarnadined . . .
 Ah, Love! still temporal, and still atmospheric,
 Teleologically unperturbed,
We share a peace by no divine divined,
 An earthly garden hidden from any cleric,
 Untrodden of God, by no Eternal curbed.

1913

The Busy Heart

Now that we've done our best and worst, and parted,
 I would fill my mind with thoughts that will not rend.
(O heart, I do not dare go empty-hearted)
 I'll think of Love in books, Love without end;
Women with child, content; and old men sleeping;
 And wet strong ploughlands, scarred for certain grain;
And babes that weep, and so forget their weeping;
 And the young heavens, forgetful after rain;
And evening hush, broken by homing wings;
 And Song's nobility, and Wisdom holy,
That live, we dead. I would think of a thousand things,
 Lovely and durable, and taste them slowly,
One after one, like tasting a sweet food.
I have need to buy my heart with quietude.

1913

The Night Journey

Hands and lit faces eddy to a line;
   The dazed last minutes click; the clamour dies.
Beyond the great-swung arc o' the roof, divine,
   Night, smoky-scarv'd, with thousand coloured eyes

Glares the imperious mystery of the way.
   Thirsty for dark, you feel the long-limbed train
Throb, stretch, thrill motion, slide, pull out and sway,
   Strain for the far, pause, draw to strength again. . . .

As a man, caught by some great hour, will rise,
   Slow-limbed, to meet the light or find his love;
And, breathing long, with staring sightless eyes,
   Hands out, head back, agape and silent, move

Sure as a flood, smooth as a vast wind blowing;
   And, gathering power and purpose as he goes,
Unstumbling, unreluctant, strong, unknowing,
   Borne by a will not his, that lifts, that grows,

Sweep out to darkness, triumphing in his goal,
   Out of the fire, out of the little room. . . .
- There is an end appointed, O my soul!
   Crimson and green the signals burn; the gloom

Is hung with steam's far-blowing livid streamers.
   Lost into God, as lights in light, we fly,
Grown one with will, end-drunken huddled dreamers.
   The white lights roar. The sounds of the world die.

And lips and laughter are forgotten things.
   Speed sharpens; grows. Into the night, and on,
The strength and splendour of our purpose swings.
   The lamps fade; and the stars. We are alone.

1913

Doubts

When she sleeps, her soul, I know,
Goes a wanderer on the air,
Wings where I may never go,
Leaves her lying, still and fair,
Waiting, empty, laid aside,
Like a dress upon a chair. . . .
This I know, and yet I know
Doubts that will not be denied.

For if the soul be not in place,
What has laid trouble in her face?
And, sits there nothing ware and wise
Behind the curtains of her eyes,
What is it, in the self's eclipse,
Shadows, soft and passingly,
About the corners of her lips,
The smile that is essential she?

And if the spirit be not there,
Why is fragrance in the hair?

1913

Clouds

Down the blue night the unending columns press
  In noiseless tumult, break and wave and flow,
  Now tread the far South, or lift rounds of snow
Up to the white moon's hidden loveliness.
Some pause in their grave wandering comradeless,
  And turn with profound gesture vague and slow,
  As who would pray good for the world, but know
Their benediction empty as they bless.

They say that the Dead die not, but remain
  Near to the rich heirs of their grief and mirth.
    I think they ride the calm mid-heaven, as these,
In wise majestic melancholy train,
    And watch the moon, and the still-raging seas,
  And men, coming and going on the earth.

The Pacific, October 1913

Sonnet
(Suggested by some of the Proceedings of the Society for Psychical Research)

Not with vain tears, when we're beyond the sun,
  We'll beat on the substantial doors, nor tread
  Those dusty high-roads of the aimless dead
Plaintive for Earth; but rather turn and run
Down some close-covered by-way of the air,
  Some low sweet alley between wind and wind,
  Stoop under faint gleams, thread the shadows, find
Some whispering ghost-forgotten nook, and there
Spend in pure converse our eternal day;
  Think each in each, immediately wise;
Learn all we lacked before; hear, know, and say
  What this tumultuous body now denies;
And feel, who have laid our groping hands away;
  And see, no longer blinded by our eyes.

1913

Waikiki

Warm perfumes like a breath from vine and tree
  Drift down the darkness. Plangent, hidden from eyes,
  Somewhere an *eukaleli* thrills and cries
And stabs with pain the night's brown savagery;
And dark scents whisper; and dim waves creep to me,
  Gleam like a woman's hair, stretch out, and rise;
  And new stars burn into the ancient skies,
Over the murmurous soft Hawaian sea.

And I recall, lose, grasp, forget again,
  And still remember, a tale I have heard, or known,
An empty tale, of idleness and pain,
  Of two that loved – or did not love – and one
Whose perplexed heart did evil, foolishly,
A long while since, and by some other sea.

Waikiki, 1913

Heaven

Fish (fly-replete, in depth of June,
Dawdling away their wat'ry noon)
Ponder deep wisdom, dark or clear,
Each secret fishy hope or fear.
Fish say, they have their Stream and Pond;
But is there anything Beyond?
This life cannot be All, they swear,
For how unpleasant, if it were!
One may not doubt that, somehow, Good
Shall come of Water and of Mud;
And, sure, the reverent eye must see
A Purpose in Liquidity.
We darkly know, by Faith we cry,
The future is not Wholly Dry.
Mud unto mud! – Death eddies near –
Not here the appointed End, not here!
But somewhere, beyond Space and Time,
Is wetter water, slimier slime!
And there (they trust) there swimmeth One
Who swam ere rivers were begun,
Immense, of fishy form and mind,
Squamous, omnipotent, and kind;
And under that Almighty Fin,
The littlest fish may enter in.
Oh! never fly conceals a hook,
Fish say, in the Eternal Brook,
But more than mundane weeds are there,
And mud, celestially fair;
Fat caterpillars drift around,
And Paradisal grubs are found;
Unfading moths, immortal flies,
And the worm that never dies.
And in that Heaven of all their wish,
There shall be no more land, say fish.

1913

The Great Lover

I have been so great a lover: filled my days
So proudly with the splendour of Love's praise,
The pain, the calm, and the astonishment,
Desire illimitable, and still content,
And all dear names men use, to cheat despair,
For the perplexed and viewless streams that bear
Our hearts at random down the dark of life.
Now, ere the unthinking silence on that strife
Steals down, I would cheat drowsy Death so far,
My night shall be remembered for a star
That outshone all the suns of all men's days.
Shall I not crown them with immortal praise
Whom I have loved, who have given me, dared with me
High secrets, and in darkness knelt to see
The inenarrable godhead of delight?
Love is a flame: – we have beaconed the world's night.
A city: – and we have built it, these and I.
An emperor: – we have taught the world to die.
So, for their sakes I loved, ere I go hence,
And the high cause of Love's magnificence,
And to keep loyalties young, I'll write those names
Golden for ever, eagles, crying flames,
And set them as a banner, that men may know,
To dare the generations, burn, and blow
Out on the wind of Time, shining and streaming. . . .
These I have loved:
                    White plates and cups, clean-gleaming,
Ringed with blue lines; and feathery, faery dust;
Wet roofs, beneath the lamp-light; the strong crust
Of friendly bread; and many-tasting food;
Rainbows; and the blue bitter smoke of wood;
And radiant raindrops couching in cool flowers;
And flowers themselves, that sway through sunny hours,
Dreaming of moths that drink them under the moon;
Then, the cool kindliness of sheets, that soon
Smooth away trouble; and the rough male kiss
Of blankets; grainy wood; live hair that is
Shining and free; blue-massing clouds; the keen

Unpassioned beauty of a great machine;
The benison of hot water; furs to touch;
The good smell of old clothes; and others such –
The comfortable smell of friendly fingers,
Hair's fragrance, and the musty reek that lingers
About dead leaves and last year's ferns. . . .

                         Dear names,
And thousand other throng to me! Royal flames;
Sweet water's dimpling laugh from tap or spring;
Holes in the ground; and voices that do sing;
Voices in laughter, too; and body's pain,
Soon turned to peace; and the deep-panting train;
Firm sands; the little dulling edge of foam
That browns and dwindles as the wave goes home;
And washen stones, gay for an hour; the cold
Graveness of iron; moist black earthen mould;
Sleep; and high places; footprints in the dew;
And oaks; and brown horse-chestnuts, glossy-new;
And new-peeled sticks; and shining pools on grass; –
All these have been my loves. And these shall pass,
Whatever passes not, in the great hour,
Nor all my passion, all my prayers, have power
To hold them with me through the gate of Death.
They'll play deserter, turn with the traitor breath,
Break the high bond we made, and sell Love's trust
And sacramented covenant to the dust.
—Oh, never a doubt but, somewhere, I shall wake,
And give what's left of love again, and make
New friends, now strangers. . . .

                   But the best I've known
Stays here, and changes, breaks, grows old, is blown
About the winds of the world, and fades from brains
Of living men, and dies.

                 Nothing remains.
O dear my loves, O faithless, once again
This one last gift I give: that after men
Shall know, and later lovers, far-removed,
Praise you, 'All these were lovely'; say, 'He loved.'

Mataiea, 1914

Retrospect

In your arms was still delight,
Quiet as a street at night;
And thoughts of you, I do remember,
Were green leaves in a darkened chamber,
Were dark clouds in a moonless sky.
Love, in you, went passing by,
Penetrative, remote, and rare,
Like a bird in the wide air,
And, as the bird, it left no trace
In the heaven of your face.
In your stupidity I found
The sweet hush after a sweet sound.
All about you was the light
That dims the greying end of night;
Desire was the unrisen sun,
Joy the day not yet begun,
With tree whispering to tree,
Without wind, quietly.
Wisdom slept within your hair,
And Long-Suffering was there,
And, in the flowing of your dress,
Undiscerning Tenderness.
And when you thought, it seemed to me,
Infinitely, and like a sea,
About the slight world you had known
Your vast unconsciousness was thrown. . . .
    O haven without wave or tide!
Silence, in which all songs have died!
Holy book, where hearts are still!
And home at length under the hill!
O mother-quiet, breasts of peace,
Where love itself would faint and cease!
O infinite deep I never knew,
I would come back, come back to you,
Find you, as a pool unstirred,
Kneel down by you, and never a word,
Lay my head, and nothing said,
In your hands, ungarlanded:

And a long watch you would keep;
And I should sleep, and I should sleep!

Mataiea, January 1914

Tiare Tahiti

Mamua, when our laughter ends,
And hearts and bodies, brown as white,
Are dust about the doors of friends,
Or scent a-blowing down the night,
Then, oh! then, the wise agree,
Comes our immortality.
Mamua, there waits a land
Hard for us to understand.
Out of time, beyond the sun,
All are one in Paradise,
You and Pupure[1] are one,
And Taü, and the ungainly wise.
There the Eternals are, and there
The Good, the Lovely, and the True,
And Types, whose earthly copies were
The foolish broken things we knew;
There is the Face, whose ghosts we are;
The real, the never-setting Star;
And the Flower, of which we love
Faint and fading shadows here;
Never a tear, but only Grief;
Dance, but not the limbs that move;
Songs in Song shall disappear;
Instead of lovers, Love shall be;
For hearts, Immutability;
And there, on the Ideal Reef,
Thunders the Everlasting Sea!
  And my laughter, and my pain,
Shall home to the Eternal Brain.
And all lovely things, they say,
Meet in Loveliness again;
Miri's laugh, Teïpo's feet,
And the hands of Matua,
Stars and sunlight there shall meet,
Coral's hues and rainbows there,
And Teüra's braided hair;

[1] Tahitian for 'fair', the name given to himself.

And with the starred *tiare's* white,
And white birds in the dark ravine,
And *flamboyants* ablaze at night,
And jewels, and evening's after-green,
And dawns of pearl and gold and red,
Mamua, your lovelier head!
And there'll no more be one who dreams
Under the ferns, of crumbling stuff,
Eyes of illusion, mouth that seems,
All time-entangled human love.
And you'll no longer swing and sway
Divinely down the scented shade,
Where feet to Ambulation fade,
And noons are lost in endless Day.
How shall we wind these wreaths of ours,
Where there are neither heads nor flowers?
Oh, Heaven's Heaven! – but we'll be missing
The palms, and sunlight, and the south;
And there's an end, I think, of kissing,
When our mouths are one with Mouth. . . .

  Taü here, Mamua,
Crown the hair, and come away!
Hear the calling of the moon,
And the whispering scents that stray
About the idle warm lagoon.
Hasten, hand in human hand,
Down the dark, the flowered way,
Along the whiteness of the sand,
And in the water's soft caress,
Wash the mind of foolishness,
Mamua, until the day.
Spend the glittering moonlight there
Pursuing down the soundless deep
Limbs that gleam and shadowy hair,
Or floating lazy, half-asleep.
Dive and double and follow after,
Snare in flowers, and kiss, and call,
With lips that fade, and human laughter,
And faces individual,

Well this side of Paradise! . . .
There's little comfort in the wise.

Papeete, February 1914

The Treasure

When colour goes home into the eyes,
   And lights that shine are shut again,
With dancing girls and sweet birds' cries
   Behind the gateways of the brain;
And that no-place which gave them birth, shall close
The rainbow and the rose: –

Still may Time hold some golden space
   Where I'll unpack that scented store
Of song and flower and sky and face,
   And count, and touch, and turn them o'er,
Musing upon them; as a mother, who
Has watched her children all the rich day through,
Sits, quiet-handed, in the fading light,
When children sleep, ere night.

August 1914

Safety

Dear! of all happy in the hour, most blest
   He who has found our hid security,
Assured in the dark tides of the world that rest,
   And heard our word, 'Who is so safe as we?'
We have found safety with all things undying,
   The winds, and morning, tears of men and mirth,
The deep night, and birds singing, and clouds flying,
   And sleep, and freedom, and the autumnal earth.

We have built a house that is not for Time's throwing.
   We have gained a peace unshaken by pain for ever.
War knows no power. Safe shall be my going,
   Secretly armed against all death's endeavour;
Safe though all safety's lost; safe where men fall;
And if these poor limbs die, safest of all.

1914

The Dead

These hearts were woven of human joys and cares,
　Washed marvellously with sorrow, swift to mirth.
The years had given them kindness. Dawn was theirs,
　And sunset, and the colours of the earth.
These had seen movement, and heard music; known
　Slumber and waking; loved; gone proudly friended;
Felt the quick stir of wonder; sat alone;
　Touched flowers and furs and cheeks. All this is ended.

There are waters blown by changing winds to laughter
And lit by the rich skies, all day. And after,
　Frost, with a gesture, stays the waves that dance
And wandering loveliness. He leaves a white
　Unbroken glory, a gathered radiance,
A width, a shining peace, under the night.

1914

The Soldier

If I should die, think only this of me:
　That there's some corner of a foreign field
That is for ever England. There shall be
　In that rich earth a richer dust concealed;
A dust whom England bore, shaped, made aware,
　Gave, once, her flowers to love, her ways to roam,
A body of England's, breathing English air,
　Washed by the rivers, blest by suns of home.

And think, this heart, all evil shed away,
　A pulse in the eternal mind, no less
　　Gives somewhere back the thoughts by England given;
Her sights and sounds; dreams happy as her day;
　And laughter, learnt of friends; and gentleness,
　　In hearts at peace, under an English heaven.

1914

Fragment

I strayed about the deck, an hour, to-night
Under a cloudy moonless sky; and peeped
In at the windows, watched my friends at table,
Or playing cards, or standing in the doorway,
Or coming out into the darkness. Still
No one could see me.

                I would have thought of them
– Heedless, within a week of battle – in pity,
Pride in their strength and in the weight and firmness
And link'd beauty of bodies, and pity that
This gay machine of splendour 'ld soon be broken,
Thought little of, pashed, scattered. . . .

                      Only, always,
I could but see them – against the lamplight – pass
Like coloured shadows, thinner than filmy glass,
Slight bubbles, fainter than the wave's faint light,
That broke to phosphorus out in the night,
Perishing things and strange ghosts – soon to die
To other ghosts – this one, or that, or I.

April 1915

Fragment of an Ode-Threnody on England

All things are written in the mind.
There the sure hills have station; and the wind
Blows   in that placeless air.
And there the white and golden birds go flying;
And the stars wheel and shine; and woods are fair;
The light upon the snow is there;
                        and in that nowhere move
The trees and lands and waters that we love.

And she for whom we die, she the undying
Mother of men
England!

In Avons of the heart her rivers run.

She is with all we have loved and found and known,
Closed in the little nowhere of the brain.
Only, of all our dreams,
Not the poor heap of   dust and stone,
This local earth, set in terrestrial streams,
Not this man, giving all for gold,
Nor that who has found evil good, nor these
Blind millions, bought and sold . . .

She is not here, or now –
She is here, and now, yet nowhere –
We gave her birth, who bore us –
Our wandering feet have sought, but never found her –
She is built a long way off –
She, though all men be traitors, not betrayed –
Whose soil is love, and her stars justice, she –
Gracious with flowers,
And robed   and glorious in the sea.[1]

She was in his eyes, but he could not see her.
And he was England, but he knew her not.

[1] This last set of jottings is not written as if they were meant to be consecutive.

Fragment of a Sonnet

The poor scrap of a song that some man tried
Down in the troop-decks forrard, brought again
The day you sang it first, on a hill-side,
With April in the wind and in the brain.
And the woods were gold; and youth was in our hands.

                    Oh lovers parted,
Oh all you lonely over all the world,
You that look out at morning empty-hearted,
Or you, all night turning uncomforted

Would God, would God, you could be comforted.

                  Eyes that weep,
And a long time for love; and, after, sleep.

Fragment of a poem about Evening

And daylight, like a dust, sinks through the air,
And drifting, golds the ground . . .
              A lark,
A voice in heaven, in fading deeps of light,
Drops, at length, home.

A wind of night, shy as the young hare
That steals even now out of the corn to play,
Stirs the pale river once, and creeps away.

Fragment of an Elegy

The feet that ran with mine have found their goal,
The eyes that met my eyes have looked on night.
The firm limbs are no more; gone back to earth,
Easily mingling . . .
           What he is yet,
Not living, lives, hath place in a few minds . . .
                      He wears
The ungathered blossom of quiet; stiller he
Than a deep well at noon, or lovers met;
Than sleep, or the heart after wrath. He is
The silence following great words of peace.

Bibliography

A Writings by Brooke

I have not attempted here to list all Brooke's published writings: this has been done admirably for all time by Sir Geoffrey Keynes in his *Bibliography* (Rupert Hart-Davis, London, 2nd Edition revised, 1954). I have omitted work which has appeared only in periodicals, but have otherwise referred all 'collected' works, both verse and prose, to the most accessible sources.

Letters from America, Charles Scribner, New York, 1916; Sidgwick & Jackson, 1916.

John Webster and the Elizabethan Drama, John Lane, New York, 1916; Sidgwick & Jackson, 1916.

Fragments (limited to 99 copies), Dunster House, Cambridge (Mass.), 1925.

Lithuania, Stewart Kidd, Cincinnati, N.D.; Sidgwick & Jackson, 1935.

Epilogue to *The Death of John Rump* in *A Number of People* by Edward Marsh, Heinemann, 1939.

The Poetical Works, ed. Geoffrey Keynes, Faber & Faber, 1946.

Democracy and the Arts, Rupert Hart-Davis, 1946.

The Prose (selected), ed. Christopher Hassall, Sidgwick & Jackson, 1956.

The Letters (selected), ed. Geoffrey Keynes, Faber & Faber, 1968; Harcourt Brace Jovanovich, New York, 1968.

B Books about Brooke

This is a selection, merely, of books (biographical and critical) which have Brooke as their main theme, or in which he makes a significant appearance.

Asquith, Herbert, *Moments of Memory*, 1937.

Bayley, John, *The Romantic Survival*, 1957.

Benson, A. C., *Memories and Friends*, 1924.

Bergonzi, Bernard, *Heroes' Twilight*, 1965.

Browne, Maurice, *Recollections of Rupert Brooke* (limited to 510 copies), 1927.

Bullough, Geoffrey, *The Trend of Modern Poetry*, 1934.

de la Mare, Walter, *Rupert Brooke and the Intellectual Imagination* (first published in a limited edition, and later revised and included in *Pleasures and Speculations*, 1940).

Drinkwater, John, *Prose Papers*, 1918.

Duncan, Joseph E., *The Revival of Metaphysical Poetry*, Minnesota, 1959.

Fairchild, Hoxie Neale, *Religious Trends in English Poetry*, vol. 5, 1962.

Forster, E. M., *G. Lowes Dickinson*, 1934.

Foster, H. C., *At Antwerp and the Dardanelles*, 1918.

Garnett, David, *Flowers of the Forest*, 1956.

Garrod, H. W., *The Profession of Poetry*, 1929.

Grant, Joy, *Harold Monro and the Poetry Bookshop*, 1967.

Guibert, Armand, *Rupert Brooke*, Genova, 1933.

Harrod, Roy, *The Life of John Maynard Keynes*, 1951.

Hassall, Christopher, *Edward Marsh : a Biography*, 1959.

Hassall, Christopher, *Rupert Brooke*, 1964.

Hastings, Michael, *The Handsomest Young Man in England*, 1967.

Holroyd, Michael, *Lytton Strachey* (vol. 1), 1967.

James, Henry, *Letters*, ed. Percy Lubbock (vol. 2), 1920.

James, M. R., *Eton and King's*, 1926.

Jerrold, Douglas, *The Royal Naval Division*, 1923.

Johnston, John H., *English Poetry of the First World War*, 1964.

Knox, Ronald, *Patrick Shaw-Stewart*, 1920.

Leavis, F. R., *New Bearings in English Poetry*, 1932.

Leslie, Shane, *The End of a Chapter*, 1916.

Marsh, Edward, *Rupert Brooke : a Memoir*, first published with the *Collected Poems*, 1918.

Marsh, Edward, *A Number of People*, 1939.

Moore, T. Sturge, *Some Soldier Poets*, 1919.

Murry, J. Middleton, *Between Two Worlds : an Autobiography*, 1935.

Phelps, W. L., *The Advance of English Poetry in the Twentieth Century*, 1919.

Potter, R. M. G., *Rupert Brooke. A biographical note 1911–1919*, Hartford (U.S.A.), 1923.

Press, John, *A Map of Modern English Verse*, 1969.

Reeves, James [ed.], *Georgian Poetry*, 1962.

Riding, L., and R. Graves, *A Survey of Modernist Poetry*, 1927.

Ross, Robert H., *The Georgian Revolt 1910–22*, 1967.

Sassoon, Siegfried, *The Weald of Youth*, 1942.

Sedgwick, Ellery, *The Happy Profession*, 1948.

Stringer, Arthur, *Red Wine of Youth*, New York, 1948.

Sturgeon, Mary C., *Studies of Contemporary Poets*, 1916.

T[ownshend], E. [ed.], *Keeling Letters and Recollections*, 1918.

Urmitzer, Klara, *Rupert Brooke*, Würtzburg, 1935.

Webb, Beatrice, *Our Partnership*, ed. B. Drake and M. I. Cole, 1948.
Wilson, Colin, *Poetry and Mysticism*, 1970.
Woodberry, G. E., *Studies of a Litterateur*, New York, 1921.
Woolf, Leonard, *Beginning Again*, 1964.

C Articles about Brooke in Periodicals

Here is the smallest fraction of the periodical literature on Brooke, but I have aimed to include the most important references.

Churchill, Winston, *The Times*, 26 April 1915.
Cornford, Frances, *Time and Tide*, 4 January 1947; *The Daily Telegraph*, 23 April 1953.
Dalton, Hugh, *The Granta*, 5 February 1910.
Dent, E. J., *The Cambridge Magazine*, 8 May 1915.
Dickinson, Patric, *Mandrake* (Oxford), Winter 1946.
Eliot, T. S., *The Egoist*, September 1911.
Erleigh, Viscount (later Lord Reading), *The Times*, 10 March 1930.
Ervine, St John, *The North American Review*, September 1915.
Fraser, G. S., *New Statesman and Nation*, 5 July 1952.
Lehmann, John, *The Listener*, 6 November 1944.
Marsh, Edward, *The Poetry Review*, April 1912.
Monro, Harold, *The Cambridge Magazine*, 22 May 1915.
Moore, J. R., *Modern Language Review*, April 1959.
Platnauer, Maurice, *Review of English Studies*, October 1943.
Pye, Sybil, *Life and Letters*, May 1929.
Schell, Sherril, *The Bookman* (U.S.A.), August 1926.
Sheppard, J. T., *The Cambridge Review*, 5 May 1915.
Thomas, Edward, *The English Review*, June 1915.
Williamson, H. R., *The Bookman*, May 1931.
Woolf, Virginia, *The Times Literary Supplement*, 8 August 1918.

DATE DUE

MAY 10 '77			
DEC 13 90			
1-5-92			
	DISCARDED		
GAYLORD			PRINTED IN U.S.A.